Using

INFORMIX-**SQL**

Using

INFORMIX-**SQL**

Second Edition

Jonathan Leffler

Informix Software Ltd
(formerly of Sphinx Ltd)

ADDISON-WESLEY
PUBLISHING
COMPANY

Wokingham, England • Reading, Massachusetts • Menlo Park, California • New York
Don Mills, Ontario • Amsterdam • Bonn • Sydney • Singapore
Tokyo • Madrid • San Juan • Milan • Paris • Mexico City • Seoul • Taipei

Cover designed by Crayon Design of Henley-on-Thames and
printed by The Riverside Printing Co. (Reading) Ltd.
Typeset by the author using Elan Eroff software on a Compaq Deskpro 386/25 running SCO Xenix 5.2.3.2 and printed on a Hewlett-Packard Laserjet III.
Printed in Great Britain by Mackays of Chatham PLC, Chatham, Kent

First edition published 1989.
Second edition printed 1991. Reprinted 1992.

British Library Cataloguing in Publication Data available

Library of Congress Cataloging in Publication Data
Leffler, Jonathan, 1960–
       Using INFORMIX-SQL / Jonathan Leffler. - - 2nd ed.
          p.   cm.
       Includes bibliographical references (p.   ) and index.
       ISBN 0-201-56509-9
       1. Relational data bases. 2. Informix-SQL (Computer program)
    I. Title.
    QA76.9.D3L4291991
    005.75′6--dc20   91-10965
                                                                  CIP

Preface

This book is a complete guide to the database product INFORMIX-SQL – it covers all aspects of the product. The introductory material in Part I gives a general description of the product, and of relational databases in general. The material in Parts II and III introduces the basic features of INFORMIX-SQL – how to create a database, put data into it and get information out of it – but much of the material in Parts IV and V is considerably more complex than what would be found in a book purporting to be an 'Introduction to INFORMIX-SQL'.

The INFORMIX-SQL product is supplied with a reference manual and a user guide, both of which are very good in comparison to the documentation provided with many other products, but they are not always easy to follow. In particular, there is a tendency to try and say everything about one part of the product in one chapter. This book takes what might be termed a spiral approach to the product. There are three chapters on each of the main components of INFORMIX-SQL – forms for data entry, SQL for retrieving data from the database and reports for producing well-formatted informative documents – but rather than present three consecutive chapters on forms, then three on SQL and finally three on reports, this book presents one chapter on each topic in turn. These nine chapters are the core of the book. The remaining chapters cover introductory material and database administration.

Throughout the book, there are examples based on one database, called the **Cars** database because it is used to store data about second-hand cars. There are sets of exercises at the end of the chapters in Parts II, III and IV of this book, and, where applicable, worked answers are provided in Appendix A. In most cases, the answer given is simply one of the many possible solutions: if your answer gives the same results, it is equivalent and therefore correct.

Order of presentation

Part I is on INFORMIX-SQL and databases, and mostly covers background material. Chapter 1 is a description of INFORMIX-SQL and the related products produced by Informix Software. Chapter 2 has two distinct parts. The first half discusses relational databases in general and emphasizes that they are easy to understand. The second half is crucial for all readers since it is a description of the **Cars** database which is used for the vast majority of the examples in the book. After these two introductory chapters, the book concentrates solely on the way in which INFORMIX-SQL can be used to create and manipulate databases.

Part II is about the basic use of INFORMIX-SQL. Chapter 3 describes how to get started with INFORMIX-SQL and continues with the methods of creating databases. Chapter 4 covers the basic aspects of single-table forms, which allow you to enter data into the database, and to carry out enquiries and to edit the data in the database. Chapter 5 describes the simpler parts of SQL – something that it is necessary to understand before it is possible to produce reports – and covers the basic elements of the SELECT statement. Reports are the subject of Chapter 6, the final chapter in Part II. This chapter covers the basic mechanics of producing a report and only deals with the simple control blocks: ON EVERY ROW, PAGE HEADER and PAGE TRAILER.

Part III is called 'Intermediate INFORMIX-SQL' and has another chapter on each of forms, SQL and reports, extending the work covered in Part II. Chapter 7 is on forms and describes multi-table forms, including master/detail relationships. Chapter 8 is on SQL and describes aggregates, sub-select statements, the GROUP BY and HAVING clauses, and the related statements INSERT, DELETE and UPDATE. Chapter 9 is on reports and covers the remaining control blocks, aggregate functions (including group aggregates) and the OUTPUT section. Chapter 10, the final chapter in Part III, is on user menus. These allow you to provide users with a complete menu-driven INFORMIX-SQL without writing any programs. This material is needed to produce good working database systems; the rest of the book is then largely optional in that many database users (as opposed to database designers and administrators) will seldom or never need to worry about the material in Part IV. The material in Part III is covered a little more quickly than in Part II.

Part IV is called 'Advanced INFORMIX-SQL'. This part assumes that you are happy with all that has gone before, so the pace picks up quite noticeably. Chapters 11–13 do a final round on forms, SQL and reports. The first of these covers some fairly esoteric parts of forms including composite joins and the detailed control available in the INSTRUCTIONS section. The next chapter covers some equally esoteric parts of SQL, notably outer joins and table aliasing. The techniques described in these two chapters will not be used all that often. Chapter 13, on reports, describes techniques that are used frequently and illustrates some of these with a report for producing address labels. This report should be easily adapted for most databases where addresses are stored, and for most layouts of the labels on printed paper.

Part V is called 'Database Administration'. Chapter 14 covers features of creating tables not covered in Chapter 3. It also discusses how the query system optimizes the enquiries made by the user, how the system of permissions can be used to control who can do what with the database and how to keep your database out of the hands of people who should not be allowed to handle the database. Chapter 15 describes the various techniques for loading and unloading ASCII data into and from the database. It also describes a set of tools which help to maintain the data in the database internally consistent, as well as some ideas for how to back up a database to protect against accidental loss of data. The final chapter, Chapter 16, covers various things that have not been covered previously. These include all the environment variables which affect INFORMIX-SQL, the command line interface to the INFORMIX-

SQL programs, the structure of the system catalogue and the various supporting tools provided with INFORMIX-SQL.

This book tries to cover all the existing versions of the product, which means that it mentions versions 1.10, 2.00, 2.10 and 4.00. In general, it treats version 4.00 as the reference version and documents the differences in the older versions. There are, however, a number of features which are only available in version 4.00, so it sometimes seems that the book uses version 2.10 as the reference version. Most of the material applies equally to INFORMIX-SE and INFORMIX-ONLINE; those parts which do not are clearly marked.

In this new edition, a few minor mistakes have been corrected and the whole book has been reset. However, the major change since the first edition is the introduction of INFORMIX-SQL version 4.00. Another change is that the database engine (either INFORMIX-SE or INFORMIX-ONLINE) is now provided separately from INFORMIX-SQL. This has meant that a lot of minor details have changed. The book has also been somewhat reorganized. Although the chapters are all roughly the same, some of the detailed information has been moved around. Chapter 3 has been substantially rewritten. In the first edition, all the data types were covered in detail in Chapter 3 and then not covered again. This has been changed so that the basic types are covered in Chapter 3, but all the types, including the new types introduced with version 4.00, are covered in Chapter 14. Similarly, information on the environment variables has been moved from Chapter 14 to Chapter 16.

Prerequisites

This book tries to assume as little background information as possible, so that it is not necessary to have an extensive working knowledge of databases in order to learn from this book. On the other hand, it cannot be denied that some background knowledge will be useful. If you have no knowledge of relational databases, you should read Chapter 2 carefully. This covers all the ideas about databases used in the book, but it is fairly concise.

The book was written on UNIX machines and generally assumes that you are working on UNIX. However, most of what is said will apply, with some small modifications, to any of the other environments which INFORMIX-SQL runs on. The knowledge of UNIX needed to use INFORMIX-SQL is limited; if you know how to login, run programs, list the files in a directory and remove files, the only other knowledge that is needed is how to use a suitable editor. Towards the end of the book, it is helpful to know rather more about UNIX. Some of the material on database administration in Part V assumes that you are working on UNIX rather than any other type of machine, and that you have a fairly good knowledge of UNIX; if you do not have this knowledge, the material will be that much harder to understand.

It is recommended, but not essential, that you have access to a machine which is running INFORMIX-SQL, if only to do the exercises. There is an immense difference between a theoretical understanding of INFORMIX-SQL and a practically based knowledge of it. You should generally try most of the exercises: the later exercises in any given set are generally harder, so if you can do them, the earlier ones are not so important.

Acknowledgements

First of all, I must thank Sphinx Ltd for permission to adapt a set of course notes originally written for customer training into this book, and for providing me with the machines on which to prepare the material, and for the unlimited supply of paper on which to print it.

There were a number of people within Sphinx who helped me with various parts of the first edition of this book. Pat Lloyd and Adrian Waters thoroughly scrutinized the various drafts and encouraged me to rewrite parts of it extensively, and also provided some technical assistance. Marianne Mayes did some of the typing for me; and Brian Willis, Carl Evans, Martin Woodward, Selwyn Castleden, Keith Asher (DEC), Robin Early and Neil Urquhart (both of Informix Software UK Ltd) also provided useful information. My thanks go to all these people.

There are some extra people who I would like to thank for their help in producing the second edition of this book. Tony Lacy-Thompson from Informix Software in the UK and Tony Rodini from Informix Software in the USA read the draft of this book and offered valuable advice on how to improve it, and both of them agreed to do it before I knew I was changing jobs to work for Informix. Nicky Jaeger at Addison-Wesley helped with all sorts of organizational problems, Stephen Bishop helped design the layout, and Debra Myson-Etherington did a superb job on the copy-editing.

As always, any remaining mistakes are my own fault. I would appreciate being told of any mistakes so that they can, perhaps, be corrected later.

Jonathan Leffler

March 1991

For simplicity, the pronoun 'he' is used to relate to both male and female throughout the book.

Contents

Part I
INFORMIX-SQL and databases

1
INFORMIX-SQL

There are many ways of answering the question 'What is INFORMIX-SQL?', all of them different, all of them correct. INFORMIX-SQL is:

1. A relational database management system (RDBMS).
2. One of a family of related products.
3. Produced by Informix Software Inc (ISI).
4. Based on the standard Structured Query Language (SQL).
5. Easily used.
6. Available on many different machines.
7. The best-selling database for UNIX machines.

SQL was originally developed by IBM and is now both an ANSI standard and an ISO standard. INFORMIX-SQL uses a superset of SQL as its database-manipulation language.

1.1 INFORMIX-SQL is an RDBMS

INFORMIX-SQL is a relational database management system or RDBMS. A relational database has a particular organization which makes it distinct from a network or hierarchical database. The organization of a relational database is described in Chapter 2; it can be regarded as a collection of tables which store the data. INFORMIX-SQL provides tools for all aspects of manipulating a relational database.

1.1.1 Create and delete databases

Before you can do anything with a database, it must be created. It is also helpful to be able to remove a database which has outlived its usefulness. Interestingly, the standard SQL does not have commands to create or delete named databases, but INFORMIX-SQL does have commands to handle named databases.

3

1.1.2 Create, alter and remove tables in a database

The information in a relational database is all stored in tables. An 'empty' database has no user-defined tables in it, only the standard system-defined tables which describe the database (the system catalogue). User-defined tables can be added, modified or removed as required, and the interactive schema editor can be used to define or modify the structure of a table.

1.1.3 Enter data from the terminal

An empty table is of little use to anyone. The simplest way of adding data to a table is to create a screen form (the system will create one automatically when told to do so) and then to use the program called PERFORM to run the form. A form is a screen layout which has fields where the user can enter data and text indicating what should be entered.

1.1.4 Make enquiries by example

PERFORM is a very powerful tool which not only allows you to add data but also allows you to retrieve data and then change or delete it. PERFORM allows you to specify which rows of data you want to look at by specifying, for example, that the date must be between 1 January and 31 January 1991. PERFORM would fetch the data, creating a list of records which could be scanned in either direction, and the individual rows of data could be deleted or changed as necessary.

1.1.5 Make complex enquiries from the database

Some enquiries are too complex to be specified using PERFORM. INFORMIX-SQL provides an interactive facility which allows arbitrarily complex SQL statements to be sent directly to the database. SQL is not just a data-retrieval language; every operation done on a database is expressed as an SQL statement. All the programs such as PERFORM translate the user's requests into SQL statements, even though the user is not aware of this.

1.1.6 Produce reports from the database

Although both PERFORM and SQL can be used to discover what is stored in the database, the user has little control over how the data is presented. ACE reports contain an SQL query and detailed formatting instructions which allow the data to be presented exactly as required, and also provide powerful facilities for summarizing the data. The results can be sent to the screen or a printer, or to a file.

1.1.7 Produce customized applications

INFORMIX-SQL provides USER MENUS which allow you to create a menu-driven application making full use of all the facilities provided by INFORMIX-SQL, and all without having to write any programs. It is perfectly feasible to arrange that, when a user logs on to a machine, the customized application is run automatically.

1.1.8 Load and unload data

INFORMIX-SQL can produce ordinary text files containing any required data from the database in a format which can be read by other programs. It can also load similar text files produced by other programs into a database. These facilities allow INFORMIX-SQL to import data from other packages when necessary, or to export data for another package to use.

1.1.9 Prevent unauthorized access to data

On multi-user systems, INFORMIX-SQL provides a set of facilities which can be used to ensure that only certain people can see particular pieces of information. Some people can be excluded completely, others can be given permission to select the data but not change it, and others can be given permission to change it too.

1.1.10 Log transactions and other integrity checks

If a database is given a transaction log, INFORMIX-SQL will record every change made to the data in the database in the log file. If necessary, this log can be used to replay the changes, so that if the database is damaged but the log is intact, a back-up copy of the database can be restored and all the changes made since the back-up can be made again (using the record from the transaction log) so that no work is lost.

1.1.11 All facilities available from one integrated program

All these facilities are provided with the purchase of INFORMIX-SQL, and are available through a single, integrated, menu-driven program. This contrasts with some other vendors' products which require you to buy multiple products with multiple interfaces just to obtain forms and reports and basic access to the database.

1.2 INFORMIX-SQL is part of a product family

INFORMIX-SQL is one of the family of products shown in Table 1.1. The Informix range of products contains four groups of products: C-ISAM on its own, the front-end

Product	Version					
C-ISAM	2.10	3.00	3.10.00	3.10.03	3.10.06	4.00
INFORMIX-SQL	1.10	2.00	2.10.00	2.10.03	2.10.06	4.00
INFORMIX-4GL	–	1.00	1.10.00	1.10.03	1.10.06	4.00
INFORMIX-4GL RDS	–	–	–	1.10.03	1.10.06	4.00
INFORMIX-4GL ID	–	–	–	1.10.03	1.10.06	4.00
INFORMIX-QUICKSTEP	–	–	–	–	–	4.00
ESQL/C	1.10	2.00	2.10.00	2.10.03	2.10.06	4.00
ESQL/COBOL	1.10	2.00	2.10.00	2.10.03	2.10.06	4.00
ESQL/ADA	–	–	–	1.10.03	–	4.00
ESQL/FORTRAN	–	–	–	–	–	4.00
INFORMIX-SE	–	–	–	–	–	4.00
INFORMIX-TURBO	–	–	–	1.10.03	1.10.06	–
INFORMIX-ONLINE	–	–	–	–	–	4.00
INFORMIX-NET	–	–	2.10.00	2.10.03	2.10.06	4.00
INFORMIX-STAR	–	–	–	–	–	4.00

Table 1.1 Versions of Informix products

tools, the embedded SQL tools and the database engines. The main products in the family are: C-ISAM, INFORMIX-SQL, INFORMIX-4GL, INFORMIX-QUICKSTEP, ESQL/C, ESQL/COBOL, ESQL/ADA, ESQL/FORTRAN, INFORMIX-SE, INFORMIX-TURBO, INFORMIX-ONLINE, INFORMIX-NET and INFORMIX-STAR.

The members of the family are continually being improved and new members introduced. Most of these products have been available in several different versions, but the version numbering for the products prior to release 4.00 did not make it completely obvious which version of, say, ESQL/C went with which version of INFORMIX-SQL. Table 1.1 summarizes which versions of each product were available concurrently. Version x.10.03 was not available on DOS, and x.10.06 was only available on DOS.

1.2.1 Two-process architecture

To understand the Informix family of products, it is helpful to understand how the products access the database. All versions of INFORMIX-SQL use a two-process architecture, also referred to as a client–server architecture, to handle the database. This means that there are two separate programs co-operating to provide a service to the user. One of these programs is the front-end. The front-end program is responsible for interacting with the user, and for translating the user's requests into statements that retrieve the correct information from the database or change the information in the database. The front-ends do not actually change the database; this is done by the other program, the back-end or database engine. The back-end is responsible for the data in the database. It handles all the complexities of where the data is stored and what is the best way of accessing the data, and some versions of

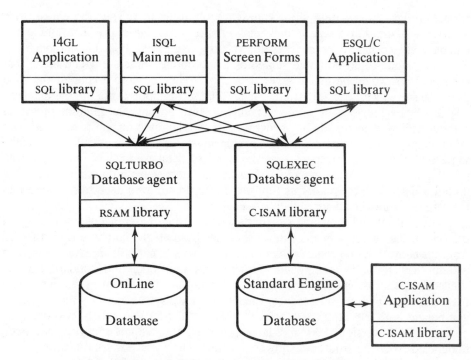

Figure 1.1 Informix two-process architecture

the back-end are designed to handle networking and other forms of distributed database when necessary.

   The two-process architecture is shown in Figure 1.1. The database engine is logically distinct from the program run by the user. On UNIX, it is a completely separate program which is run automatically by the user's program, and the user's program communicates with the database engine through two pipes (one-way communication channels). Every time the user's program needs to fetch some data from the database, it sends a suitable message to the database engine and waits for a response. Meanwhile, the database engine is waiting for a message, reads it, does whatever it is told to do and sends back an appropriate response.

   There are several reasons for organizing the database access this way. Firstly, it guarantees that the database is always treated in the same way. In particular, it means that the permissions are treated uniformly, and also that locking always operates uniformly. It also means that the same front-end program can work with different back-ends, and one back-end provides a service for all sorts of front-end programs. Secondly, all programs using the database benefit from the optimizations that the database engine performs when interpreting the database requests. Thirdly, the database engine can have special privileges. In particular, the Standard Engine needs to be able to create very large files, but on UNIX ordinary users can only create moderately large files. If every program had to have the special privileges, an unscrupulous programmer could quickly subvert the entire security system (and a careless programmer would allow knowledgeable users to subvert the entire UNIX security system), but because only one program has these privileges, only the database engine has to be checked for security loopholes. Fourthly, although the database engine could be implemented as a subroutine library, it would mean that each program would be much larger than it is already because a copy of the code would be stored with each program. Finally, and most important of all, the database engine can be replaced by a new version (or even an entirely different program) without having to recompile any programs. If the database engine is replaced by a different program, the new database engine must obey the same rules – use the same communications protocol – as the standard database engine. As long as the new engine is always used to handle a particular database from the time it is created until it is destroyed, the programs run by the user do not even need to be aware that they are not using the standard database engine.

The front-end tools and programs written using the embedded SQL tools all use one of the database engines to access a database. If the database is transferred from the control of one engine to another, the programs can still access the database without having to be recompiled. Up until version 4.00, the Standard Engine, INFORMIX-SE, was automatically provided with INFORMIX-SQL (and also with INFORMIX-4GL and all the products except INFORMIX-TURBO). This meant that if you bought both INFORMIX-SQL and INFORMIX-4GL, you also bought two database engines. With version 4.00 and later products, the database engine has been unbundled from the front-end software, so that when you buy INFORMIX-SQL and INFORMIX-4GL, you are not also supplied with two copies of the database engine. However, it does mean that when a machine is being set up initially, you must buy both INFORMIX-SQL and either INFORMIX-SE or INFORMIX-ONLINE.

1.2.2 Informix C-ISAM

C-ISAM is the odd man out in the family because it is not an SQL product; it operates at a lower level than SQL. INFORMIX-SE (Standard Engine) uses C-ISAM as the basic data-access package. The name stands for Indexed Sequential Access Method in C. It implements indexed sequential files using two operating system files to represent one indexed sequential file. It deals with fixed-length data records only. The product is actually a library of subroutines for use by C programmers, so end-users never use C-ISAM directly – they always run a program which uses C-ISAM.

1.2.3 INFORMIX-SQL

INFORMIX-SQL provides the non-programming user with a complete set of tools for handling databases, as already described. The facilities it provides are described in detail in the rest of the book.

1.2.4 INFORMIX-4GL

INFORMIX-4GL is a fourth-generation language built upon SQL. It uses the same basic style of forms and reports as INFORMIX-SQL, but it allows the programmer to write code to do all sorts of things that simply cannot be expressed in INFORMIX-SQL. It has procedural statements (IF/THEN/ELSE) like a third-generation language, which can be used to do very complex validation of data that cannot be done in INFORMIX-SQL, but it also has non-procedural statements to handle menus, input from the screen and scroll arrays displayed on the screen. It actually makes use of an extended version of ESQL/C as an intermediate language – that is, the INFORMIX-4GL compiler produces ESQL/C code, then invokes a special version of the ESQL/C compiler to produce C and finally invokes the system C compiler to produce the executable program. It can make use of any of the facilities offered by the operating system because it can call C functions directly.

There are two other products available to the INFORMIX-4GL programmer. The first of these is the INFORMIX-4GL Rapid Development System, RDS. The other INFORMIX-4GL system converts the INFORMIX-4GL code into C (which does not take long) and then links the object code with a number of large libraries (which does take a long time). The RDS does not create C code but generates a pseudo-code instead, and the pseudo-code programs are then interpreted by the RDS, which means that there is no linking phase and the programs can be tested much more quickly, simply because the programmer spends less time waiting for the linker. The final programs can be compiled into C in the traditional way, or they can be left in pseudo-code. One advantage of the pseudo-code is that the same pseudo-code program can be run on any machine for which there is an RDS interpreter, so there is no difficulty moving an RDS application between machines. The only disadvantage of the RDS is that, because it is interpreted, it is slightly slower than a compiled system. The difference is not noticeable if there is any user interaction in the program, and other factors (such as the ability to share one copy of the text segment of the interpreter between all the users on the machine) generally mean that the advantages outweigh any disadvantages.

The second product, which is closely related to the RDS, is a symbolic debugger for INFORMIX-4GL applications running under RDS called INFORMIX-4GL Interactive Debugger, ID. It allows programmers to monitor what is happening to an RDS program while it is running, and it operates at the source-code level. This means that the programmer can see what is happening in terms of what he has written, rather than having to be able to interpret assembler, pseudo-code or C. The ease of debugging code with this tool is more than sufficient to justify using RDS and ID in preference to compiled INFORMIX-4GL.

1.2.5 The embedded SQL tools

ESQL/C allows an application written in C to embed SQL statements in the program. These are then converted into suitable declarations and function calls making use of libraries. Among other advantages, this allows the application to make use of a graphical user interface (GUI) and still access an Informix database. This will become less important when the graphical version of INFORMIX-4GL is released. It is also possible to provide customized versions of both PERFORM and ACE. ESQL/COBOL provides analogous facilities for COBOL, ESQL/ADA for Ada and ESQL/FORTRAN for FORTRAN.

INFORMIX-SQL is intended for use by semi-technical people, and is a valuable prototyping tool for professional software developers. INFORMIX-4GL is designed for professional programmers to use to generate highly customized applications for unsophisticated end-users. The embedded SQL products are for institutions with a significant investment in third-generation language software and skills that want to be able to use relational databases without having to abandon the languages they already know well.

1.2.6 The database engines

There are two main database engines in the product range, namely INFORMIX-SE and INFORMIX-ONLINE, which organize the databases on disk in totally different ways.

The Standard Engine, INFORMIX-SE, is the original database engine. The actual program is called `sqlexec`, and it provides databases which are handled simply and reliably, and which do not require any special facilities to maintain them. INFORMIX-SE uses C-ISAM to organize the data files, so it uses ordinary files provided by the operating system. Databases can be created at any time, providing there is enough space on the hard disk. It does not require any special areas on the disk to be reserved for the databases. Because this product requires almost no maintenance, it is still the preferred database engine for many installations, particularly for small and medium sites, and especially where the users are naïve. Additionally, many products have been written using C-ISAM for the main processing work, but which have a set of definitions available which allows INFORMIX-SQL to access the same data files. (These are seldom entirely satisfactory because the database is never as secure as if the application used just the database engine to access the data, and there is no possibility of making the product work with any other engines.)

In contrast, the other database engines, INFORMIX-TURBO and INFORMIX-ONLINE, require considerably more care and attention, both to set them up and to keep them going, but the pay-off is that the database runs considerably faster than under INFORMIX-SE. They are especially useful in large installations with many users and on-line transaction processing requirements. The actual program is called `sqlturbo` for both INFORMIX-TURBO and INFORMIX-ONLINE, and it uses a different method of organizing the disks (using so-called *raw* disks) instead of using the files provided by the operating system. It also uses shared memory, which means that all the simultaneously running INFORMIX-ONLINE engines normally co-operate, with only one of them fetching a given page of data from the disk and then making the data available to all the others automatically. Both these features help to make

INFORMIX-ONLINE much quicker than INFORMIX-SE, especially on a heavily loaded machine with many users accessing the same database. There are two consequences of this other than speeding up database operations: first, it is not possible to use C-ISAM to access the data since it is no longer stored in C-ISAM files; and second, the database requires more loving attention on the part of the database administrator to keep it working smoothly. The latest versions of the Informix products are able to use either INFORMIX-SE or INFORMIX-ONLINE without really being aware of which engine is in use, and without being recompiled.

One of the most valuable features of INFORMIX-ONLINE is that it is designed for 24-hours a day, 7-days a week operation; the system can be backed up with the database still active (and a coherent back-up is produced) and extra disk space can be added at any time. It also features a software disk-mirroring system which means that there can be two independent copies of the database on separate disk drives. If one of the two drives fails, the database will continue to operate on the other drive, and when the failed drive is made available again, it will automatically be brought up to date. INFORMIX-ONLINE also features an enhanced query optimizer which improves the system performance. In addition, it supports variable-length data types, which are not available with any of the other engines, called VARCHAR, BYTE and TEXT. The latter two are known collectively as *blobs* (for *b*inary *l*arge *ob*jects) and can be used to hold chunks of data of arbitrary sizes such as bit-mapped images and text documents.

INFORMIX-TURBO is a predecessor of INFORMIX-ONLINE; the technology in them is similar, but the INFORMIX-ONLINE product is considerably better than INFORMIX-TURBO in many ways. If there is a choice between INFORMIX-TURBO and INFORMIX-ONLINE, use INFORMIX-ONLINE every time.

There are a collection of products which allow database access over networks. This is an area which changes rather rapidly, but there are two main products, INFORMIX-NET and INFORMIX-STAR. INFORMIX-NET allows an application running on machine A to use a database on machine B, providing distributed processing, but not distributed databases. It provides a substitute for the normal INFORMIX-SE program which communicates over the network with a server on the remote machine (called `sqlexecd`), which starts up a standard `sqlexec` and leaves the two programs communicating over the network. There are a number of network types which are supported, including TCP/IP, PC NFS, X.25 using SLIP, and StarLAN.

INFORMIX-STAR provides the distributed database facility. It only works with INFORMIX-ONLINE (and hence only on version 4.00 and later), and makes use of INFORMIX-NET components too. Basically, INFORMIX-STAR allows a single Informix application to communicate with several different servers on several different machines simultaneously and transparently. (The transparency means that the users and programmers need not be aware of the details of where the databases are located; only the administrators need worry about it, and they can change the database locations without recompiling the applications.) This is a facility which will be extended greatly and made more powerful and general in future releases of the products.

1.2.7 Other products

The standard report facilities in both INFORMIX-SQL and INFORMIX-4GL are very powerful, but some people who are not full-time database programmers find it difficult to produce really neat and tidy reports. INFORMIX-QUICKSTEP provides an easy-to-use interface which allows you to produce professional quality reports interactively, using pull-down menus and dialogue boxes, even on a 'green-screen' terminal. The resulting report can be saved for reuse. INFORMIX-QUICKSTEP can also be useful to developers because the report can be converted to INFORMIX-4GL code, which can then be modified by hand if necessary.

As well as these database products, ISI provides a number of other products. The most important of these products are SmartWare and Wingz. SmartWare is an integrated package offering word processor, database management, spreadsheet, business graphics and communications facilities. It is available on DOS and UNIX.

Wingz is a 'presentation spreadsheet'; it offers a massive spreadsheet with the ability to include high quality, 3-dimensional graphics and text in the spreadsheet. It also includes a powerful programming language called HyperSheet which allows you to do many things, including retrieve data from Informix databases. This is available on the Apple Macintosh (under Finder and AU/X), on DOS with Windows 3.0 and on OS/2 with Presentation Manager, and Wingz is promised on UNIX with X-Windows.

1.3 INFORMIX-SQL is produced by ISI

INFORMIX-SQL is produced by Informix Software Inc (ISI) in California, USA. It was started in 1980 as Relational Database Systems Inc (RDS), a name which was retained until December 1986 when it was changed to Informix Software to reflect the name of the products by which it was best known. The first product produced by RDS was C-ISAM which was made available on UNIX and DOS. This quickly established itself as a *de facto* standard for indexed sequential files and is used, for example, by MicroFocus in its Level II COBOL product when running on UNIX systems. The X/Open group is a consortium of computer manufacturers who produce machines which run UNIX. It has defined a Common Applications Environment (CAE) which should be available on all the members' machines which run UNIX so that programs developed on one X/Open system using only X/Open features should transfer to any other X/Open system with a minimum of fuss. The CAE was defined by selecting between various existing UNIX standards, and C-ISAM was chosen as the indexed sequential file-handling package. C-ISAM is widely used for implementing things such as accounts packages, and of course it is the basis for ISI's own INFORMIX-SE.

In 1982, RDS introduced Informix, an RDBMS which evolved into INFORMIX 3.3. It was a complete database system which used C-ISAM to store the data. INFORMIX 3.3 had a number of component programs, including: `formbuild` to compile forms and `perform` to run them, allowing the user to add data to the database, or to make enquiries on existing data and then change or delete it as necessary; and `aceprep` to compile reports and `acego` to run them, allowing the user to produce all sorts of neatly formatted printouts of the data in the database. Many developers found the set of tools and libraries provided with INFORMIX 3.3 for programmers very attractive. Many applications have been developed which use an INFORMIX 3.3 database to store the data and these have programs written using either C-ISAM or the library routines provided with INFORMIX 3.3. One of the many advantages of this is that users can be given the schemas for the database so that they can write ACE reports in addition to the reports provided by the application writer. The current version of INFORMIX 3.3 is 3.30.14 and it is now a static product – there is no development work being done on it. It is not ported on to new machines unless someone specifically requests a port. INFORMIX 3.3 was a fine product for its time and established RDS's reputation.

By 1984, it was becoming clear that SQL was going to be a significant force in the database market-place, and RDS responded by introducing INFORMIX-SQL which used SQL as its query language. A significant portion of the ideas developed for INFORMIX 3.3 were transferred to INFORMIX-SQL: `formbuild` became `sformbld`, `perform` became `sperform`, but the basic ideas and syntax of the forms themselves were essentially unchanged and anyone familiar with INFORMIX 3.3 forms could quickly pick up the new system; similarly, `aceprep` became `saceprep`, `acego` became `sacego` and the formatting section of a report was virtually unchanged. On the other hand, the organization of the database underwent a radical change. With INFORMIX 3.3, all the information about the structure of the database was contained in a single non-C-ISAM file. With INFORMIX-SQL, the database as a whole was stored in a directory and the information about the structure of the database was held in a set of system-controlled C-ISAM files that were indistinguishable from tables created by the user. This change, which was certainly fundamental, was a consequence of discarding the INFORMIX 3.3 query language and adopting SQL instead. The method of building databases and tables in INFORMIX-SQL is very different from that in INFORMIX 3.3, and the change of query language particularly affected the part of a report which selected the data to be printed. One of the tools provided with INFORMIX-SQL was a tool to convert an INFORMIX 3.3 database into an INFORMIX-SQL database with the equivalent structure and the same data as the INFORMIX 3.3 database. INFORMIX-SQL is written using ESQL/C, so ESQL/C was also made available at the same time.

When version 2.00 of INFORMIX-SQL was released in mid-1986, the programming language INFORMIX-4GL version 1.00 was released too. This has many valuable features for helping to develop applications rapidly, over and above those provided by ESQL/C. Most notably, it can handle all aspects of screen management and input, including ring menus, forms, reports and (with INFORMIX-4GL version 1.10) a windowing facility. Other parts of the Informix family have become available at different stages. ESQL/COBOL was available very quickly, while INFORMIX-TURBO was announced in 1987 (though it did not become available until 1988), and the RDS and the Interactive Debugger were added in 1988. Also in 1988, ISI took over Innovative Software Inc and began to absorb the SmartWare products (which had been successful on DOS) into the range of products available for UNIX. Version 4.00

of the Informix range of products was released in April 1990, replacing INFORMIX-TURBO by the enhanced INFORMIX-ONLINE product, and adding INFORMIX-STAR, INFORMIX-QUICKSTEP and ESQL/FORTRAN.

1.4 INFORMIX-SQL is based on standard SQL

Until the mid-1980s, almost all mainframe databases used either hierarchical databases or network databases. Hierarchical systems were first developed in the early 1960s, and network systems during the late 1960s and early 1970s. Both types of database are difficult to use, especially for non-programmers. They place a premium on having every single part of the database design correct before data is added to the database because it is difficult to change the database structure; both systems store the addresses of other related records, so if a record address changes, many other records must also be changed to reflect the new location. Both types of system are still used extensively because commercial versions of relational databases did not become available until the mid-1980s, and there is a lot of money invested in the older systems.

In 1970, E. F. Codd wrote a paper called 'A relational model of data for large shared data banks' (Codd, 1970), which first described the theory of relational databases. He was then working for IBM. IBM subsequently began developing a prototype relational database system called System R and one part of that system was a query language called Sequel, which was subsequently renamed Structured Query Language – SQL – which is reputedly still pronounced 'sequel' although most people say 'ess-cue-ell'. It became clear that IBM would use it as the query language in a commercial version of System R, and in 1981, SQL/DS was released for DOS/VSE and subsequently for VM/CMS, and DB2 was released in 1983 for MVS/370 and MVS/XA machines, and both systems did indeed use SQL. Such is the power of IBM that many other companies announced the use of SQL as a query language for their relational database systems, either as a replacement for their proprietary language or as an alternative to it.

It was quickly evident that there would be a multitude of dialects of SQL unless something was done, and in 1983, ANSI set up a committee given the title X3H2 to define an ANSI standard SQL language. Standards always take time to produce, and the final standard was approved by ANSI in 1986 as X3.135-1986. It was adopted by ISO as IS-9075-1987. The standard is not ideal; in particular, although it defines how tables can be created and altered, there is no command for creating a named database, and there are many similar minor problems. RDS got around this by creating RDSQL as a superset of SQL, and this language is used in all the Informix products, though the name RDSQL has now been dropped in favour of plain SQL.

Relational database theory has been refined and developed. One key feature which is required is called 'referential integrity', which is to do with making sure that the data in a database is self-consistent, and doing so automatically. Referential integrity is not a part of IS-9075-1987, but ISO standards also evolve with time, and this standard now has an extra section called the 'referential integrity addendum', IS-9075-1987/AD1. This is called SQL1 – the ANSI X3H2 committee is now working on improvements to SQL1 and there are two new versions of SQL under development called SQL2 and SQL3 which significantly extend the facilities of SQL1. It is difficult to predict when either SQL2 or SQL3 will become a standard.

1.5 INFORMIX-SQL is easy to use

It is easy to use INFORMIX-SQL to create a database and the tables in the database; creating the database involves little more than specifying its name, and there is the schema editor to help create the tables. A set of forms can be generated to allow the user to enter data into the database, to make enquiries about the data in the database, and to change or delete the existing data. Similarly, a set of default reports can be generated for producing printouts of the data in the database. Finally, a menu system can be created to guide the user when using the database. This whole process could take as little as an hour if the design had been largely decided in advance and the default forms and reports were used exclusively, and all this without any programming of any sort.

The default forms and reports would need to be customized for continued use. The data to be entered would be validated and extra, related, information would be shown on the screen to help the user. The report formats would need tidying up, with proper page headers and trailers and totals and so on. This is a more time-consuming operation and requires a better knowledge of INFORMIX-SQL, but it is still well within the capabilities of most users. This simple application could be used for a while to establish whether it does what the users need it to do, and many of the small changes that seemed desirable (such as changing the position of a field on a form) could be made by the user who really uses the form. If it proves necessary, this application can become the basis for creating a more complex application using INFORMIX-4GL.

If the database holds data which is crucial to the success of the company, the application will often be designed and created by data-processing staff, because to do so thoroughly requires an understanding of database principles and an ability to consider all the procedures necessary to ensure that the database is kept secure. For example, the data-processing staff will be able to advise on back-ups of the database, and security in general, and on the best design of the tables which hold the data. INFORMIX-SQL provides a lot of tools to make this job easy; in particular, it allows for rapid prototyping of the user interface. It is also particularly simple to modify the structure of the database; if the initial design is not quite right, it is trivial to modify the existing schema, or (slightly less trivial) it is possible to redesign the database from scratch, if necessary. However, the details of access permissions, special user logins, installation, back-ups and audit trails are likely to be overlooked by inexperienced users.

Anyone can use a database application created using INFORMIX-SQL. The ease of use depends on the skill with which the application was designed, but feedback from users can usually be incorporated quickly even if the application has been in use for some time.

1.6 INFORMIX-SQL is widely available

INFORMIX-SQL is available on a very large number of different machines of all sizes and running on many different operating systems. The number of different machines on which it is available is continually growing too.

The smallest machines which run INFORMIX-SQL are IBM PCs and compatibles running DOS – either PC-DOS or MS-DOS. This requires a hard disk and the full 640K of memory. The DOS version does not have all the security features because DOS does not recognize the concept of users – it is a single-user, single-tasking system which means that only one user can use a machine at one time, and the user can only have one program running at one time. There are versions available for networked DOS machines too. These implement record locking because more than one person may be accessing the data at a time over the network. INFORMIX-SQL is also available on machines running OS/2.

One of the main strongholds of INFORMIX-SQL is in the small-to-medium size of multi-user machines. A typical example would be a Compaq Deskpro 386/25 with 70 MB or more disk, running Xenix or one of the other versions of UNIX for the Intel 80386 chip. INFORMIX-SQL is also available on many other machines of comparable size using the Motorola chips (and many other architectures) instead of the Intel chips.

INFORMIX-SQL is also available on larger machines, including Amdahl IBM plug-compatible mainframes running UTS (a variant of UNIX), and even Cray-2 supercomputers running UNICOS (another variant of UNIX). In total, the availability list shows several hundred different machines, but the total number of machines is greater because of the multiplicity of clones and badge-engineered machines.

1.7 Different versions of INFORMIX-SQL

There have been four main versions of INFORMIX-SQL: versions 1.10, 2.00, 2.10 and 4.00. The basic operation of INFORMIX-SQL has not changed between these versions, but numerous details have changed. This book will not cover versions 1.10 or 2.00 in much detail. For most purposes, versions 2.00 and 2.10 are very similar, and version 4.00 has some extra features. Because there are numerous small differences between different versions of the product, you will find a number of places in the text marked with tags such as:

> Version 4.00.
> Version 2.10 and earlier.
> Standard Engine.
> OnLine.

These indicate that the next paragraph (or, occasionally, sentence) applies to the designated versions of the product. There are also a number of places where the text describes differences between the versions without using these markers.

1.8 Summary

This chapter has tried to answer the question 'What is INFORMIX-SQL?'. It is a relational database management system produced by Informix Software Inc as one member of a family of products which can all work together. It provides a complete set of tools for manipulating relational databases, and it uses a version of SQL based on the ANSI standard as the language which actually changes the database. It uses a two-process architecture which ensures that the integrity of the database is maintained carefully, and permits applications to be flexible about where the database is located. It also means that the database engine can be changed completely without the end-user being aware of the change. It is an easily used product which is available on an extremely large number of different types of computer, ranging from single-user personal computers up to the largest mainframes.

2
Relational databases

This chapter has three purposes: to introduce the basic ideas behind a relational database, to clarify the terminology used throughout the book and to introduce the database used for examples. If you feel comfortable with the basic ideas of a relational database and understand what is meant by table, column, row and join, by all means skip to Section 2.6 which introduces the database that will be used for most of the examples in this book.

2.1 What is a database?

There are many possible definitions of a database, but one definition is:

- a database is a collection of *data*
- kept in *long-term storage*
- which is *structured* so that
- *information* can be retrieved from it.

Each of the italicized terms is important. Many other definitions would specify that a database is kept on a computer; this seems unnecessarily restrictive, though this is the only chapter where non-computerized databases will be considered at all.

2.1.1 What is meant by data?

Data are[1] facts – any facts – and are raw, unstructured information. The data may have come from many different places, but ultimately someone, somewhere, will have decided which facts should be stored in the database, and will have ensured that the data are collected, organized and entered into the database storage.

---

1. 'Data' is strictly a plural noun, and I have treated it as a plural noun here, but in common with most computer people, I treat it as a mass noun – eg the data is structured – when convenient.

2.1.2 What is long-term storage?

The term *database* implies some well-defined purpose for the collection of data, and that in turn implies that the data will be kept for a considerable period of time. Even if some of the data changes frequently (for example, the number of seats available on a plane flight), the database as a whole is a permanent repository for the data.

2.1.3 What does structured mean?

If the contents of a filing cabinet were thrown all over the floor and then collected back together without ordering the sheets of paper and without collecting related sheets together and then replaced in the drawers, the filing cabinet would still contain the same data as before this drastic reorganization (disorganization), but it would not contain the same information because the relationships between the different facts would have been lost completely. The data would also be completely unusable; the letter you sent to your solicitor confirming that you agreed to the sale of your house and the solicitor's response would probably be in different drawers, and the only way of finding either would be by an exhaustive search of each drawer, which would probably take hours to do, unless you were very lucky. In comparison, before the disaster you could simply have gone to the third drawer and opened the folder marked 'house' and found the letter in a matter of moments.

Just as a filing cabinet has to be carefully organized, a database also has to be organized if people are to get useful information out of it. As far as a naïve user is concerned, the database imposes the order on the data, but the database designer knows that a lot of effort goes into designing the database. In the same way, a manager can find the information in the filing cabinet if he has an efficient secretary, but the secretary knows how hard it is to keep the filing cabinet in order.

2.1.4 What is information?

Information can be defined as the basis for making decisions. It is also, almost invariably, processed data; it is derived from raw facts (or other information), and summarizes or correlates these facts. The primary distinction between information and data is that information is immediately useful to the person studying it, whereas data has to be processed in some way before it becomes information. Thus, what is information to the financial accountant of a company is data to the financial director, and what is information to the financial director is probably just data to the managing director. This means that information is an elusive thing; its value keeps changing depending on who it is given to. The volume of raw data stored in a database is often too large to be comprehensible. The data stored in an accounting database describes the individual transactions made by a company – the sales and the purchases – but the data has to be summarized before the management can tell whether the company is making a profit or a loss. When the data has been appropriately summarized, the information can be used to decide whether to declare a dividend or to call in the official receiver to close the business.

In fairness, it must be pointed out that some books regard data and information as synonyms, but it seems worth keeping the distinction. After all, it is a database that stores facts, but the software which extracts information from a large-scale database system in a big corporation is called a 'management *information* system', not a 'management *data* system'.

2.1.5 An example of a database

An example of a database is the card-index catalogue in an old-fashioned library. The facts stored are the names of authors, books, publishers, classification number and numerous other details. These facts are organized so that each card contains the facts about one book, and duplicated copies of the cards are then organized in several different ways. For example, the author index has one copy of each card stored in alphabetic order of the name of the author of the book; if you want to find out which books by, say, Roger Lancelyn Green are in the library, this is the place to look. On the other hand, if you want to find out about all the books the library has on Ancient Egypt, the author index is a very bad place to look; you would have to go through each card to see what the book is about, because the data is not organized to answer this sort of enquiry. The correct way to find a list of the books on Ancient Egypt is to look in the subject index under 'Egypt, Ancient' to find the classified number for the subject and then to look in the classified index using that number to find all the books on the subject. An alternative trick is to find the classified number and then go and look on the shelves directly, but this will not tell you which books are currently on loan.

The important thing about this example is that it shows how the data has to be organized in different ways to allow users to retrieve the information they require, and that the different organizations are suitable for answering some enquiries and not for answering others.

The card-index catalogue in a library is not computerized: some authors would automatically exclude it from the category 'databases' simply because it is not computerized. (Of course, many libraries do have fully computerized – or partially computerized – catalogues.)

2.2 Databases, tables, rows, columns

Computer-based databases can be organized in a number of different ways. There are at least four such ways in common use which are called hierarchical, network, inverted index and relational. Of these, relational databases are the easiest to understand, and they are also at least as powerful as any of the others. INFORMIX-SQL is a relational database, so nothing more will be said about the others.

To the user, a relational database appears to store the data as a set of tables. All the information in the database, and all the information about the database, is

Maker	Model	Details	Engine Capacity
Vauxhall	Cavalier	1.6 GL	1600 cc
		2.0 SRi	2000 cc
Ford	Escort	1.4 L	1400 cc
		RS Turbo	1600 cc
	Granada	2.0 GL	2000 cc
		2.8 Ghia	2800 cc
	Sierra	2.8i Ghia 4x4 Estate	2800 cc
BMW	Series 3	3.2.0i	2000 cc
	Series 7	7.3.5	3500 cc

Table 2.1 Models of cars

stored in tables within the database. Even if the underlying storage system on the computer is not purely tabular (for example, it might store some data about the links between two tables), the ordinary user does not see the relational database as anything other than a collection of tables.

Each table is very simple: it is a collection of columns, with headings which identify what information appears in each column, and there are rows of data underneath the headings which represent different objects. For example, consider the table of cars shown in Table 2.1. The column heading **Maker** tells us that the values in the rows underneath identify the company which makes the car, the column heading **Engine Capacity** tells us that the values in the rows underneath should be a numerical value approximating to the capacity of the engine, and so on. Each row identifies one type of car: the first row describes a Vauxhall Cavalier 1.6 GL, whereas the last row describes a BMW 7.3.5.

2.3 Joins

Another table needed in the **Cars** database is the prices of second-hand cars. A simple version of this table is shown in Table 2.2. Clearly, by looking at the **Models** table and the **Prices** table, we can see that a Vauxhall Cavalier 1.6 GL has a nominal engine capacity of 1600 cc, and a 1989 model would cost between £4500 and £5300. How do we do this? Mentally (and very quickly) we equate the values in the **Maker**, **Model** and **Details** columns of the two tables and choose all the relevant details. As we will see later, the notation *table.column* is used to identify a particular column, and to retrieve the information about a 1989 model Vauxhall Cavalier 1.6 GL, we could write a statement such as:

```
CHOOSE  Models.Maker, Models.Model, Models.Details, Prices.Year, Prices.Price
JOINING Models.Maker    WITH Prices.Maker
   AND Models.Model    WITH Prices.Model
   AND Models.Details WITH Prices.Details
  GIVEN Models.Maker   = "Vauxhall" AND Models.Model   = "Cavalier"
   AND Models.Details = "1.6 GL"   AND Prices.Year    = 1989.
```

Maker	Model	Details	Year	Price	
				Low	High
Vauxhall	Cavalier	1.6 GL	1990	£5600	£6600
			1989	£4500	£5300
			1988	£3500	£4250
			1987	£2800	£3400
Ford	Escort	1.4 L	1990	£4880	£5500
			1989	£4075	£4700
BMW	Series 3	3.2.0i	1990	£9900	£11200
			1989	£8475	£9650
			1988	£6775	£7900

Table 2.2 Prices of second-hand cars

Note: this is deliberately not the same syntax as INFORMIX-SQL uses. The process of selecting values from two tables where some of the fields in each table are the same is called *joining*.

2.4 Some rules

There are four basic rules that all tables in a relational database must follow and these are listed and discussed below. Although there are a number of other rules which it is a good idea to follow, they are not discussed here. The four basic rules about tables are:

1. A table may contain no lists; only a single value may be stored in any row under any one column.
2. The meaning of the data must not depend on the order of the columns in a table.
3. The meaning of the data must not depend on the order of the rows in a table.
4. Each row in a table must be distinct from every other row in the same table.

The first rule means that a row in a table cannot contain an entry such as 'Ford: Sierra/Escort/Granada/Fiesta' to indicate that Ford makes Sierras, Escorts, Granadas and Fiestas. Instead, it must be written out in full: Ford makes Sierras, Ford makes Escorts, Ford makes Granadas and Ford makes Fiestas.

The second rule means it does not matter whether the list of cars looks as it did in Table 2.1 or as it does in Table 2.3 – the table stores the same information. The first table is certainly easier to read, but the information has not changed.

Similarly, the third rule means that there is no significance to the order in which the lines occur in the table. If there is some ordering of the information (such as the order of preference or the order in which the models were announced), then that information should be stored in the table explicitly (probably in an extra column).

Engine Capacity	Model	Details	Maker
1600 cc	Cavalier	1.6 GL	Vauxhall
2000 cc		2.0 SRi	
1400 cc	Escort	1.4 L	Ford
1600 cc		RS Turbo	
2000 cc	Granada	2.0 GL	
2800 cc		2.8 Ghia	
2800 cc	Sierra	2.8i Ghia 4x4 Estate	
2000 cc	Series 3	3.2.0i	BMW
3500 cc	Series 7	7.3.5	

Table 2.3 Alternative layout for the table of cars

The fourth rule merely indicates that if two rows are identical in every column, one of them is redundant and can be deleted.

2.4.1 More complicated rules

This section can be omitted when first reading this chapter. It briefly discusses the extra rules alluded to earlier, and tries to describe the idea of primary keys and foreign keys quite simply.

Because each row in a table is distinct, a row of data can be identified by quoting the value stored in each column of the row. For example, to identify the row describing the Cavalier 1.6 GL, it is sufficient to quote 'the maker is Vauxhall, the model is Cavalier, the details are 1.6 GL and the engine capacity is 1600 cc'. Often, however, a subset of the columns is sufficient to identify the row. In the case of the Cavalier, the engine size is not necessary; the model is identified without specifying that value. There is always at least one set of columns in a table which can be used to identify any row in the table uniquely (because by quoting a suitable set of values for each of these columns, at most one row of data will be defined), and this group of columns is called the *primary key*.[2] The extra rules help to keep the database self-consistent. The extra rules can be summarized as:

- All the non-primary-key columns in a table should say something about the primary key, the whole primary key and nothing but the primary key.

For example, suppose the **Models** table was extended to include the address of the manufacturer as shown in Table 2.4. Now when Ford moves its headquarters to

---

2. This is a simplification. There can be more than one such set of columns, and each such set is called a candidate key. One of these candidate keys is chosen to be the primary key, and the others become alternate keys (as well as being candidate keys). For a more rigorous definition of a primary key (and foreign keys), see Date (1986, 1990).

Maker	Town	Model	Details	Engine Capacity
Ford	Dagenham	Escort	1.4 L	1400 cc
Ford	Dagenham	Escort	RS Turbo	1600 cc
Ford	Dagenham	Granada	2.0 GL	2000 cc
Ford	Dagenham	Sierra	2.8i Ghia 4x4 Estate	2800 cc

Table 2.4 The **Models** table extended with an address

another place (say Eastleigh, near Southampton), all the Ford rows have to be changed because otherwise the user can obtain different answers to the question 'Where are Ford's headquarters in the UK?'. The reason the trouble arises is that the address column breaks the rule specified. The primary key in this table is the combination **Maker, Model, Details**. The **Town** column says something about the primary key (it says that the UK headquarters of the company that makes this model are in Dagenham), but it does not say something about the whole key (because the UK headquarters of Ford are in Dagenham regardless of whether this model is a Ford Escort or a Ford Sierra).

One of the important tasks when designing a database is to eliminate such problems as having the address in the wrong place. This process can be made mathematically rigorous (it is called *normalization theory*), but an intuitive approach such as that outlined here will suffice for many purposes.

One of the important properties of relational database theory is that it has a sound mathematical basis. Each of the rules mentioned is also a consequence of the mathematical theory (primarily *set theory*) on which relational databases are built. It also means that there are alternative nomenclatures for the objects described as tables, columns and rows, as outlined in Table 2.5.

2.5 Further reading on database design

This book does not try to teach anything more than the merest outline of how to design a database. To do the job properly would take far more space than is available, and would lead us well away from the subject of INFORMIX-SQL. However, this is not to say that database design is not important! On the contrary, it is crucial to the success of the database, and is probably as important as which package is used to implement the database.

Mathematical Term	Ordinary Name	Alternative Name
Relation	Table	File
Attribute	Column	Field
Attribute value	Value	Value
Tuple	Row	Record
Domain	Column type	Field type

Table 2.5 Alternative terms for tables, columns and rows

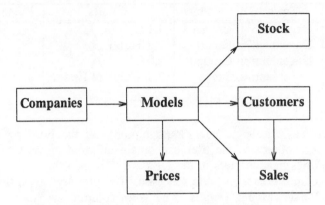

Figure 2.1 Relation diagram for the **Cars** database

There are many books which discuss database design with varying degrees of lucidity. The ones which I have found most helpful are listed below. The full bibliographical details are given in Appendix D.

Date (1990): This book gives a good general introduction to databases in general and the theory of how databases are organized. It is presented informally and does not require a degree in mathematics to understand it.

Date (1986): This book is also very interesting and presents its material very differently to the previous book. It tends to assume familiarity with the ideas in Date (1990), but it has a pragmatic chapter on database design.

Fleming (1989): This book concentrates exclusively on database design. It gives a comprehensive set of steps with worked examples which, if followed, should lead to a sound database design. It too avoids being mathematically rigorous.

NCC (1986): The SSADM design method is widely used in the UK, especially in the government sector. The manual splits the method into a set of tasks, outlining what must be achieved, and a set of techniques which help to achieve it. Data-flow diagrams, logical data structure diagrams and entity life-history diagrams are all valuable tools, particularly for the early stages of the design. Informix has announced an SSADM-based CASE tool for delivery during the first half of 1991.

I apologize to those whom I have offended by listing these books and omitting dozens of other books which are equally valuable.

2.6 The Cars database

This book uses the **Cars** database for almost all its examples, and this section describes its structure. The database is used by a car dealer, ABC Cars Ltd, which deals mainly in second-hand cars. The database consists of six tables, each of which joins with at least one other table, as shown in Figure 2.1.

Column Name	Purpose
Maker	Identifying number
Company	Name of company
Address1	1st line of address
Address2	2nd line of address
Address3	3rd line of address
Postcode	Postcode
Phone	Telephone number
Notes1	Free text
Notes2	Free text

Table 2.6 Columns in the **Companies** table

2.6.1 The Companies table

The **Companies** table is a list of car manufacturers; it has the columns shown in Table 2.6. The primary key of this table is the **Maker** column. The chances are that the dealer will seldom make use of the address information; the primary purpose of the table is to provide the list of manufacturer names. This table has a particularly simple relationship with the other tables in the database because it is only related with the **Models** table (there is a sensible join between the **Companies.Company** column and the **Models.Maker** column), and it does not cross-reference any other table in the database.

2.6.2 The Models table

The **Models** table is a list of the models made by manufacturers and has the columns shown in Table 2.7. It defines all the car models known to the database. The **Modelname** is used to define the generic model, such as Cavalier or Escort; the **Details** column stores the rest of the information needed to distinguish between models – details such as '1.6 GL 5dr' to identify a particular type of Cavalier.

The primary key of this table is the **Model** column. As can be seen from Figure 2.1, this table is crucial in gluing the database together. The **Models** table joins with every other table in the database – it is the most important table in the database. All the other tables cross-reference the **Models** table using the **Models.Model** column.

A *foreign key* is a set of columns in a table which cross-references the primary key of another table (or the same table). If the foreign key is a single column, the value in the column must match the primary key of one row in the table it cross-references. If the foreign key consists of more than one column, then the primary key it matches must have the same number of columns, the types of the columns must be the same and the composite value of the foreign key must match exactly one row in the table it cross-references.

The **Models** table contains one foreign key; the **Models.Maker** column cross-references the **Companies.Company** column, and the database is corrupt if any

Column Name	Purpose
Model	Identifying number
Maker	Company making model
Modelname	Generic name of model
Details	Details of model
Price	List price for new car
Maxspeed	Maximum speed (mph)
Accel	Time to accelerate from 0–60 mph
Enginesize	Nominal engine size (cc)
Urban	Fuel consumption – simulated urban
Mpgat56	Fuel consumption – steady 56 mph
Tanksize	Tank capacity (gallons)

Table 2.7 Columns in the **Models** table

row in **Models** has a value in the **Maker** column for which there is no corresponding row in the **Companies** table. Whenever a user goes to delete a row from the **Companies** table, the action should be rejected if any row in the **Models** table cross-references it; a deletion from the **Companies** table is restricted by the **Models** table.

2.6.3 The Prices table

The **Prices** table is a list of the current guide prices for models from different years of manufacture; it has the columns shown in Table 2.8. This table stores information about the guide prices to be used for pricing a second-hand car when it is offered for sale by a customer. There might be an entry in this table indicating that a Vauxhall Cavalier 1.6 GL built in 1986 should sell between £700 and £2400. Any given model will be listed many times in this table.

This table has a composite primary key formed from the **Model** and **Year_made** columns. The table contains one foreign key; the **Prices.Model** column cross-references **Models.Model**, and the database is corrupt if there is a row in **Prices** which has a value stored in the **Model** column for which there is not a corresponding row in the **Models** table. If the user deletes a row from the **Models** table, all the corresponding rows in the **Prices** table should be deleted; a deletion from the **Models** table cascades to the **Prices** table.

Column Name	Purpose
Model	Model number
Year_made	Year when model was built
Lo_price	Lower guide price for model
Hi_price	Higher guide price for model

Table 2.8 Columns in the **Prices** table

Column Name	Purpose
Registration	Registration
Model	Model number
Colour	Colour of car
Condition	How well kept the car is (coded)
Datebought	When car was bought
Boughtfor	Price the car was bought for
Mileage	How far the car has travelled
Notes1	Free text
Notes2	Free text

Table 2.9 Columns in the **Stock** table

2.6.4 The Stock table

The **Stock** table is a list of the cars on the forecourt at ABC Cars Ltd; it has the columns shown in Table 2.9. It stores information such as the registration number, model number and condition, and the mileage on the car when it was bought.

One of the simplifying assumptions made is that all the cars in stock have a registration number, so the registration number is unique and can be used as the primary key for this table. The other data gives some rudimentary information about the car; one noticeable but deliberate omission is a record of who it was bought from. This probably corresponds very accurately to the average, uncomputerized second-hand car dealer but is not necessarily appropriate for a computerized system like this. The condition is a simple, one-character code: 'X' means excellent, 'V' means very good, 'G' means good, 'A' means average and 'P' means poor.

The table has one foreign key; the **Stock.Model** column also cross-references the **Models.Model** table, and, as usual, the database is corrupt if any row in **Stock** has a value in the **Model** column which does not correspond to the model number of a row in **Models**. The user should not be allowed to delete a row from the **Models** table if there is a record in **Stock** which cross-references it.

2.6.5 The Customers table

The **Customers** table is a list of the people who have bought cars from ABC Cars Ltd, or who have made enquiries about cars, or anyone with whom ABC Cars Ltd has had contact. It has the columns shown in Table 2.10. The information includes the name, address and phone number of the customer, a brief resumé of the customer's last contact with ABC Cars Ltd and also an estimated spending power. This means that ABC Cars Ltd should be registered under the Data Protection Act 1984 (in the UK), as otherwise the company is liable to be prosecuted under that act.

The **Enquiry** column records whether the last contact with the customer was a sale 'S' or an enquiry 'Q', which means that the customer got in contact with ABC

Column Name	Purpose
Number	Identifying number for customer
Salutation	Prefix to name – Mr, Mrs, Miss, Ms, Sir, Dr, etc
Firstname	Christian or given name
Surname	Family name
Address1	1st line of address
Address2	2nd line of address
Address3	3rd line of address
Postcode	Postcode
Phone	Telephone number
Maxmoney	Estimated spending power
Enquiry	Type of contact
Lastmodel	Last model bought
Contactdate	Date of last contact

Table 2.10 Columns in the **Customers** table

Cars Ltd, or a contact 'C', which means that ABC Cars Ltd made the effort to get in contact with the customer.

The primary key of the table is the **Number** column. Using a number avoids many of the problems caused by people's names and addresses. The alternative to using a number is a composite key; this would need to include the salutation, firstname, surname and all the address fields, and still would not distinguish between Mr John Smith and his son, Mr John Smith, who lives with his parents. Using a number as the primary key reduces the amount of data in the primary key (which both simplifies and speeds up joins with the **Customers** table), but it means that two entries (with different numbers) can easily be created to represent one customer of ABC Cars Ltd.

This table contains one foreign key; the **Lastmodel** column contains the model number that was involved in the last contact; it need not correspond to the last model that the customer bought unless the last contact was also a sale, in which case, of course, the model number in the **Customers** table should agree with the model number in the **Sales** table. As usual, the database is corrupt if any row in **Customers** has a value in the **Lastmodel** column which does not correspond to the model number of a row in **Models**. If the user deletes a model from the **Models** table, any records in the **Customers** table which cross-reference the model should have the **Lastmodel** field set to null.

This is the third of the three types of action which can occur when a row in a table is deleted when there are other tables with identified foreign keys which cross-reference the table. In case you missed them, the delete could be restricted (disallowed) or cascaded (delete the matching rows), or the delete could nullify the cross-references. The same actions can be applied to an update. In general, the default behaviour for deletes should be restricted, while the default behaviour for updates should be cascaded. This sort of control, which is called *referential integrity*, should be implemented by the database engine (for Informix, either `sqlexec` or

Column Name	Purpose
Registration	Car registration number
Customer	Customer number
Model	Model number
Soldfor	Price car was sold for
Datesold	When was it sold
Terms	How did the customer pay
Colour	Colour of the car
Condition	Condition of car
Datebought	When car was bought
Boughtfor	Price car was bought for
Mileage	Mileage when bought
Notes1	Free text
Notes2	Free text

Table 2.11 Columns in the **Sales** table

sqlturbo), but it is not yet part of ANSI standard SQL so it is not actually implemented by Informix yet, but it will be included in some future release of the Informix range of products.

2.6.6 The Sales table

The **Sales** table is a record of the cars which have been sold by ABC Cars Ltd; it has the columns shown in Table 2.11. The information stored includes which car, what type it was, how much ABC Cars Ltd paid for it, how much the customer paid for it, when each event occurred and so on.

Much of the data is a copy of the information that was in the **Stock** table prior to the time the sale was made. The information here is rudimentary but allows the company to produce a basic analysis of the profits made on the sales. The **Terms** column indicates whether the customer paid in cash, or with Access or Barclaycard, or under the terms of a hire-purchase agreement arranged by ABC Cars Ltd. Note that this table cannot make the assumption that any given car registration is unique: ABC Cars Ltd might sell the same car on several different occasions. This table does assume that the same car would not be sold twice in one day – not unreasonable since the sales and stock data might well be checked for consistency at the end of the day (or overnight), and the sale would not be regarded as permanent until this night-time job had been run.

This table has two foreign keys; it cross-references two tables. The **Sales.Model** column cross-references the **Models.Model** column, and, as usual, the database is corrupt if any row in **Sales** has a value in the **Model** column which does not correspond to the model number of a row in **Models**. By the same token, if there is a row in **Sales** which has a value in the column **Customer** which does not occur in **Customers.Number**, the database is corrupt. It should not be possible to delete a row from either **Models** or **Customers** if there is a row in **Sales** which cross-references that row.

2.6.7 Points to note

The names of tables can be singular (**Model**) or plural (**Models**); sometimes scripts read better if the names are singular, sometimes if plural. In this book, the tables have been given plural names. Either naming convention can be used, but it is probably better to use singular names, if only because they are almost invariably shorter than the plural equivalents.

The naming of columns is generally easy, but you will perhaps have noticed that the company name column is not **Companies.Name**, nor is the model name column **Models.Name** when this is the obvious naming convention. Of itself, INFORMIX-SQL does not prohibit the use of these names, but this database is also intended to work with INFORMIX-4GL and NAME is a reserved word in INFORMIX-4GL. This means that if the company name was stored in **Companies.Name**, INFORMIX-4GL programs would not compile, hence the column names **Companies.Company** and **Models.Modelname**.

Where two tables join, the joining columns normally have the same name, so for example, **Models.Model** joins with **Prices.Model**, **Stock.Model** and **Sales.Model**. This is generally the best system for naming the fields. There is one exception to this rule in the **Cars** database: **Customers.Lastmodel** joins with **Models.Model**.

There are two other ways of naming the columns in a table. One of these is to give all the columns in any table a two- or three-character prefix which identifies the table, followed by a name which is mnemonic for what the column contains. Thus, the columns in the **Models** table could have the prefix 'mo', while the columns in the **Stock** table could have the prefix 'st', and so on. This technique more or less had to be used with INFORMIX 3.3 since every column in the database had to have a unique name, and many databases which have since been converted to INFORMIX-SQL retain this naming convention.

The other way of naming columns (which works best when the table names are singular rather than plural) is to make the name of the serial column **Model.Number**, for example, so that **Stock.Model** cross-references **Model.Number**. On small databases where much effort is spent in getting the names correct, this can be very effective, but experience shows that it is both difficult to get the names correct and it tends to lead to confusion (even anarchy) in a large database, partly because the cross-referencing columns are frequently given inconsistent mnemonics. Because of these dangers, this technique is not recommended.

It is important to note that not all fields with the same name join, so **Sales.Notes1** does not join with **Stock.Notes1**, nor with **Companies.Notes1**, nor with **Models.Notes1**. Nevertheless, fields with the same name generally store the same sort of data, so all the fields called **Notes1** have a similar purpose – to allow the user to make comments about an entry.

Column Name	Nulls?	Purpose
Number	No	Serial number for address
Building	Yes	Name of building
Street	No	Address within street
District	Yes	Area smaller than post town
Town	No	Main post town
Region	No	Area larger than post town
Postcode	Yes	Postcode, zip code, etc
Country	No	Country

Table 2.12 A schema for addresses

The **Stock** and **Sales** tables contain very similar information – the **Sales** table contains all the information in the **Stock** table as well as some extra information relating to the date of sale and so on. It would be possible to combine these tables into one provided two conditions were met. First, the columns which cannot be filled in until a sale is made would have to allow null values (a null value indicates that the value is unknown), and second, there would need to be a way of handling the possibility that a particular car may be sold several times. The existing primary key on the **Sales** table would not do, so the simplest solution would be to add a stock item number to the combined record which would be the primary key of the new table. If this scheme was adopted, the users would regularly want to know which cars were in stock. A relational database provides a facility called a *view* which allows the database designer to create an object which looks like a table but which restricts the rows and columns of a table which the user can see. If the **Sales** and **Stock** tables were combined, it would be useful to have a view defined which only showed the cars still on the forecourt.

There are a couple of repeating structures in the tables, the most striking example being the fields **Address1 .. Postcode** in both the **Customers** and the **Companies** tables. There is a further problem with these addresses; it is almost impossible to do any geographical analysis because the fields have no particular meaning. Some instances of **Address3** in the example database have as many as three lots of data in them: the major postal town, the county and the country. An alternative scheme for handling addresses is to create a table with its own serial column which stores nothing but addresses. A suitable schema for this is shown in Table 2.12. The **Building** field contains the name of the building, as distinct from the number in the street – it is optional. The **Street** field would contain the number of the building and the name of the street, and it is mandatory. The **District** is optional and often omitted; it is the part of the town (or the village) where the address is found. The **Town** column stores the main postal town and is mandatory. The **Region** is a county in the UK; it would be a state in the USA, *département* in France and so on. The **Postcode** is whatever is used to speed mail on its way; it has to be optional because not everyone knows their postcode. The **Country** would probably be coded and would be given a suitable default value. The scheme outlined is flexible; it is occasionally necessary to twist the meanings of the **Building**, **Street** and **District** columns, but the others do not cause trouble. The address table can be extended to contain phone, telex and fax numbers if required.

Every table that needs to store an address now stores the serial number of the address record which actually contains the required address. There is one major advantage to this: all tables have exactly the same address structure. This means that the manufacturers, clients and everybody are put on the same basis. If the application was written using INFORMIX-4GL, it should definitely also use a standard function to create and validate new addresses.

This scheme was not adopted in the **Cars** database for the simple reason that it would have made the examples more complicated than was necessary. However, in a working database where there is a requirement for geographical analysis of addresses, a scheme of this sort is probably necessary because it imposes uniformity on the addresses.

2.7 Summary

This chapter has explained the basic ideas behind a relational database and pointed you in the direction of some books which will explain a lot more about relational databases. It has described the **Cars** database which will be used for most of the examples in this book. It is important that you become familiar with this database and, in particular, the interconnections between the tables. Note that virtually all the meaningful connections have been described. (There is a sort of connection between the **Stock** and **Sales** tables because they contain very similar information.) A relational database system does not stop you making meaningless connections, such as connecting the columns **Prices.Model** and **Customers.Customer**; it is up to you to know which connections are sensible. As an aid, Appendix B contains a complete description of the tables used in the **Cars** database.

The rest of this book will demonstrate how to build the **Cars** database, how to create screen forms to enter data into the database and retrieve data from the database, how to write reports to summarize the state of the business and how to piece it all together to build a menu-driven application.

Part II
Basic INFORMIX-SQL

3
Creating a database

This chapter has two main parts. The first describes the basic use of INFORMIX-SQL and, in particular, the environment variables that must be set up before the product can be used. For some people, this information will be crucial – they are in charge of the machine and need to set it up correctly. For others, this information can be largely ignored because the system administrator has already done the necessary work. It also includes a description of the INFORMIX-SQL main menu and the options available from it.

The remainder of the chapter covers some necessary background information which you need to be aware of as a preliminary to building a database, followed by two methods for creating a database. One of these methods is essentially interactive and is very useful for novice users of INFORMIX-SQL, whereas the other uses the SQL language in a batch mode of operation and is generally preferred by more experienced users, particularly if the database is going to be rebuilt periodically. The chapter finishes up with some miscellaneous operations on a database, such as how to load data into the database and how to check how much data is in the database.

3.1 Setting up INFORMIX-SQL

The method of installing INFORMIX-SQL is described in Section 16.4; this chapter assumes that the software is installed on your system. There are four environment variables which may need to be set up in order for INFORMIX-SQL to work correctly. Two of these are general-purpose variables (PATH and TERM) which *must* be set correctly; the other two, INFORMIXDIR and INFORMIXTERM, are specific to Informix products and can often be left unset. There are also several other environment variables which affect the behaviour of INFORMIX-SQL, all of which have names which start with the letters 'DB'. These are discussed fully in Chapter 16; you may like to look ahead and see what DBMONEY and DBDATE do.

If you use any programs other than Informix which use the full screen and you are working on UNIX, the TERM environment variable will almost certainly be set up already. This means that you can ignore the section on the TERM environment variable. Unless you are using version 4.00, you can also ignore the section on INFORMIXTERM. The information in this section is rather detailed because it is crucial to getting the system to work at all, but once it is working correctly, you can forget it until you get a new terminal or operating system.

3.1.1 INFORMIXDIR

The first step towards using INFORMIX-SQL is to know where the programs are stored. All the programs distributed with INFORMIX-SQL (or any other members of the Informix family) are stored in a set of sub-directories under one parent directory. Unless it is told otherwise, INFORMIX-SQL assumes that the parent directory is /usr/informix on UNIX (C:\informix on DOS). If the product has been installed somewhere else (eg /u/informix), then INFORMIX-SQL *must* be told by setting the environment variable INFORMIXDIR so that it contains the name of the parent directory where the Informix products are installed.

How is this set? It depends...

It depends on which operating system you are using, and if you are using UNIX, it also depends on which shell you are using. If you are using UNIX and either the Bourne shell (**sh**) or the Korn shell (**ksh**), the syntax is:

```
INFORMIXDIR=/u/informix; export INFORMIXDIR
```

If you are using the C shell (**csh**), the syntax is:

```
setenv INFORMIXDIR /u/informix
```

If you are using DOS (MS-DOS or PC-DOS), the syntax is:

```
set INFORMIXDIR=C:\u\informix
```

Hereafter, all the examples will only be expressed in terms of the Bourne/Korn shell syntax. It is a nuisance to have to do this manually every time you use INFORMIX-SQL, so if your system administrator does not set it for you, you should modify your .profile (**sh** or **ksh**) or .login (**csh**) or AUTOEXEC.BAT (DOS) to set it when you login on UNIX or boot the machine on DOS. This will apply to all the environment variables mentioned in this book.

Note: although INFORMIXDIR does not have to be set if INFORMIX-SQL was installed in the default location, it is a good idea to do so.

3.1.2 PATH

Setting INFORMIXDIR is the first crucial step to using INFORMIX-SQL. The second is to make sure that the command interpreter or shell knows where to look for the Informix commands. All the commands are stored in $INFORMIXDIR/bin (eg /u/informix/bin), and the shell must be told to look in that directory too by adding the directory to the path, or the list of places where the shell looks for commands. The reliable way to do that is to add $INFORMIXDIR/bin to the path if INFORMIXDIR is set to a non-null string; otherwise, add /usr/informix/bin to the path. In the Bourne shell, this translates to:

```
PATH=$PATH:${INFORMIXDIR:-/usr/informix}/bin; export PATH
```

3.1.3 INFORMIXTERM

Version 4.00. In common with most UNIX-based products, INFORMIX-SQL will work with almost any type of terminal, provided that it is told which terminal you are using and which control sequences clear the screen, move the cursor, change into reverse video, and so on. There are two systems for telling programs about which control sequences do which jobs. One version is called **termcap** and is used on older versions of UNIX (prior to UNIX System V) and on versions derived from BSD (Berkeley) UNIX. The other system is called **terminfo** and is used on UNIX System V systems. The two systems are closely related even though they differ in detail.

   Prior to version 4.00, all Informix products used the **termcap** system regardless of whether the version of UNIX normally used **termcap** or **terminfo**. Version 4.00 will use **termcap** unless told otherwise. If you have version 4.00 and wish to use **terminfo** instead of **termcap**, you must set the environment variable INFORMIXTERM:

```
INFORMIXTERM=terminfo; export INFORMIXTERM
```

3.1.4 TERM

As well as telling Informix which system of terminal handling it should use, you must also explicitly tell it which type of terminal you are using. For example, if you are using a Wyse 50 terminal, set the TERM variable using:

```
TERM=wy50; export TERM
```

For INFORMIX-SQL to work, you must set TERM to an appropriate value. INFORMIX-SQL will let you know if it cannot find a description for your terminal. If you have any difficulty, consult your system administrator; if you are the system administrator, consult Section 16.1 for more details, or your operating system manuals, terminal manuals, Strang (1989) or your supplier.

3.2 Using INFORMIX-SQL

With INFORMIXDIR, PATH, INFORMIXTERM and TERM set correctly, it is possible to use INFORMIX-SQL. The program which will be used most frequently (by a large margin) is called **isql**. This is a menu-driven program which allows the user to use almost all the facilities provided by INFORMIX-SQL. In this book, it will normally be referred to as ISQL.

```
INFORMIX-SQL:  [Form] Report Query-Language User-menu Database Table Exit
Run, Modify, Create, or Drop a form.

--------------------------------------------- Press CTRL-W for Help --------
```

Figure 3.1 The INFORMIX-SQL main menu

To run this program, simply type **isql** at the command-line prompt:

```
$ isql
```

When the program is run, it first produces a screen which identifies the product, version and serial number, and then it offers the ring menu shown in Figure 3.1.

3.2.1 Ring menus

The menu shown in Figure 3.1 is a ring menu. In case you have not seen one of these before (they are used in Lotus 1-2-3, to name one among many other products), a ring menu shows its options on one line. The letters at the left-hand end identify the menu. One of the options is highlighted, shown by the square brackets '[ ]' in the figure; this is the option which would be selected if the RETURN key is hit. The description on the second line summarizes what the option will do. The highlight can be moved by using the space bar, the arrow keys or the backspace key. If you keep hitting the space bar, the highlight will move round to the **Exit** option and then flip back to the **Form** option, and if you go backwards from the **Form** option, the highlight will jump to the **Exit** option; it is as if the options form a loop or ring – hence the name 'ring menu'.

As well as moving the highlight and hitting RETURN, there is another mechanism for choosing options. Each option starts with a different letter and by typing the initial letter (it doesn't matter whether you use an upper-case or lower-case letter), you can select any option without using the arrow keys to highlight the option. This is a very useful shorthand technique, and most experienced users use it continually. In almost every menu, there is an **Exit** option. This is useful because it is consistent: typing a sequence of 'E's will normally get you out of the program you are in.

There are two other important keys used in INFORMIX-SQL. The ESCAPE key (ESC, also known as the ACCEPT key) is used to terminate input. There are many places where this is used. It always means that what has been entered is correct. The other important key is the INTERRUPT key. This is normally the DELETE (DEL) key on UNIX and CONTROL-C on DOS. This is used to stop something if you have made an error.

There are many places where help is available; when help is available, the CONTROL-W key is used to show the help information. This takes the form of a full page of help which overwrites what was on the screen, and it has a menu at the top which offers the options **Screen** and **Resume**. If there is more than one page of help, the **Screen** option will show the next page, and while there is more help, this will be the default option. The **Resume** option cancels any remaining help and returns you to whatever you were doing. There can be no harm in asking for help; at worst the program will beep at you.

One other facility which is occasionally useful is that CONTROL-R redraws the screen; if it has got scrambled, typing CONTROL-R normally sorts it out again.

3.2.2 The INFORMIX-SQL main menu options

After that digression on what a ring menu is, we can look at the options on the main menu. The menu shown in Figure 3.1 is for INFORMIX-SQL versions 2.00 and later; the main menu for INFORMIX-SQL version 1.10 was very different and is illustrated in Section 16.6.

The **Form** option is used to run forms and to create or modify them. It leads to a sub-menu which is described in detail in Chapter 4. Forms are used to enter data into the database, to modify or delete data already in the database, and to make *ad hoc* enquiries.

The **Report** option is similar to the **Form** option except that it works with reports. Reports are used to produce neatly formatted enquiries, which implies that the enquiries are not *ad hoc*. The sub-menu is discussed in detail in Chapter 6.

The **Query-Language** option allows the user to make enquiries on the database using SQL, or to do any other operation supported by SQL, which means that databases can be created and destroyed and tables added or deleted, permissions granted and so on. The sub-menu is discussed briefly in this chapter and in detail in Chapter 5.

The **User-Menu** option allows the user to modify or run an application built solely out of INFORMIX-SQL commands or programs (though non-Informix commands could be used if required). This is discussed in Chapter 10. The **Database** option is used to choose a database to work with, or to create or destroy one. It is discussed later in this chapter.

The **Table** option is used to create, modify or destroy tables in a database; it too is discussed later in this chapter.

The **Exit** option hardly needs explaining: it will stop ISQL running and leave you with the operating system prompt.

3.3 The steps in creating a database

The sequence of steps used to build a database is fairly clearly defined:

1. Design the database.
2. Create an empty database.
3. Create the tables in the database.
4. Load any fixed data into the database.
5. Create the indexes on the tables.

6. Grant database users the necessary permissions.
7. Start the transaction log or audit trails.
8. Back up the initial database.
9. Release the database for use.

Some of these steps are more important than others, while some steps can be (and often are) omitted. The order of some of the steps can be varied.

The first step in building a database is to design it. The design is crucial to the success of the database, and the importance of making sure that the design is both reasonably complete and flexible cannot be overemphasized. New tables can be added without affecting existing software, minor details such as the length of character fields can be adjusted after the initial design without difficulty, and adding extra columns to a table does not cause much trouble; but, if the structure of the database must be changed so that the tables are connected in different ways from the original design, you will have to do a lot of work to get the database operational again, with much of the time spent altering or recreating the forms and reports. With INFORMIX-SQL, it is almost possible to design the database as you build it, but this cannot be done reliably without considerable experience, and those with sufficient experience normally design the database on paper first to make sure that they know what they are doing. Chapter 2 considered the design of the **Cars** database in some detail; this chapter only illustrates how to turn the outline design of a table into a table in the database.

After the database has been designed, you must create an empty database and then build some or all of the tables that go in it. You can create the indexes on each table immediately after you create the table, but, if the database has any data to be loaded, it is usually quicker to load the tables before creating the indexes. Steps 6–8 are often treated very casually; they will not be discussed again until Chapters 14 and 15. The last step is normally trivial; the database is made available for use when the program that created it stops running. It may be necessary to set the UNIX permissions to let other people get at the database; again, see Chapter 14 for information on both Informix and UNIX permissions.

One of the biggest advantages of a relational database (compared with other types of database) is that it can be designed and built in stages. It is possible to create the database and the first few tables and put that version of the database into general use. Some time later, extra tables can be added without any difficulty and the existing tables can normally be modified without affecting anything except the forms and reports which use the modified tables.

3.4 Building the database

There are two main ways of building a database. The interactive method is especially useful for novice users because it requires no knowledge of the syntax of SQL. It uses a completely menu-driven system for defining (and editing) the structure of the database tables.

```
DATABASE: Select  Create  Drop [Exit]
Return to the INFORMIX-SQl Main Menu.

--------------------- cars ----------------- Press CTRL-W for Help --------
```

Figure 3.2 After creating or selecting a database

However, experienced users generally find that the batch method using SQL is preferable because the scripts developed can be reused to rebuild a database, whereas to rebuild a database of, say, 100 tables using the interactive method would be unbearably tedious. Additionally, the scripts can be used to form part of the documentation of the database; they can have comments in them about the primary keys and foreign keys, and also information about the ranges of acceptable values in a column and so on.

The remainder of this section describes how to create the database itself; it also introduces the SQL menu and discusses what a database looks like when the standard operating system tools are used to look at it. Section 3.5 describes how to convert the outline design of a table such as those in Chapter 2 into a complete table description, and how to create the table using either the schema editor or SQL.

3.4.1 Creating the database interactively

The simplest way to create a database is to use the **Database** option from the ISQL main menu. This menu offers the options shown in Figure 3.2: **Select**, **Create**, **Drop** and **Exit**. When **Create** is chosen, the database name should be entered and ISQL will create the database. This takes a little while, so ISQL prints a message:

```
Running . . .
```

at the bottom of the screen. When the database is created, it is selected as the current database and ISQL will use this database until told to change. The name of the current database is shown on the screen as illustrated in Figure 3.2.

The **Select** option is used to make an existing database the current database. ISQL will show the list of databases it can find, but you can also enter the full path name of a database that it cannot otherwise see.

The **Drop** option is used to delete a database and all the data in it. Although only authorized people (such as the person who created it) can drop a database, and although it asks you to confirm that this is what you intend to do, it is an option that is seldom used because of the danger it represents. If you are using INFORMIX-TURBO or INFORMIX-ONLINE, you can only drop a database using this option or the equivalent SQL statement:

```
DROP DATABASE cars;
```

```
RDSQL:  [New] Run  Modify  Use-Editor  Output  Choose  Save  Info  Drop  Exit
Enter new RDSQL statements using the RDSQL editor.

---------------------- cars ------------------- Press CTRL-W for Help --------
```

Figure 3.3 The **Query-Language** menu

but most experienced people who wish to drop an INFORMIX-SE database use the raw UNIX command to achieve the same effect:

    rm -fr cars.dbs

3.4.2 The SQL menu

The previous section discussed creating the database interactively; this section describes how to create the database using SQL and the batch mode of operation. The database and its tables may be created using the **Query-Language** option of the main menu. The menu shown in Figure 3.3 is correct for versions prior to version 4.00. For version 4.00, the menu title changed from RDSQL to SQL.

One of two options can be used to create an SQL script file, namely **New** or **Use-Editor**. If **New** is chosen, the built-in editor will be used, which is not very powerful but is very convenient. The built-in editor has two modes of operation, namely overwrite mode, in which what you type replaces what is already on the screen, and insert mode, where the characters you type are placed before the cursor, moving the other characters along the line. The CONTROL-A key is used to toggle between the overwrite and insert modes, with the editor starting off in overwrite mode. The cursor keys can be used to move the cursor around. The CONTROL-X key deletes the character under the cursor; the CONTROL-D key deletes all the text from the cursor up to the end of the line. Typing CONTROL-X after the last character on a line deletes the newline and joins the next line to the current line. There is no input wrapping at the end of a line. The ESC key is used to terminate an editing session.

If **Use-Editor** is chosen, you will be asked to specify which editor you wish to use. One of the system editors will be offered as the default: on UNIX, the default is usually **vi**, on DOS, it is **edlin**. You may use any editor you wish, but it must accept the name of the file to be edited as a command-line argument.

An SQL script file consists of one or more SQL statements separated by semicolons. The layout of the statements is free: spaces, tabs and newlines can be mixed at will. The text can be in any mixture of upper and lower case, but one good convention is to use upper case for SQL keywords and lower case for table names and column names. Another frequently used convention is to use lower case for everything. The convention used in this book is to use upper case for keywords and an initial capital letter for table names and column names.

When the SQL script is finished, exit from the editor (remembering to save the file) and use the **Run** option to run the script. As the script is run, each completed statement will be identified at the bottom of the screen with messages such as 'Table created'. If there are any errors, use either the **Modify** or the **Use-Editor** option to edit the script. The script will contain the error message, which can be deleted if you wish; however, it need not be removed since ISQL will remove the error message automatically. If you use the built-in editor, the help system can give you guidelines on the correct syntax for a statement. The full workings of the **Query-Language** option are discussed in Chapter 5.

Beware: if the script creates several tables and there is an error in one of the later SQL statements, you should convert those statements which have succeeded into comments. Comments are pieces of text enclosed by braces '{}', a style of comment that can extend over several lines if necessary.

```
{ This is a .sql file comment }
```

The error can then be corrected and the script run again. When it is all working correctly, the comments can be removed and the script saved. The name you type in response to the prompt will be given the extension '.sql'.

Version 4.00. There are two additional types of comments, both of which make the text from the starting symbol up to the end of the line into a comment. One type is started by the hash character '#', while the other type, which is the ANSI standard type, is started by the two characters '--'.

```
#  In version 4.00, this is a comment.
-- This is also a comment in version 4.00.
```

3.4.3 Creating a database using SQL

The syntax of the SQL statement for creating a database is illustrated by:

```
CREATE DATABASE Cars;
```

If the database is created successfully, that database will be the current database and will continue to be the current database until it is closed or the program stops. As with the interactive method of creating a database, the name of the current database is shown on the same line as the 'CTRL-W for help' message.

This simple statement can be used to illustrate the point made earlier that the language is case-insensitive except inside quoted strings, and that spaces are not significant except inside quoted strings. This means that the above statement could have been typed as:

```
cReAte
          dAtabaSE
cARS;
```

and it would have exactly the same effect as the previous statement. Also, the semi-colon ';' is optional when a single statement is being executed. However, if several statements are being executed, the statements must be separated by semicolons.

3.4.4 Selecting a database

When the database you wish to work with already exists, you can make it the current database by executing the command:

```
DATABASE Cars;
```

This will work whether there is a database active or not. You should generally close the current database before changing to the new one, although it is not absolutely necessary unless the database is on a remote machine.

```
CLOSE DATABASE;
DATABASE Other_cars;
```

If you ever wish to work on a database and ensure that no one else is using it at the same time, you can use a variant form of the DATABASE statement:

```
DATABASE Cars EXCLUSIVE;
```

This will fail if anyone else is already using the database, but once you have executed this statement, no one else can use the database until you close it again, or until you stop using it and terminate ISQL.

3.4.5 What is an Informix database?

Standard Engine. Now that you have seen the two methods of creating a database, what is it that has been created? The operating system sees an Informix database as a collection of C-ISAM data and index files contained in a directory. The directory name consists of the database name you specified followed by the extension '.dbs'. On UNIX, the database name can be up to 10 characters long, whereas on DOS, the limit is eight characters. The characters in the name should be alphabetic or numeric, and the first character should be alphabetic. If the name is specified in upper case, ISQL will convert the name to lower case. This book will be using a database called **Cars** for its examples, so the database directory will be:

```
cars.dbs
```

The database directory will contain a number of C-ISAM files, each of which consists of a pair of operating system files. Each pair of files represents a table in the database and consists of a '.idx' file and a '.dat' file with the same prefix. (The extensions are normally pronounced as *dot-eye-dee-ex* and *dot-dat*.) The '.dat' file contains the data records; the '.idx' file contains information about the structure of the file as well as index information which allows INFORMIX-SE to find records more quickly than it would by scanning the data file sequentially.

Even an empty database contains a number of tables which hold the information about the tables in the database, the columns in those tables, who is allowed to use the database and so on. These tables are called the *system catalogue*. All these tables have names starting with *sys*, and their names are shown below. The four files marked with a dagger '†' are new with version 4.00.

```
syscolauth.dat      syscolauth.idx
syscolumns.dat      syscolumns.idx
sysindexes.dat      sysindexes.idx
systabauth.dat      systabauth.idx
systables.dat       systables.idx
sysdepend.dat       sysdepend.idx
syssynonym.dat      syssynonym.idx
sysusers.dat        sysusers.idx
sysviews.dat        sysviews.idx
sysconstra.dat†     sysconstra.idx†
syssyntabl.dat†     syssyntabl.idx†
```

As well as the system catalogue files, there will be one C-ISAM file for each table in the database. The name of the table must not be longer than 18 characters. On UNIX, the names of the C-ISAM files consist of the first seven characters of the table name followed by a three-digit serial number; on DOS, the file name is five characters plus a three-digit number. The serial number is used to identify the table throughout the system catalogue, with the numbers for user tables starting at 100. If the table name has fewer than seven characters, such as the table **Stock** in the **Cars** database, the name is padded with underscore characters:

```
stock__103.dat      stock__103.idx
```

OnLine. The INFORMIX-ONLINE and INFORMIX-TURBO database engines store all the data for a database in the chunks of disk allocated to it, but there are no visible files for the user to examine. Internally, there are some similarities to the way the data is organized (there are recognizable index and data pages), but there are also many major differences.

3.5 Creating a table

In Chapter 2, the skeletal structure of the **Models** table was given in Table 2.7, which is repeated in Table 3.1 overleaf. The detailed structure of the table must now be specified in terms that INFORMIX-SQL can understand. This means specifying the data type of each column, whether a column will allow the user to omit data when adding a new row to the table and which columns should be indexed. To be able to do this, we must know something about what data types are available, what nulls are and which columns should be indexed.

3.5.1 Data types

Each column in each table in the database stores data of one type. As the type must be specified when the table is created, you need to know something about these types before trying to build the database. INFORMIX-SQL recognizes a large number of data types. This section only covers the simpler data types, all of which are available

Column Name	Purpose
Model	Identifying number
Maker	Company making model
Modelname	Generic name of model
Details	Details of model
Price	List price for new car
Maxspeed	Maximum speed (mph)
Accel	Time to accelerate from 0–60 mph
Enginesize	Nominal engine size (cc)
Urban	Fuel consumption – simulated urban
Mpgat56	Fuel consumption – steady 56 mph
Tanksize	Tank capacity (gallons)

Table 3.1 Columns in the **Models** table

with both INFORMIX-SE and INFORMIX-ONLINE, and with all the versions of the product. All the data types, including the more complex ones and the new ones made available with version 4.00, are described fully in Section 14.1.

CHAR

The CHAR data type is used to store text: names, alpha-numeric codes and similar things. The maximum number of characters to be stored in a CHAR column is fixed when the table is created and must be specified in parentheses – CHAR(20). The maximum permitted number of characters in one string is 32767. The CHAR(1) data type is frequently used to store flag values as it uses less disk space than even a small integer.

INTEGER and SMALLINT

The INTEGER and SMALLINT data types are used for storing whole numbers. An INTEGER uses 4 bytes of disk space and can store values in the range -2147483647 .. 2147483647. Similarly, a SMALLINT uses 2 bytes of disk space and can store values in the range -32767 .. 32767.

SERIAL

The SERIAL type is a special case of INTEGER. When the value zero is inserted into a SERIAL column, the value actually stored is one greater than the maximum number previously inserted into the table. It is possible to specify the first serial number to be assigned to a SERIAL column by enclosing the number for the first row in parentheses – SERIAL(1000). A SERIAL column gives a simple way of generating a unique number for each row of data. It is, of course, possible to insert a value other than zero (but not by using PERFORM – only by using SQL); if this happens, the value is stored in the SERIAL column unchanged, and if the number is higher than the previous maximum value, the maximum value is changed accordingly. The schema editor (see Section 3.5.5) ensures that the numbers stored in a SERIAL column are unique within the table by creating an index which prohibits duplicate entries. If you create a table using SQL, you should create a UNIQUE INDEX on the SERIAL column. There can only be one SERIAL column in any one table.

DECIMAL and MONEY

The DECIMAL and MONEY types are used for storing floating-point values to a guaranteed accuracy. Internally, they use the same data type, but PERFORM and ACE both display a MONEY column with a currency symbol whereas a DECIMAL column is displayed as a pure number.

The DECIMAL and MONEY types can have a precision and scale specified using the notation DECIMAL(p, s), where p represents the precision and s the scale. The scale is optional. The precision is the number of decimal digits preserved, while the scale is the number of digits after the decimal point. Note that the precision is the total number of digits preserved, including those after the decimal point. One very common mistake is to think that DECIMAL(6,2) can store all values less than one million; it can only store values less than ten thousand. The maximum number of digits is 32, with the default being 16. If no scale is specified, the number is floating point rather than fixed point. The default scale for MONEY is 2 – that is, there are two digits after the decimal point. Section 14.1 discusses the FLOAT and SMALLFLOAT types which can also be used to store floating-point numbers.

DATE

The DATE type should be used whenever dates are stored. INFORMIX-SQL provides a powerful collection of facilities for formatting and converting dates when needed. A DATE is stored internally as an INTEGER (actually the number of days since 31 December 1899, so that 1 January 1900 is day 1), and therefore occupies 4 bytes of disk space. (There is a DATETIME type available with version 4.00 which can store both a date and a time in a single column – see Section 14.1.)

3.5.2 Nulls

In INFORMIX-SQL (and in ANSI standard SQL), there is the concept of a *null* data value. A null data value can be stored in a database column and means that either the value that belongs in the column is unknown or that the value is not applicable to the particular row of data. For example, if the database stored information about employees, there would be a null value stored in the leaving date column for all the current employees.

When nulls are stored in a table, it can be more difficult to retrieve data from the database because selection criteria have to allow for the possibility that a column may store nulls. On the other hand, if nulls are not allowed, a value may have to be specified to indicate that the data for this column is unknown. If the database was collecting market intelligence about contracts won by competitors, for example, the chances are that much of the information would be missing. If some columns did not allow null values, it would be difficult to enter any intelligence data.

When a table is created, each column in the table can allow or disallow nulls to be stored, independently of whether any other column allows nulls or not. In general terms, it is better not to allow nulls if possible, but when the data to be entered will not always be known, or if a column like the employee's leaving date is included in the table, nulls have to be allowed.

There is a further discussion of nulls in Section 8.4 on the SELECT statement. The references Date (1986), Date (1989) and Codd (1990) all have extensive discussions on nulls, although the conclusions reached by Date and Codd are somewhat different.

3.5.3 Indexes

Indexing is a complicated subject which is covered in outline here and in more detail in Section 14.4. There are two main reasons for creating indexes on a table. One reason is to ensure that there are no rows of data in a particular table with duplicate values in a particular column (or set of columns). This type of index is called a *unique* index (because the SQL statement to create such an index starts CREATE UNIQUE INDEX). Every table has a primary key – there cannot be two rows in the table with the same set of values in the columns which form the primary key – so each table should have at least one unique index on it to enforce the uniqueness of the primary key. In version 4.00, you can use a UNIQUE CONSTRAINT instead. See Section 14.6 for more information on these.

The other reason for using indexes is to improve performance. An INFORMIX-SQL database will work without any indexes on any of the tables, but it will also be unbearably slow unless the database is trivially small. Indexes are used to speed up the search process on tables, but they occupy extra disk space, and every time a row of data changes, the index file has to be kept accurate as well as the data file, which slows down any operation that changes the data in the table. (This loss of speed is small and is normally more than outweighed by the extra speed of retrieving the data.) The guidelines given by Informix for creating indexes are:

- Index columns which are used in many enquiries.
- Index columns used to order a report.
- Index columns used in join operations.
- Index only tables of more than 200 rows.

In Chapter 14, there is a more detailed discussion of how the database agent makes use of indexes. Note that because primary keys are used in most joining operations, it is a good idea to create an index on them because it both enforces the uniqueness of the primary key and speeds up enquiries. Similarly, but less importantly, indexes on foreign keys can help speed up enquiries. It is unusual for the index on a foreign key column to be unique.

The argument for only having indexes on large tables is that it takes time to open and use an index, and if the table is small, this time offsets the speed advantage of the index. However, this ignores the use of indexes to enforce uniqueness. Even small tables need a unique index on their primary key (unless you can guarantee that the data does not change, or that when it does change, the person changing it knows that duplicate entries must be avoided).

When you are creating a table, you should create a unique index on the primary key and a duplicates (non-unique) index on any foreign key columns (those which will be used in joining to other tables). You may also decide to create indexes on the columns most likely to be searched in enquiries – columns such as **Companies.Company** and **Models.Modelname**. Most tables will only need two or three indexes; simple definition tables usually only need one.

Indexes can be added to or removed from the database at any stage in the life of the database, so it is not necessary to create an index as the database is being created. It is generally better to regard the indexes created when you create the table as permanent indexes, but remember that extra indexes can be added later if they turn out to be necessary. Superfluous indexes can also be removed later if required. If data has to be loaded into the database, it will generally speed things up if you create the skeletal table, load the data into the table and only then create the indexes.

3.5.4 Design of the Models table

Given this information, we can now design in detail the **Models** table. For example, the **Model** column is to be the primary key and is to be an identifying number; this makes it a natural candidate for being the SERIAL in this table. It will not allow nulls and will need a unique index on it. The **Maker** column is a foreign key which references the **Companies** table, which means that the column should have the same type as the primary key of the **Companies** table. That column will itself be SERIAL, and a column which cross-references a SERIAL should always have the type INTEGER. Since the column is involved in joins, there should be an index on it, but the index must allow duplicates because the **Models** table will contain several entries for each manufacturer. The **Modelname** column needs to contain text so it will be a CHAR field; we will choose to allow 20 characters for this. This field will be frequently searched (every time we need to know about a particular model), so it too should be indexed with a duplicates index. None of these three columns can accept nulls: every model must have a number and a maker, and we must give every model some sort of name.

The **Details** column is also going to be a CHAR field for which we will allow 40 characters. This field will not be searched so often, so it will not be indexed. Note that this will not stop us from searching for all the cars with the letters 'GL' in the **Details** column; it just means that some of these enquiries may not be as efficient as they would be if the column was indexed. The list price for a car is a monetary value, so the column should be a MONEY value; we are not going to worry about pennies, so the scale can be zero, and the cars we deal with are unlikely to exceed £999 999, so the precision can be set at six digits. The maximum speed is a numeric quantity, but is only quoted to the nearest mile per hour, so it can be an integer quantity. As cars do not reach 30 000 mph, this column can be a SMALLINT. The **Accel** column is the time taken to reach 60 mph from standing still; this will be about 10 seconds and is often quoted to the nearest tenth of a second, so this should be a DECIMAL(3,1) column. The tank size is quoted in gallons and tenths of gallons, and should have the same type as **Accel**. The fuel consumption figures are quoted in

Table: Models			
Column Name	**Type**	**Index?**	**Nulls?**
Model	SERIAL(1)	Unique	No
Maker	INTEGER	Duplicates	No
Modelname	CHAR(20)	Duplicates	No
Details	CHAR(40)	No	Yes
Price	MONEY(6,0)	No	Yes
Maxspeed	SMALLINT	No	Yes
Accel	DECIMAL(3,1)	No	Yes
Tanksize	DECIMAL(3,1)	No	Yes
Urban	DECIMAL(3,1)	No	Yes
Mpgat56	DECIMAL(3,1)	No	Yes
Enginesize	SMALLINT	No	Yes

Table 3.2 Detailed design of the **Models** table

miles per gallon and can also have one decimal place; so far, cars do not achieve more than 100 mpg so, again, a DECIMAL(3,1) column can be used for these two columns. The engine size is always quoted to the nearest cubic centimetre, and there are no cars with 300 litre engines, so a SMALLINT will be able to hold the engine size. None of these fields needs an index unless it can be shown that such an index will speed up a number of enquiries, and all these columns can accept nulls. These decisions lead to the table design shown in Table 3.2.

3.5.5 Creating tables using the schema editor

Version 2.00 and later. There must be at least one table in the database before any useful data can be stored in it. The easiest way for a novice user to create tables is to exit from the **Database** menu and select the **Table** option from the main menu. This brings up the menu shown in Figure 3.4. The **Create** option is used to create a new table; the **Alter** option allows you to alter an existing table; the **Info** option allows you to discover which columns and indexes are present on the table, and what privileges different users have on the table; and the **Drop** option deletes a table and all its data (after you have confirmed that you intend to do so).

```
TABLE:  [Create] Alter  Info  Drop  Exit
Create a new table.

---------------------- cars ------------------ Press CTRL-W for Help --------
```

Figure 3.4 The **Table** menu

```
CREATE TABLE stock :  Add  Modify  Drop  Screen  Exit
Adds columns to the table above the line with the highlight.

----- Page 1 of 1 ----- cars ------------------ Press CTRL-W for Help --------

  Column Name                     Type           Length   Index   Nulls

  [registration      ]            Char                7   Unique  No
  model                           Integer                 Dups    No
  colour                          Char                8           Yes
  condition                       Char                1           Yes
  datebought                      Date                            No
  boughtfor                       Money             8,2           No
  mileage                         Integer                         Yes
  notes1                          Char               60           Yes
  notes2                          Char               60           Yes
```

Figure 3.5 The schema editor

When creating a table, you should choose the **Create** option. ISQL asks for a table name and then runs the schema editor. The schema editor offers the options shown in Figure 3.5, which shows the schema editor with a complete specification of the table **Stock**. You should select the **Add** option. You can now enter the details of the table you have designed. Each column will have a name and a type. The type is specified via a multi-level menu. For versions 2.00 and 2.10, the top level looks similar to that shown in Figure 3.6. With version 4.00, this menu is extended to include several extra options to cope with the extra types available with version 4.00. For details of these types, see Chapter 14. The changes to the menu are easily coped with. For any of the numeric types other than MONEY, choose the **Numeric** option, which brings up yet another sub-menu, offering the choice illustrated in Figure 3.7. If you choose the **Float** option, a final layer of menu gives a choice between FLOAT and SMALLFLOAT. To back out of one of these menus, hit the INTERRUPT key. For the CHAR, MONEY and DECIMAL types, you must specify the length of the column; the default length for a CHAR column is 20, the default precision for DECIMAL is 16 digits floating point and the default precision for MONEY is 16 digits with two decimal places. The starting number for a SERIAL column can be specified as something other than the default of 1.

The schema editor can create an index on any single column you tell it to, but it cannot create composite indexes on several columns at once. The indexes may be unique or they may allow duplicates. It is a good idea to put a unique index on the primary key of a table. If any of the indexes for the database must involve more than one column, these need to be created individually using the **Query-Language** option of the main menu; they cannot be created with the schema editor. It is also possible to specify that any column must have a value stored in it by specifying no nulls in the column on the schema editor. The screen in Figure 3.5 shows what the screen

```
ADD TYPE stock : [Char] Numeric  Serial  Date  Money
Permits any combination of letters, numbers, and symbols.

----- Page 1 of 1 ----- cars ------------------ Press CTRL-W for Help --------
```

Figure 3.6 Schema editor – types menu

```
ADD NUMERIC stock : [Integer] Smallint Decimal Float
Permits whole numbers in the approximate range -2 billion to 2 billion.

----- Page 1 of 1 ----- cars ------------------ Press CTRL-W for Help --------
```

Figure 3.7 Schema editor – numeric types menu

looked like when all the data for the **Stock** table was entered.

To get back to the first level of the schema editor menu, you need to hit the INTERRUPT key. To create the table, select the **Exit** option, which gives you a choice of **Build-new-table** and **Discard-new-table**. When the build option is chosen, ISQL creates the table. This process can be repeated for every table in the database.

Version 2.00 only. The schema editor asked for the name of a script file before it created the table, and it would save a copy of the statements used to create the table and its indexes in the file which started with the name you entered and ended with the extension '.ise'. In principle, this was a useful form of documentation; in practice, the documentation became obsolete as soon as the table was altered. With version 2.10 and later, there is a tool called **dbschema** (described in Section 16.5) which will produce the schema of a database from the information in the database, so the '.ise' files are no longer necessary and are no longer saved for the user.

3.5.6 Creating a table using SQL

Version 1.10. The schema editor was not available with this version, so all tables had to be created using SQL as described in this section.

The syntax of the SQL statement for creating a table is illustrated by:

```
CREATE TABLE Stock
(
        Registration      CHAR(7)        NOT NULL,
        Model             INTEGER        NOT NULL,
        Colour            CHAR(8),
        Condition         CHAR(1),
        Datebought        DATE           NOT NULL,
        Boughtfor         MONEY(8,2)     NOT NULL,
        Mileage           INTEGER,
        Notes1            CHAR(60),
        Notes2            CHAR(60)
);
```

The types used are those listed earlier (eg INTEGER, MONEY). The type may be followed by the keywords NOT NULL to indicate that a proper value must always be entered in this column.

3.5.7 Creating an index using SQL

The syntax of the SQL statement to create an index is illustrated by:

```
CREATE UNIQUE INDEX Pk_stock ON Stock(Registration);
CREATE INDEX F1_stock ON Stock(Model);
```

The index name you use is arbitrary but must be unique within the database. The only time you need to know the name of an index is when you want to delete the index later on. The section enclosed in parentheses is a list of one or more columns separated by commas. If there is more than one column, the index is called a *composite* index.

The optional keyword UNIQUE may be used between CREATE and INDEX, and disallows duplicate entries in the indexed columns. There should always be a unique index on a SERIAL column, and this must be created explicitly when using the batch method to create the database.

3.5.8 Loading data into the database

The normal way of adding data to a database is to enter the data manually using a screen form, which is the subject of the next chapter.

For an example database such as this one, there is already a certain amount of data available in ASCII text files. These were unloaded from an existing copy of the **Cars** database using the UNLOAD statement, which is described in Chapter 15. The LOAD command is used to load previously unloaded data back into a database table. This provides a way of restoring and transporting a database since the unloaded file is ASCII text. Alternatively, the data may have been generated from somewhere other than an Informix database, in which case it may be loaded into the INFORMIX-SQL database as long as it has the same format as an unloaded file.

An unloaded file contains one line of data for each row of data. A line consists of a sequence of fields delimited by a distinct character, which is by default the pipe '|' character. There must be one delimiter for each column in the table to be loaded, and if there is no value in a particular column, this is shown by two adjacent delimiters.

The syntax for the LOAD command is illustrated by:

```
LOAD FROM "stock.unl" INSERT INTO Stock;
```

Strictly, the file name should be enclosed in double quotes, but SQL does not object if they are missing. There is no rule about the extension used on the file name, but '.unl' is often used for an unloaded data file.

3.5.9 Checking the status of a table

The INFO statement allows various types of information pertaining to a table to be obtained. This may include such details as the structure of the table, the amount of data stored in the table, who is allowed to access the data and details of any indexes that have been created for the table. The SQL command to obtain information about the amount of data stored in a table is:

```
UPDATE STATISTICS;
INFO STATUS FOR Stock;
```

Alternatively, the same information may be obtained by selecting the **Info** option from the **Table** or **Query** menus.

In both cases, you should execute the UPDATE STATISTICS statement before obtaining the status information to ensure that the information returned is up to date. For example, if a LOAD statement is executed that causes 10 000 rows of new data to be inserted into a table, and it is immediately followed by an INFO statement, the information will not reflect the new number of rows in the table.

Various different forms of the INFO statement can be used to obtain other information. Instead of the word STATUS, the word COLUMNS would list the columns in the table, the word INDEXES would list the indexes on the table and the word PRIVILEGES would show who could do what to the table.

3.6 Summary

This chapter has covered a lot of material. Before INFORMIX-SQL can be used, there are a few environment variables that must be set up, and these were described, followed by how to run INFORMIX-SQL and how to use the main menu.

The rest of the chapter outlined how to build a database. It described both the interactive and batch methods of building a database. It explained how to convert the outline design of a table into a table schema which can be created in the database using either the interactive schema editor or SQL. This included a brief description of the available data types, the significance of nulls and why indexes are useful. It also explained how the operating system stores an σE database. The chapter finished with a brief description of how to load data into the database and how to check on the status of the database.

Exercises

No answers have been provided for these exercises.

1. Create a database called **Cars**.

2. Use the schema editor to create the **Companies** table with the schema shown below.

Table: Companies			
Column Name	**Type**	**Index?**	**Nulls?**
Maker	SERIAL(1)	Unique	No
Company	CHAR(15)	Duplicates	No
Address1	CHAR(25)	No	Yes
Address2	CHAR(25)	No	Yes
Address3	CHAR(25)	No	Yes
Postcode	CHAR(10)	No	Yes
Phone	CHAR(16)	No	Yes
Notes1	CHAR(60)	No	Yes
Notes2	CHAR(60)	No	Yes

3. Use an SQL script to create a table called **Stock** with columns as below:

Table: Stock			
Column Name	**Type**	**Index?**	**Nulls?**
Registration	CHAR(7)	Unique	No
Model	INTEGER	Duplicates	No
Colour	CHAR(8)	No	Yes
Condition	CHAR(1)	No	Yes
Datebought	DATE	No	No
Boughtfor	MONEY(8,2)	No	No
Mileage	INTEGER	No	Yes
Notes1	CHAR(60)	No	Yes
Notes2	CHAR(60)	No	Yes

4. Create the other tables in the database, **Customers, Models, Sales** and **Prices,** using either the schema editor or an SQL script as you prefer. There should be a composite unique index on the columns **Sales.Registration** and **Sales.Datesold,** and another on the columns **Prices.Model** and **Prices.Year_made**; you will have to create these using SQL.

Table: Prices			
Column Name	**Type**	**Index?**	**Nulls?**
Model	INTEGER	Duplicates	No
Year_made	SMALLINT	No	No
Lo_price	DECIMAL(6,0)	No	No
Hi_price	DECIMAL(6,0)	No	No

Table: Customers			
Column Name	**Type**	**Index?**	**Nulls?**
Number	SERIAL(1000)	Unique	No
Surname	CHAR(15)	Duplicates	No
Firstname	CHAR(10)	No	Yes
Salut	CHAR(5)	No	Yes
Address1	CHAR(25)	No	Yes
Address2	CHAR(25)	No	Yes
Address3	CHAR(25)	No	Yes
Postcode	CHAR(10)	No	Yes
Phone	CHAR(16)	No	Yes
Enquiry	CHAR(1)	No	No
Maxmoney	MONEY(6,0)	No	Yes
Lastmodel	INTEGER	No	Yes
Contactdate	DATE	No	Yes

Table: Models			
Column Name	**Type**	**Index?**	**Nulls?**
Model	SERIAL(1)	Unique	No
Maker	INTEGER	Duplicates	No
Modelname	CHAR(20)	Duplicates	No
Details	CHAR(40)	No	Yes
Price	MONEY(6,0)	No	Yes
Maxspeed	SMALLINT	No	Yes
Accel	DECIMAL(3,1)	No	Yes
Tanksize	DECIMAL(3,1)	No	Yes
Urban	DECIMAL(3,1)	No	Yes
Mpgat56	DECIMAL(3,1)	No	Yes
Enginesize	SMALLINT	No	Yes

Table: Sales			
Column Name	**Type**	**Index?**	**Nulls?**
Registration	CHAR(7)	Unique	No
Customer	INTEGER	Duplicates	No
Model	INTEGER	Duplicates	No
Soldfor	MONEY(8,2)	No	No
Datesold	DATE	No	No
Terms	CHAR(4)	No	No
Colour	CHAR(8)	No	Yes
Condition	CHAR(1)	No	Yes
Datebought	DATE	No	No
Boughtfor	MONEY(8,2)	No	No
Mileage	INTEGER	No	Yes
Notes1	CHAR(60)	No	Yes
Notes2	CHAR(60)	No	Yes

4

Perform screen forms

This is the first of three chapters on forms. It covers three main topics. The first describes how to generate a default form and also describes the options in the ISQL **Form** menu; the second discusses how to customize forms; and the third describes how to use a form.

This chapter only covers the simpler parts of form handling; Chapter 7 in Part III covers the multi-table forms and master/detail relationships, and Chapter 11 in Part IV covers anything not covered in the other two chapters. The forms in this chapter are exclusively single-table forms; they only manipulate the data from one table.

4.1 What is a form?

Forms are the primary method of interacting with a database. Forms can be used to add data to the database, to delete or amend data, and to make enquiries from the database without needing to know the database query language SQL. It is fair to say that most users of the database will spend more of their time using forms than any other single type of object in INFORMIX-SQL.

There are two programs which work directly with forms: FORMBUILD which compiles forms and PERFORM which runs them. Although most users will spend most of their time using PERFORM, most of the text in this book will be spent discussing the syntax and semantics of forms so that you, the reader, will be able to create useful forms for yourself and others to use. A form is created in a readable source file and then compiled into an interpretable object file. It is very easy to modify the layout of a form or to change the attributes of the data that may be entered via the form using any convenient text editor.

Physically, a form is stored in two files. The source file for a form will be given the extension '.per', while the compiled version will be given a '.frm' extension, so the source file for a form named customers would be contained in the file customers.per, and the object would be kept in a file called customers.frm.

```
FORM:  [Run]  Modify  Generate  New  Compile  Drop  Exit
Use a form to enter data or query a database.
---------------------- cars ------------------ Press CTRL-W for Help --------
```

Figure 4.1 The **Form** menu

4.2 The Form menu

Normally, ISQL is used to handle forms although it is possible to compile and run forms from the UNIX (or MS-DOS) command line. Assuming that you are using ISQL, to do anything with a form, select the **Form** option from the ISQL main menu, which gives you a screen that looks something like Figure 4.1.

4.2.1 Menu options

The **Run** option

The **Run** option runs PERFORM on an existing compiled form. When this option is selected, ISQL presents a list of all the forms it can find. It finds forms in the current directory and in directories in the list specified by the environment variable DBPATH. You can choose which form to run by: using the cursor keys to move the highlight up and down (or across) the list of forms; typing the name of one of the forms on the list; or typing the full path name of a form not on the list.

The **Modify** option

The **Modify** option is used to change an existing form. The same selection process as for the **Run** option allows you to specify which form should be edited. If you have not specified an editor with the DBEDIT environment variable, you will be prompted to specify which one to use; on UNIX the default is **vi**, on MS-DOS the default is **edlin**. Once you have made a choice for the session, you will not be asked a second time – if you used the **Report** or **Query-Language** options first and specified an editor there, you will not be asked again here.

Inside the editor, you may modify the form in whatever manner you wish, and when you have finished, you exit from the editor, remembering to save the file if it is not saved automatically. The details of the ways in which a form can be modified constitute the third part of this chapter plus all of Chapters 7 and 11, so the details will not be discussed further now.

When you exit the editor, ISQL offers you a choice of actions, the default one of which is to compile the form. The alternatives are to save the form as it is or to discard the changes made since the form was last saved. It does not matter if you completely spoil a form; you are always editing a copy of the original and you get the opportunity to discard any changes you have made. If you do not choose the **Compile** option, you will be returned to the **Form** menu.

If you choose the **Compile** option, the form will be compiled. Often, you will have made a mistake, and FORMBUILD will have produced a file containing your form specification and also its error messages. You are given a choice between correcting your mistakes and exiting; if you exit, you can compile, save or discard the form as before. If you choose to correct the form, the editor will be run for you and you may need to find the error messages, which are on lines starting with a hash symbol '#'. If you are using **vi**, ISQL invokes it in such a way that it always goes to the first error message, which is useful. When you have corrected the errors, there is no need to remove the error messages (although it does no harm if you do) because ISQL does that automatically for you. When you exit from the editor, you are given the option to compile, save or discard again. This cycle is very convenient indeed; the default option is almost always the correct one to use.

When you are satisfied with the form, or want to test it, save the compiled form and then use the **Run** option to run it. You will find that the form you were modifying is automatically highlighted as the default choice.

The **Generate** option

The simplest way to create a new (default) form is to use the **Generate** option. When this is selected, ISQL first checks whether a database has been selected, and if not, asks you to choose one. It then prompts for the name of the form to be generated. This should be a file name without any extension – ISQL will add the correct extension automatically.

After that, ISQL prompts for the list of tables to be included in the form. It gives a list of the tables that are in the database, and these can be chosen either by typing the name of the table or by using the arrow keys to highlight the required table and then pressing RETURN. After each choice of table, ISQL prompts with the choices **Table-selection-complete**, **Select-more-tables** and **Exit**. The **Exit** option abandons the form generation process, **Table-selection-complete** indicates that the generation process can be run and **Select-more-tables** allows another table to be chosen, which will therefore create a multi-table form. (Multi-table forms are the subject of Chapter 7.) When all the tables have been selected, ISQL generates a form and compiles it. The form can then be run.

The **New** option

The New option allows you to create a new form (from scratch). It asks for the name of the form and then gives you an empty file in which to create the form. Apart from the fact that you have to do a lot of typing, this makes it difficult to get the field sizes correct, so this is not the recommended way of creating a form. When you finish editing the form, ISQL treats you as if you had modified an existing form.

The **Compile** option

The **Compile** option is used to compile an existing form. You are offered a choice of which form to compile, and if the compilation fails, you are treated as if you were modifying a form which had failed to compile.

The **Drop** option

The **Drop** option deletes a form – both the source and the object versions of the form if it can find them both. It gives you a list of forms which you can drop, and when you have selected one, asks for confirmation that you really intend to drop it.

```
database cars
screen
{
customer          [f000      ]
salut             [f001 ]
firstname         [f002     ]
surname           [f003         ]
address1          [f004              ]
address2          [f005              ]
address3          [f006              ]
postcode          [f007     ]
phone             [f008         ]
maxmoney          [f009     ]
enquiry           [a]
lastmodel         [f010      ]
contactdate       [f011     ]
}
end
tables
customers
attributes
f000 = customers.number;
f001 = customers.salut;
f002 = customers.firstname;
f003 = customers.surname;
f004 = customers.address1;
f005 = customers.address2;
f006 = customers.address3;
f007 = customers.postcode;
f008 = customers.phone;
f009 = customers.maxmoney;
a = customers.enquiry;
f010 = customers.lastmodel;
f011 = customers.contactdate;
end
```

Figure 4.2 The default form for the **Customers** table

4.3 Structure of a form file

The example default form shown in Figure 4.2 is for the **Customers** table in the **Cars** database. A form file has a fixed structure. It consists of a DATABASE section, a SCREEN section, a TABLES section, an ATTRIBUTES section and optionally an INSTRUCTIONS section. Of these, the two most important sections are the SCREEN section (the part between curly braces in Figure 4.2 which is more or less what the user will see on the screen) and the ATTRIBUTES section, which relates the fields in the screen section to the columns in the database. A default form (or a default report) is produced in all lower-case letters by ISQL. One of the first things I do to a default form is to reformat it with a program that converts keywords to upper-case letters.

The DATABASE section consists of the keyword DATABASE followed by the name of the database which the form uses. This can have the attribute WITHOUT NULL INPUT added to it. This means that PERFORM will not insert null values into the database but will insert blank strings for character fields and zeros for numeric fields and dates. This is not normally used unless the database was originally built using INFORMIX-SQL 1.10 and was subsequently converted to a more recent version, and if the conversion specified that the converted database should not accept null values. If the database is of this type, then all the forms used with it must have the WITHOUT NULL INPUT option specified.

The SCREEN section consists of one or more screen layouts, followed by the keyword END. Each screen layout consists of the keyword SCREEN followed on the next line by an open brace '{', one or more lines to be displayed on the screen and a close brace '}' on a line on its own. Each display line consists of text optionally interspersed by display fields. The text will be displayed on the screen exactly as it appears in the form file. The layout of the default form consists of the column names in the selected table(s) followed by a field delimited by square brackets '[ ]'. If a character field is too long to fit on one line, it will automatically be split across two or more lines. If the table is very large, it may be split across more than one screen.

The display fields consist of a field tag and spaces enclosed by square brackets. Each display field must have a unique tag which must be cross-referenced in the ATTRIBUTES section. The sum of the number of spaces between the square brackets and the number of characters in the tag denotes the amount of space available to display the data. If this does not match the length of the corresponding column in the database, ISQL will clip or pad the data as necessary. (One reason for using a generated form as the starting point for a customized form is that the length of the fields will be correct.) The tag must start with a letter, but can be followed by any combination of alpha-numeric characters or the underscore '_'. The case of the letters is not relevant: `alpha` and `ALPHA` refer to the same field tag.

The TABLES section consists of the keyword TABLES followed by a list of tables separated by spaces and optionally followed by the keyword END. Any table contributing data to the form must be listed. It is not necessary for every column of every listed table to be used on the screen.

The ATTRIBUTES section is the most important section, and is often the most complex section too. (If it is not the most complex section, the INSTRUCTIONS section is.) It consists of the keyword ATTRIBUTES followed by a list of field tags and their properties, followed by the keyword END. (If there is an INSTRUCTIONS section, the keyword END is optional.) Each of the field tags defined in the SCREEN section must be referenced in the ATTRIBUTES section, and vice versa. The simplest form of an ATTRIBUTES section follows each field tag with an equals sign '=', the name of the corresponding column in a table and finally a semicolon. The more complex forms of the attributes are discussed later.

The INSTRUCTIONS section, if present, consists of the keyword INSTRUCTIONS followed by a set of instructions and the keyword END. The only simple instruction is DELIMITERS. This is followed by a quoted string containing two characters which will be used to mark the ends of the display fields on the screen. A common use for this is to change the delimiters from '[ ]' to ' ' (two spaces). The MASTER OF instruction is left until Chapter 7, and all the more complex instructions are deferred until Chapter 11.

4.4 The ATTRIBUTES section

The ATTRIBUTES section is very important in determining the usefulness of a form. The order of the field tags in the ATTRIBUTES section determines the order in which data is entered using the form. When the form is generated, the fields are listed in the order in which the columns occur in the table, but this can be changed when the form is customized.

The ATTRIBUTES section also allows the form designer to specify a number of different types of input validation (termed *input* or *validation* attributes), and also the way in which the data should be displayed (via the *display* attributes). The input attributes govern what the user can enter into the field, while the display attributes control the appearance of the data in the database after the user has entered the data. Any number of attributes can be applied to any of the fields on the screen.

Some of the attributes are discussed in this chapter and the remainder are covered in Chapter 7, as shown in the table . Those marked with a dagger '†' are only available with version 4.00. In the table, type I means an input attribute, D a display attribute, and B means both input and display.

	Attribute	Type	Attribute	Type
	UPSHIFT	I	DEFAULT	I
	DOWNSHIFT	I	AUTONEXT	I
Chapter 4	COMMENTS	I	NOENTRY	I
	INCLUDE	I	FORMAT	D
	REQUIRED	I	REVERSE	D

	Attribute	Type	Attribute	Type
	NOUPDATE	I	QUERYCLEAR	D
Chapter 7	PICTURE	I	RIGHT	D
	LOOKUP	B	COLOR†	D
	VERIFY	I	WORDWRAP†	D
	ZEROFILL	D	COMPRESS†	I

4.4.1 Input attributes

UPSHIFT and DOWNSHIFT

These two attributes ensure that the data entered into the form is in upper or lower case respectively. If the user types data in the wrong case, it is automatically converted to the correct case and displayed in the correct case. They are used to make it easier to do searches, because they guarantee that the data is in one case. These attributes cannot both be used in one field. The syntax is illustrated by:

```
a = customers.enquiry, UPSHIFT;
```

COMMENTS

The COMMENTS attribute is used to specify a one-line message which will be displayed when the cursor is in the field identified by the tag, when either inputting or updating data. The comment will be displayed at the bottom of the screen. It is normally used to give information to the user. It is often used in conjunction with the INCLUDE attribute to tell the user what values are acceptable. The syntax is illustrated by:

```
a = customers.enquiry, UPSHIFT,
      COMMENTS = "Q enquiry, S sale, C contact";
```

INCLUDE

The INCLUDE attribute is used to specify the acceptable values for a field. The list of values is surrounded by brackets and the individual items are separated by commas. The syntax is illustrated by:

```
a = customers.enquiry, UPSHIFT,
      COMMENTS = "Q enquiry, S sale, C contact",
      INCLUDE = ("Q", "C", "S");
```

For numeric fields in particular, a range notation may be used to specify the acceptable values. This is illustrated by:

```
f008 = customers.maxmoney,
         INCLUDE = (NULL, 2000 TO 100000);
```

Ranges can be applied to character fields but may not have the desired effect. For example, suppose the character field was four characters long and the INCLUDE specification was:

```
abcd = table1.column1, INCLUDE = ("A" TO "M");
```

The user could enter the values such as 'A', 'B' and 'M' as was probably intended, but could also enter 'Aaaa', 'Azzz' and 'Lzzz' (but not 'Ma' because that comes after 'M'). It is theoretically possible to leave the quotes off a character field unless it contains a punctuation character, but it is strongly discouraged.

REQUIRED

The REQUIRED attribute is used to insist upon an entry for the corresponding field. It means that the user must actually enter data for the field. It also means that a default value cannot be specified. The syntax is illustrated by:

```
a = customers.enquiry, UPSHIFT, REQUIRED,
      COMMENTS = "Q enquiry, S sale, C contact";
```

DEFAULT

The DEFAULT attribute is used to display a default value for the corresponding field. This value is displayed immediately when the form is used to add data, update or query. It is often used with date fields and the special keyword TODAY to set the default date to today's date. This is illustrated by:

```
f010 = customers.contactdate, DEFAULT = TODAY;
```

Symbol	Interpretation
mm	Month as two digits
mmm	Month as three-letter abbreviation
dd	Day of month as two digits
ddd	Day of week as three-letter abbreviation
yy	Year as two digits
yyyy	Year as four digits

Table 4.1 Format symbols for DATE fields

Note that a field cannot have a default and also be required. If both attributes are specified, the default value satisfies the required data-entry criterion.

AUTONEXT

The AUTONEXT attribute means that when a field is filled (that is, the cursor was on the last character of the field and the user has just entered a character), the cursor should immediately go on to the next field in the ATTRIBUTES section. This is particularly useful when the field is either a single character or part of an extended character field. The syntax is illustrated by:

```
a = customers.enquiry, UPSHIFT, AUTONEXT,
    COMMENTS = "Q enquiry, S sale, C contact",
    INCLUDE = ("Q", "C", "S");
```

NOENTRY

The NOENTRY attribute is used to indicate that no entry is allowed in a field using the **Add** option. It is automatically applied to a serial field – you cannot either specify a serial number during input or update it once it is in the database. NOENTRY can be applied to any column of any type. One convenient use for NOENTRY is to supply a default which the user cannot change. This is done by specifying both a DEFAULT value and NOENTRY, thus:

```
f009 = customers.contactdate, DEFAULT = TODAY, NOENTRY;
```

4.4.2 Display attributes

REVERSE

The REVERSE attribute means that the field will be displayed in reverse video, which normally means it is displayed in black text on a white background. If used carefully, it is very useful, but it can be over-used. The syntax is illustrated by:

```
f008 = customers.maxmoney, REVERSE,
       INCLUDE = (NULL, 2000 to 100000);
```

FORMAT

The FORMAT attribute is used to specify the appearance of DECIMAL, FLOAT, SMALLFLOAT and DATE fields. It is not allowed with MONEY fields.

For the numeric types; the hash (or pound) symbol is used to denote a digit, and a single decimal point (period '.') may also be specified. Thus, a string '*###.##*' will produce up to three places to the left of the decimal point and exactly two after it. The number will be right-justified and blank-padded if necessary. Numbers are rounded before they are displayed.

For the DATE type, the symbols shown in Table 4.1 are recognized. The syntax of this attribute is illustrated by:

```
f010 = customers.contactdate, DEFAULT = TODAY,
       FORMAT = "ddd, dd mmm yyyy", NOENTRY;

f999 = mystery.decfield, FORMAT = "####.######";
```

The length of the display field must be exactly as long as the format string; if it is not, FORMBUILD will complain.

The FORMAT attribute is a display attribute. The user is not constrained by the format when the data is entered, but when the cursor moves out of the field, what the user types will be reformatted to conform to the format specification.

4.5 Using the attributes

The modified version of the form `customers.per` would now look as shown in Figure 4.3. All the attributes discussed above are used in the form.

4.6 Using a form

You now know a great deal about how to design a form, but how do you use it? The normal way of using a form is to select the **Run** option from the **Form** menu. ISQL then asks you which form you want to run and offers you a list of the available forms. You can either type in the name or use the arrow keys to select the form and then hit RETURN. ISQL then runs the PERFORM program **sperform**. The alternative is to run the form direct from the UNIX command line.

Version 2.10 and later. PERFORM gives you a large ring menu which extends on to a second page, as shown in Figures 4.4 and 4.5. The appearance of PERFORM in version 2.00 and earlier is shown in Section 16.7. The ellipsis (the three dots '. . .') on the first page indicates that there are additional menu items available on the second page. The ellipsis on the second page indicates that there are additional menu items on the previous page.

As shown in Figures 4.4 and 4.5, the options available are **Query, Next, Previous, Add, Update, Remove, Table, Screen, Current, Master, Detail, Output** and **Exit**. With version 4.00, there is also a **View** option for looking at blobs, and it appears between the **Previous** and **Add** options. The **Table, Screen, Master** and **Detail** options are only relevant to multi-table forms, and the **Current** option is most useful in multi-table forms, so these will be discussed in Chapter 7, which is about multi-table forms.

```
{
    @(#)custom3a.per    5.2 91/03/07
    Form for table Customers in database Cars
}

DATABASE Cars

SCREEN
{

            Customer details

    Number  [f000]
    Name    [f001 ][f002       ][f003              ]

    Address [f004                      ]
            [f005                      ]
            [f006                      ]
    Post code[f007   ]

    Phone number [f008              ]

    Type of enquiry            [a]
    Spending power (estimated) [f009      ]
    Model bought               [f010]
    Last contact date          [f011     ]
}
END

TABLES
Customers

ATTRIBUTES
```

Figure 4.3 Fully customized **Customers** form

4.6.1 Menu options

The **Query** option

The **Query** option is used to do 'query-by-example' database enquiries. When a query is executed, it will produce a list of rows which can then be manipulated. The **Query** option is a very flexible way of finding data from the database.

To find any particular row of data, enter sufficient information in the fields to identify the rows you are interested in. If the enquiry results in more than one row being returned, the **Next** and **Previous** options will allow you to step through the selected rows. Any data fields left blank will not influence the choice of rows, and a completely blank form will select all the rows in the table.

There are a number of control characters which can be used to make the enquiry more general. They are shown in Table 4.2. If a field is left blank during an enquiry, it does not participate in the condition. To match a null value, it is necessary to use the '=' operator in the first character of the field. To match a field which only contains a '=', use '\='. To match a '\', use '\\'.

The wild-card character matches zero or more characters – any characters. It is rather like the '*' character in the UNIX Bourne shell. If the first character is an equals sign, the wild card loses its special meaning.

```
f000 = Customers.Number;
f001 = Customers.Salut,
       COMMENTS = "Mr Mrs Miss Ms or blank",
       INCLUDE = ("Mr", "Mrs", "Miss", "Ms", NULL);
f002 = Customers.Firstname;
f003 = Customers.Surname, REQUIRED;
f004 = Customers.Address1, AUTONEXT,
       COMMENTS = "Enter address";
f005 = Customers.Address2, AUTONEXT,
       COMMENTS = "Enter address";
f006 = Customers.Address3, AUTONEXT,
       COMMENTS = "Enter address";
f007 = Customers.Postcode, UPSHIFT,
       COMMENTS = "Enter post code",
       PICTURE = "AXXX #AA";
f008 = Customers.Phone, DOWNSHIFT,
       COMMENTS = "STD code, number and extension";
a    = Customers.Enquiry, UPSHIFT, AUTONEXT,
       COMMENTS = "Q enquiry, S sale, C contact",
       INCLUDE = ("Q", "C", "S");
f009 = Customers.Maxmoney, REVERSE,
       COMMENTS = "2000 to 100000, or blank",
       INCLUDE = (NULL, 2000 TO 100000);
f010 = Customers.Lastmodel;
f011 = Customers.Contactdate, DEFAULT = TODAY,
       FORMAT = "ddd, dd mmm yyyy",
       NOENTRY;
END

INSTRUCTIONS
DELIMITERS "  "
END
```

Figure 4.3 (*cont.*)

Version 4.00. The '?' character matches any one character. It can be used in conjunction with '*'. There is some evidence of it working in some earlier versions, but there are no other versions of PERFORM where it works 100% reliably, which is presumably why it is not documented for them. Also new with version 4.00 is the '. .' operator, which is a synonym for the ':' range operator.

The '|' operator was introduced with version 2.10, but might be available in version 2.00 on some machines; it is always worth trying new features like this in old versions, but since they are not documented, they are unsupported, and if they do not work, there is nothing anyone can (or will) do except say 'tough'.

The **Next** and **Previous** options

The options **Next** and **Previous** are used once a list of rows has been retrieved using **Query**. If several rows of data were selected by the query, these options can be used to navigate through the list. If you type '13N', then the cursor will move forward 13 rows of data; similarly, '2P' will move back two rows of data. The data selected is not in any particular order. The order normally corresponds to the physical order of the records in the data file, which need not be the same as the order the records were added if some records have been deleted and then others added.

```
PERFORM: [Query] Next  Previous  Add  Update  Remove  Table  Screen  ...
Searches the active database table.              ** 1: customers table**
customer            [           ]
salut               [    ]
firstname           [        ]
surname             [          ]
address1            [                ]
address2            [                ]
address3            [                ]
postcode            [      ]
phone               [         ]
maxmoney            [      ]
enquiry             [ ]
lastmodel           [       ]
contactdate         [      ]
```

Figure 4.4 PERFORM menu

```
PERFORM:  ... [Current]  Master  Detail  Output  Exit
Displays the current row of the current table.  ** 1: customers table**
customer            [           ]
salut               [    ]
firstname           [        ]
surname             [          ]
address1            [                ]
address2            [                ]
address3            [                ]
postcode            [      ]
phone               [         ]
maxmoney            [      ]
enquiry             [ ]
lastmodel           [       ]
contactdate         [      ]
```

Figure 4.5 PERFORM menu – the second page

The **View** option

Version 4.00. The **View** option is used to allow you to inspect the contents of any blobs in the table. For details about blobs, look in Chapter 14. When this option is selected, the cursor moves to the first blob field. The arrow keys can be used to move around the form and the exclamation mark '!' can be used to start up the program which allows you to view the blob.

Character	Interpretation	Applies to
=	Equal to	All
<>	Not equal to	All
>	Greater than	All
<	Less than	All
>=	Greater than or equal to	All
<=	Less than or equal to	All
:	Range	All
..	Range	All
*	Wild card	CHAR only
?	Any single character	CHAR only
<<	Lowest value	Indexed columns
>>	Highest value	Indexed columns
|	OR operator	All

Table 4.2 Query option meta-characters

The **Add** option

The **Add** option is used to add data to the database. When you select the **Add** option, the fields in the form are usually cleared, except for any with default values specified by the form. Data for the new entry can be entered by typing data in each field. The return and tab characters take you to the next field. The backspace character goes back a space, and will move to the first character of the previous field if you backspace from the first character position. The arrow keys may also be used. Unless you use the arrow keys, data is overwritten. When all the data is entered, use the ESCAPE (ESC) key to enter the data. If you need to abandon the entry before pressing ESC, use the INTERRUPT key. If you have already pressed ESC, use the **Remove** option.

When you are entering data, PERFORM makes the most basic checks on what you type; a numeric field will not accept alphabetic characters, and dates must be valid. If the form has been customized, there will usually be some extra validation done while the data is entered, and if you have made a mistake, you will get a message indicating what you have done wrong. Some validation is performed field by field, but some validation can only be done when the ESC key is pressed.

The **Update** option

The **Update** option is used to alter the data in the row currently on display. It is the same as the **Add** option except that the row of data already exists in the database. PERFORM is not really suitable for large-scale, systematic updates of the database. The SQL statement UPDATE (see Chapter 8) is more appropriate, provided the same operation has to be done on each row (eg all prices are increased by 10%). On the other hand, if each price has to be increased, but the increases cannot be specified systematically, PERFORM is the best way of making the changes.

```
FORM OUTPUT FILE:  [Append] Create
Adds new data to an existing output file.      ** 1: customers table**
```

Figure 4.6 The FORM OUTPUT FILE menu in PERFORM

```
FORM OUTPUT FILE LIST:  [Current-list] One-page
Write current list to the file.                ** 1: customers table**
```

Figure 4.7 The FORM OUTPUT FILE LIST menu in PERFORM

```
OUTPUT FORMAT:  [Unload-format] Screen-format
Writes the selected output in ascii format.    ** 1: customers table**
```

Figure 4.8 The OUTPUT FORMAT menu in PERFORM

The **Remove** option

The **Remove** option deletes a row of data from the database. It asks you to confirm that you wish to remove the record. As with bulk data updates, PERFORM is not really a suitable mechanism for deleting many rows of data; use the DELETE command from SQL, which is discussed in Chapter 8, for removing large quantities of data.

The **Output** option

The **Output** option is used to produce a screen dump of the data area of the form (this means the 20 lines in the middle; the top two lines are reserved for the menu, and the bottom two lines are reserved for comments and error messages) to a file. When you select this option, PERFORM will ask a series of questions: what is the name of the file to be used; should it be created or should the dump be appended to the end of the file if it already exists (Figure 4.6); and should it dump just the current record or the whole current list (Figure 4.7)? There are a series of defaults (file name `perform.out`, append, current list) which can be used by just hitting RETURN in answer to each question.

Version 4.00.   The **Output** option has been extended so that you can now specify either unload format or screen format (whereas previously there was only screen format), using the menu shown in Figure 4.8.

The **Exit** option

The **Exit** option is a signal to PERFORM to stop. You are returned to where you left off. If you were in the ISQL menu, you will be returned to the **Form** menu; if you were working at the UNIX command line, you will be returned to your shell prompt; and if you were in a user menu, you will be given a chance to choose another option.

4.7 Summary

This chapter described the **Form** option of the ISQL main menu which is used to create, modify, compile and run forms, and showed a default (generated) form. The structure of a form was described and the techniques used to modify a form were illustrated. Some of the attributes used to control the input and display of data in a form were described. The other ones are left to Chapter 7. Finally, the basic options used in PERFORM were described, leaving the other options to be described in Chapter 7. All the forms in this chapter used one table.

Exercises

1. Generate a form for table **Companies** in the **Cars** database. Revise the layout. Give better names to the fields. Give the screen a title. Add attributes to the display fields.

    Use the form to find out about companies whose name contains the letter **r**. Use the form to add your own company. Use an enquiry to check the data you entered.

2. Generate and customize a form for each of the other tables in the **Cars** database. Be prepared to make major changes to them after reading Chapter 7, because most of the forms will work better (ie they will be easier for people to use) if they are made into multi-table forms.

5

Basic database enquiries

Did you say 'Why on earth is he doing the query language next?'. It's a fair question, but there is a good reason for doing it. SQL must be taught next because the subject after this is reports, and reports have to use SQL to get the data out of the database before it is formatted. So, until you understand the basic operation of the SELECT statement, which is the subject of this chapter, there is little point in moving on to the next.

The first section of this chapter discusses the SQL (or **Query-Language**) menu in detail. The rest of the chapter is about the SELECT statement, which is the only way of getting data out of the database. A SELECT statement can be a very large and complicated piece of logic, or it can be as simple as three words and a star '*'. This chapter covers the simplest SELECT statements, basic selection criteria, joining tables and sorting the output. This is sufficient to understand the reports in the next chapter; anything more complicated is left until Chapters 8 and 12. These facilities allow both *ad hoc* and standardized enquiries to be made, but the output format is rudimentary. Fine control of the format is achieved using an ACE report.

5.1 Using the Query-Language menu

Although the **Query-Language** option of the ISQL main menu (which is shown again in Figure 5.1) has already been used, some of the options were not described. All the options will therefore be discussed again fully. There is always a current set of SQL statements (which may be empty). The menu options allow you to manipulate the current set of statements in a variety of ways.

5.1.1 Menu options

The **New** option
This is used to create a new set of SQL statements. It uses a built-in editor which is modeless like most word processors, and unlike **vi**. It is a convenient tool for small

```
RDSQL:  [New] Run Modify Use-Editor Output Choose Save Info Drop Exit
Enter new RDSQL statements using the RDSQL editor.

-------------------- cars ------------------- Press CTRL-W for Help --------
```

Figure 5.1 The **Query-Language** or SQL menu

pieces of editing, but is less satisfactory if there is a lot of major editing to do because it lacks the pattern-matching facilities of an editor like **vi**.

Note that unless you explicitly save them, the current SQL statements are lost when you exit the ISQL main menu, or when you select the **New** or **Choose** options. If you exit from the **Query-Language** option and do some work with forms, say, and then return, the current statements are kept as they were when you left the menu.

The **Run** option

This option runs the current set of statements. As each statement completes, a progress message is displayed at the bottom of the screen. If the statement is a SELECT statement, the results are displayed on the screen, with an elaborate scrolling mechanism to ensure that you do not miss any of the information.

The **Modify** option

This uses the same editor as the **New** option. If there was an error, the cursor will be positioned at the point where the error was detected (which is not necessarily the same place as where the error occurred), and a message will be shown describing the error. Some of the messages are rather imprecise; one of the favourites is number −201 − a syntax error has occurred. (Incidentally, all error messages from INFORMIX-SQL have a negative number. A fuller explanation of each message is supplied in the INFORMIX-SQL reference manual.)

The **Use-Editor** option

This option allows you to use your favourite system editor to edit the current set of SQL statements. If there was an error in the statements, the error message will be embedded in the file after the line where the error was detected. The error can be corrected, and the revised file saved, and ISQL will remove the error message if you did not do so.

The **Output** option

This option runs the current set of statements and can send the output to a file (append or create), pipe it to a program or send it to the printer; all these may be done with or without headings.

The **Choose** option

This allows you to choose the contents of a file ending with the '.sql' extension as the current set of SQL statements. Once the contents of the file have been chosen, there is no further connection between the current statements until you save them. Editing the current statements does not change the contents of the file.

The **Save** option

This option saves the current set of statements – regardless of whether they are syntactically correct or not – in a file with the '.sql' extension. If you chose a file (used the **Choose** option), the default file name will be the name of the chosen file, but it is possible to change that name simply by typing a new one.

The **Info** option

The **Info** option is very useful when there is an error in your SQL script caused by a reference to a table or column which is not known to the database. It can be used to find the names of the tables in the database and the names of the columns in any table. It also allows you to find out the type of data stored by the columns, what indexes there are on a table and the access privileges (see Chapter 14).

The **Drop** option

This simply deletes a '.sql' file; you get the opportunity to say which one, and you have to confirm that you mean to get rid of it.

5.2 SELECT statement – syntax

The SELECT statement is the most useful and most complex SQL statement. It is used to fetch data from the database. The full syntax for the statement is:

```
SELECT select-list
    FROM table-list
    [WHERE condition]
    [GROUP BY group-list]
    [HAVING condition]
    [ORDER BY column-list]
    [INTO TEMP table-name]
```

The square brackets indicate optional elements. The order of the elements is mandatory: the FROM clause must precede the WHERE clause, which must precede the GROUP BY clause, and so on. As you will see in Chapter 8, SELECT statements can be used in the WHERE clause, giving nested SELECT statements which are usually called *sub-queries*. This chapter covers the SELECT clause, the FROM clause, the WHERE clause (but not everything about it) and the ORDER BY clause. The other parts will be left for the other chapters on SQL.

5.3 SELECT statement – mandatory parts

There are two mandatory parts to a SELECT statement: the SELECT clause with the *select-list* and the FROM clause with the *table-list*. Every single SELECT statement will have at least these two parts, even if it has nothing else. For example, to list the salutation, first name and surname of all the customers in the **Customers** table of the **Cars** database, the SELECT statement would be:

```
SELECT Salut, Firstname, Surname FROM Customers;
```

```
RUN: [Next] Restart  Exit
Display the next page of query results.

--------------------- cars ------------------ Press CTRL-W for Help --------

salut firstname  surname

Mr    Colin      Askestrand
Mr    R.         Bycroft
Mr    P.         Tinkler
Mr    J.         Goodman
Mr    T.A.       Janetta
Mr    Richard    Plumb
Mr    B.         Jevons
Mr    E          Hewett
Mr    G.W.       Randal
Mr    Peter      Jacobson
Mr    G.         Brys
Mr    M.J.R.     Hunter
Mr    S.E.       Haug
Mr    W.         Merritt
```

Figure 5.2 The output from a SELECT statement

The output from this enquiry would be a list of names on the screen, with the column names printed at the top of the screen, as shown in Figure 5.2. Since the output from this enquiry occupies several pages, ISQL uses a menu to go on to the next screen, stop the enquiry or restart it. The headings are carried over for each page.

The *select-list* is normally a list of column names (or expressions involving column names). The *table-list* is the list of tables that will be used to make the enquiry. The column names must be unambiguous, so if several tables are involved, the column name may be prefixed by the table name and a dot to make it absolutely clear which column is being referred to. When writing working code, it is good practice to use the *table.column* notation everywhere in the SELECT statement unless the SELECT statement only uses one table. It is possible to include a constant such as 3 or a string literal (`"A string literal"`) in the *select-list* or, more usefully, USER or TODAY to find out who is running the SQL script or what today's date is. The shorthand notation '*' can be used to select all the columns in a table:

```
SELECT * FROM Customers;
```

This would list all the columns in the **Customers** table of the database. Because there is too much data to fit across the screen (unlike the first example), the output would now be down the screen, as shown in Figure 5.3.

5.4 SELECT statement – WHERE

The unqualified form of SELECT is seldom used. Usually, only rows which satisfy one or more conditions are required. These conditions are specified by the WHERE clause. Assuming that the **Maxmoney** column contains the maximum price of car

```
RUN: [Next] Restart  Exit
Display the next page of query results.

--------------------- cars ----------------- Press CTRL-W for Help --------

customer    1001
salut       Mr
firstname   Colin
surname     Askestrand
address1    6 Warwick Court
address2    Maldon
address3    ESSEX
postcode
phone       0419 805142
maxmoney    #7500
enquiry     S
lastmodel   92
contactdate 24/01/1984
```

Figure 5.3 The alternative layout for the output

that the customer is willing (or deemed able) to afford, this statement will select all those customers for whom the maximum price has been specified:

```
SELECT Salut, Firstname, Surname FROM  Customers WHERE Maxmoney > 0;
```

The WHERE clause has a second purpose, namely to specify joining conditions. These are just a special case of selection condition, and will be discussed again later in this chapter.

All the normal comparison operators listed in Table 5.1 can be used in a WHERE clause, and can also be used to compare two strings or two dates or two numbers. The condition can be made more complex by compounding the expressions using the keywords AND, OR and NOT, and by using brackets to group conditions together. An example of this would be:

```
SELECT Model FROM Models WHERE  Price < 8000 AND Mpgat56 > 45;
```

This selects those models for which the price is less than £8000 and the fuel consumption at 56 mph is better than 45 mpg. In addition, SQL provides the following operators. In each case, the keyword NOT is optional and negates the condition:

```
expr [NOT] BETWEEN expr1 AND expr2
expr [NOT] IN (expr-list)
columnname [NOT] LIKE "string"
columnname [NOT] MATCHES "string"
columnname IS [NOT] NULL
```

Operator	Interpretation
<	Less than
<=	Less than or equal to
=	Equal to
!=	Not equal to
<>	Not equal to
>	Greater than
>=	Greater than or equal to

Table 5.1 Numeric comparisons

5.4.1 BETWEEN/AND operator

The BETWEEN/AND operator is used to select items in a given range. The example selects the models which cost between £3000 and £4500.

```
SELECT Model FROM Models WHERE Price BETWEEN 3000 AND 4500;
```

It *does* matter which of the expressions *expr1* and *expr2* is the larger; *expr1* must be smaller than *expr2*. This means that BETWEEN/AND is a shorthand for:

```
SELECT Model FROM Models WHERE Price >= 3000 AND Price <= 4500;
```

5.4.2 IN operator

The IN operator ensures that the expression is one of the values in the *value-list*. The values may be variables or constants (or another SELECT statement, but that is covered in Chapter 8). The example lists all the Escorts, Cortinas and Granadas in the **Models** table:

```
SELECT Modelname, Details FROM Models WHERE Modelname IN ("Escort", "Cortina", "Granada");
```

5.4.3 LIKE and MATCHES operators

The relational operators in Table 5.1 can be used for simple comparisons between strings as well as between numeric fields, but they are case sensitive. The LIKE and MATCHES operators also compare string columns, but they both provide a set of meta-characters to provide a fuzzy matching capability. The LIKE operator uses '%' and '_' (percent and underscore). The underscore represents any one character, while the percent represents a string of zero or more characters. The MATCHES operator uses the set of meta-characters listed in Table 5.2 and is much more powerful than LIKE. The meta-characters are closely related to those used by the UNIX shells.

The LIKE keyword is part of the ANSI standard SQL, but MATCHES is an Informix extension. The following examples both select all the customers whose surname derives from Smith (including Smythe and Smithyman), but one uses LIKE

Meta-character	Interpretation
*	Zero or more characters
?	Any one character
[a-z]	Any lower-case letter
[a0-2-]	Match 'a' or '0' or '1' or '2' or '-'
[^a-zA-Z]	Anything which is not a letter
\	The next character has no special meaning
*	Match an asterisk
\\	Match one backslash

Table 5.2 Meta-characters for the MATCHES operator

and the other uses MATCHES:

```
SELECT Salut, Firstname, Surname FROM Customers WHERE Surname MATCHES "*Sm?th*";
```

```
SELECT Salut, Firstname, Surname FROM Customers WHERE Surname LIKE "%Sm_th%";
```

5.4.4 IS NULL operator

The IS NULL operator is used to check whether the special null value is stored in the column. Null is used to indicate that no value has been specified for a particular column. This can be useful when the value is unknown, either because the value is intrinsically unknowable (such as the leaving date of an employee) or because the value has not yet been supplied (such as the total value of a sale when the deal has not been finalized). A null value cannot be tested except by using the IS NULL operator since it always causes the condition to fail. The full details of this are described in Section 8.5, and also in Section 2 of the INFORMIX-SQL reference manual. The example selects those customers for whom a maximum spending power has not been specified:

```
SELECT Salut, Firstname, Surname FROM Customers WHERE Maxmoney IS NULL;
```

5.5 SELECT statement – joins

It is also possible to select from several tables at once. Suppose that we wish to find out which cars are in stock and what model they are. The simplest way of doing this is to choose the model name and details from the **Models** table and the registration from **Stock**. This could be written as:

```
{ This SELECT statement should not be run }
SELECT Models.Modelname, Models.Details, Stock.Registration FROM Models, Stock;
```

The column names have all been specified in full, even though there is no ambiguity in this example. Since the values come from two different tables, both tables must be listed in the FROM clause.

There is just one snag with this statement: it does not produce the answer we want. Unless we specify a *join* condition, the SELECT statement will produce what is called the *Cartesian product* of the set of tables listed in the FROM clause. In the Cartesian product of two tables (call them A and B), each row from table A is matched with every row in table B. Each of the resulting rows consists of all the columns in A plus all the columns in B. This means that if **Models** has *n1* rows in it and **Stock** has *n2* rows, the number of rows produced by the SELECT statement will be $(n1 \times n2)$. So, when it is run, the example above matches each row in the table **Models** with each row in the table **Stock** and selects the model name and car registration number for each composite row in the Cartesian product.

The rows we are interested in are those in which the value in **Stock.Model** is equal to the value in **Models.Model**, which is written algebraically as:

```
Stock.Model = Models.Model
```

This looks very like the conditions we have already been using in the WHERE clause, the only difference being that it compares two quantities stored in the database instead of comparing a quantity in the database with a literal value, and, in fact, such joining conditions are allowed and are used very extensively. When selecting from *n* tables, it is necessary to include at least $(n - 1)$ conditions to ensure that the only rows selected from the Cartesian product are those where the values in one table are correctly joined to those in another. In the example, there are two tables, so we need one join condition to make the example work as we want it to. To get the result we require, we need to specify the join condition that the model number in the **Stock** and **Models** tables must be identical. This results in the statement:

```
SELECT Models.Modelname, Models.Details, Stock.Registration
   FROM  Models, Stock
   WHERE Models.Model = Stock.Model;
```

This does not tell us the manufacturer, so we really need to select from three tables with two join conditions as below:

```
SELECT Company, Modelname, Details, Registration
   FROM  Models, Stock, Companies
   WHERE Models.Model = Stock.Model
     AND Models.Maker = Companies.Maker;
```

Obviously, it is very important to identify which columns in which tables join to each other when the database is designed. You may have noticed the emphasis on the connections between the tables in the **Cars** database in Chapter 2: this is because they are crucial when it comes to getting useful information out of the database.

Note: although the set of rows produced by a SELECT statement with a join can be found by forming the Cartesian product of the joined tables and then removing all the unwanted rows, this is not the way that Informix produces the answer. The database agent has a built-in query optimizer which avoids doing any more work than is necessary. The optimizer is a very important component of any relational database system; indeed, it governs the performance of the database more than almost anything else. The details of how the Informix optimizer works are discussed in more detail in Chapter 14. It is not something that users can alter, and the details only matter when trying to squeeze the utmost performance out of a system. For the time being, it is sufficient to know that although the correct answer can be produced by the brute-force approach of producing the Cartesian product and then deleting the unwanted entries, the actual method is much more efficient.

5.6 SELECT statement – ORDER BY

So far, the order in which items have come out of the database has not mattered and has been left to the order in which the data was found in the database. It is possible to specify the order in which items are selected by using the keywords ORDER BY. For example, to list the models in stock in decreasing order of cost, the SELECT statement would be:

```
SELECT Company, Modelname, Details, Registration, Boughtfor
    FROM    Models, Stock, Companies
    WHERE   Models.Model = Stock.Model
    AND     Models.Maker = Companies.Maker
    ORDER BY Stock.Boughtfor DESC;
```

There is one important restriction on the ORDER BY clause: the columns named must also be named in the *select-list*. It is possible to order by an expression such as 'Tanksize * Urban' by using one or more numbers to indicate which items in the *select-list* should be used for sorting. Thus, the following SELECT statement will list the stock in decreasing order of range on one tank of fuel:

```
SELECT Company, Modelname, Details, Tanksize, Urban, Tanksize * Urban
    FROM    Models, Stock, Companies
    WHERE   Models.Model = Stock.Model
    AND     Models.Maker = Companies.Maker
    ORDER BY 6 DESC;
```

It is possible to use a *display label* anywhere in the select list to give a new name to a column. A display label is a name following a column name or expression in the *select-list* and is separated from the column name or expression by a space rather than a comma. ISQL normally uses the name of the column as the heading which identifies the data on the screen, but if there is a display label, it uses that instead, which allows different aggregates to be identified on the screen. It is also possible to order by a display label, as shown below:

```
SELECT Company, Modelname, Details, Tanksize, Urban, Tanksize * Urban Range
    FROM    Models, Stock, Companies
    WHERE   Models.Model = Stock.Model
    AND     Models.Maker = Companies.Maker
    ORDER BY Range DESC;
```

5.7 Summary

This chapter has covered the use of the **Query-Language** option of the ISQL main menu and the simpler parts of the SELECT statement. In particular, it has discussed the *select-list* (what is to be shown), the *table-list* (the list of tables used by the query), the WHERE clause (both simple conditions on one column and joining conditions relating columns from two tables) and the ORDER BY clause. This is sufficient for you to be able to move on to the next chapter without having to wonder what on earth a SELECT statement is.

Exercises

1. List all the models in stock.

2. List the models which cost more than £10 000.

3. List the vehicles in stock giving the name of the maker, the name and details of the model, and the registration number of the vehicle.

4. Imagine that the **Lastmodel** field in the table **Customers** indicates the model that a customer wishes to purchase. List those customers whose order can be satisfied from stock, giving the customer's name, the name of the car and the name of the maker.

5. List the customers in decreasing order of importance. Important customers buy expensive cars, and expensive cars cost more than £10 000.

6. List all models available in stock which have a top speed in excess of 100 mph and can accelerate from 0 to 60 mph in less than 10 seconds. Include the manufacturer's name for each model.

6
Ace reports

This chapter is the first of three about reports. It explains what a report is and why it was necessary to read Chapter 5 before doing reports, and covers the basic operations of a report. It leaves until Chapter 9 some more complicated topics such as the PRINT USING clause, the BEFORE GROUP OF block and aggregate functions. Chapter 13 covers the use of variables and the use of the INPUT section of a report.

Throughout this chapter, we are going to be assembling a report that lists all the customers in the **Customers** table and also lists their address, the amount of money we estimate that they can afford to spend and the car they showed an interest in. At the end, the complete report is shown, together with the first page of output from the report.

6.1 What is a report?

A report is used to produce neatly formatted results from an enquiry made on an INFORMIX-SQL database. The formatted data may be sent to the screen, to a file, to the printer or to another program. As well as defining how all the data should appear, a report can define details such as the shape of the page and the information that should go at the top and bottom of the page. Many reports are created once and used regularly; for example, a weekly summary of sales or a monthly summary of accounts. Other reports are created for one special job and will only be used once; for example, a mail shot for a selected group of customers. In this case, the format would be organized once and for all, but the selection of customers would change from time to time. This would require the report to be altered and recompiled.

Physically, a report consists of a source file and a compiled report file. The source file ends with a '.ace' extension and contains ordinary text which can be changed using a text editor such as **vi**. The compiled version of a report has a '.arc' extension and its contents are intelligible only to the ACE program **sacego**.

```
REPORT: [Run] Modify  Generate  New  Compile  Drop  Exit
Run a report.

--------------------- cars ----------------- Press CTRL-W for Help --------
```

Figure 6.1 The **Report** menu

6.2 The Report menu

Normally, ISQL is used to handle reports. To do anything with a report, select the **Report** option from the ISQL main menu, which will give you a screen which looks somewhat like Figure 6.1. All the options are substantially identical to those in the **Form** menu.

6.2.1 Menu options

The Run option
The **Run** option runs ACEGO on an existing compiled report. When it is chosen, ISQL presents a list of all the reports it can find and you can choose the one to be run with the cursor keys or by typing its name.

The Modify option
The **Modify** option is used to change an existing report. You choose the report to be modified from the list presented by ISQL, edit the report, and when you exit from the editor, you normally compile it, although it could be saved instead. The **Report** menu gives the same edit–compile–correct cycle as the **Form** menu does, except that it works with reports.

The Generate option
The simplest way to create a report is to use the **Generate** option from the **Report** menu in ISQL. When this is selected, ISQL first checks whether a database has been selected, and if not, asks you to choose one. It then prompts for the name of the report to be generated. The name entered should be a file name without any extension – ISQL will add the correct extension automatically. After that, ISQL prompts for the table to be reported on. It gives a list of the tables that are in the database and these can be chosen either by typing the name of the table or by using the arrow keys to highlight the required table and then pressing RETURN. Once the table has been selected, ISQL generates and compiles it. The report can then be run.

The layout of the output from the default report depends on how wide the columns in the table are. If they can be printed across the paper, they will be printed like that; otherwise, the columns will be listed down the left-hand edge and the data appended afterwards. Each row of data will be separated from the last by a couple of lines. The layout of the report needs to be customized and then the report must

```
database cars end

select
     number,
     salut,
     firstname,
     surname,
     address1,
     address2,
     address3,
     postcode,
     phone,
     maxmoney,
     enquiry,
     lastmodel,
     contactdate
from customers end

format every row end
```

Figure 6.2 Default report for the **Customers** table

be recompiled. An example of a default report is shown in Figure 6.2 for the **Customers** table in the **Cars** database.

The **New** option

Frankly, the **Generate** option is not very useful. Almost all reports will need a more complex SELECT statement than one that selects everything from one table, and the format section will normally be more complicated than the default too. A better way of generating a report is to:

1. Use the **Query-Language** option to create a SELECT statement (or sequence of SELECT statements) which produces the correct data on the screen.
2. Save the statements in a '. sql' file.
3. Get out of the **Query-Language** option and into the **Report** option. Choose the **New** option.
4. Read the saved SQL file into the report (use ': r' in **vi**).
5. Write in the missing default bits of the report by hand.

The missing default bits are the DATABASE section and the FORMAT section.

```
DATABASE Cars END
```

goes before the SELECT statement, and

```
END

FORMAT
     EVERY ROW
END
```

after the SELECT statement. If this is too much typing, you could of course generate the report, edit out the supplied SELECT statement and edit in the one that was saved. This gives you a report which will print the data that will appear in the final version of the report, but the layout will be in the default style.

The **Compile** option

The **Compile** option is used to compile an existing report. You are offered a choice of which report to compile, and if the compilation fails, you are treated as if you were modifying a report which had failed to compile.

The **Drop** option

The **Drop** option deletes a report – both the source and object versions of the report. You are offered a list of reports, and when you have selected one, you have to confirm that you mean to drop it.

6.3 Structure of a report file

A report file has a fixed structure consisting of the following six sections: DATABASE, DEFINE, INPUT, OUTPUT, SELECT and FORMAT. The sections must be in the order shown. Only the DATABASE, SELECT and FORMAT sections are mandatory.

6.3.1 DATABASE section

The DATABASE section consists of the keyword DATABASE followed by the name of the database that the report uses, followed by the keyword END (which is mandatory). It is the first section of the report.

```
DATABASE Cars END
```

The statements in a report are all free format; this means that white space (blanks, tabs and newlines) is only significant as separators between keywords. Provided each keyword is separated from the next by at least one white space character, the layout is immaterial to the program. You should make use of this to lay out your reports in a neat and readable fashion. For example, you could write the DATABASE section as:

```
DATABASE
    Cars
END
```

This does not use up very much space and is possibly more readable. (With a statement as simple as this, it is not very relevant which format is used, but when it comes to the SELECT section or the FORMAT section, it is vital to use a good layout.)

6.3.2 DEFINE, INPUT and OUTPUT sections

The DEFINE, INPUT and OUTPUT sections are described fully in Chapters 9 and 13. Briefly, the DEFINE section allows variables to be defined. Variables can be initialized via the PROMPT statement in the INPUT section or manipulated by calculations within the report and printed as required. The INPUT section prompts the user for values for variables; the values can be used to modify the data selected by the SELECT section, or to modify some of the information printed on the report. The OUTPUT section is used to define the page dimensions for the report.

6.3.3 SELECT section

The SELECT section retrieves the data to be printed from the database. It uses the SELECT statement, which is why report writing was deferred until after Chapter 5. Many reports require several SELECT statements to fetch the data from the database, but these SELECT statements use a clause – INTO TEMP – which has not been covered yet (see Chapter 8), so this chapter only discusses the simple SELECT statement.

There are very few constraints on the complexity of the SELECT statement in a report, but only the selected columns can be printed. The selected columns may be given display labels; indeed, sometimes it is *necessary* to give them display labels. For example, if both the customer address and the company address fields were being selected, it would be necessary to use display labels to make the names unambiguous. The names used to identify the columns when printing the report will be the display labels, if they were defined, or the column names if not. The notation *table.column* may be used in the SELECT statement, but not in the FORMAT section of the report.

If an ORDER BY clause is used in a SELECT statement, the sorted column names may not have a table prefix (that is, the notation *table.column* is not permitted). If a column is not unique, define a display label and use that in the ORDER BY clause and the FORMAT section of the report.

This example of a SELECT section does not need to use display labels, but it does show an ORDER BY clause which cannot use the *table.column* notation:

```
SELECT  Companies.Company, Models.Modelname, Models.Details, Customers.*
    FROM     Companies, Models, Customers
    WHERE    Customers.Lastmodel = Models.Model
    AND      Models.Maker = Companies.Maker
    ORDER BY Company, Modelname, Details, Surname, Firstname
END
```

The only difference between this SELECT section and an ordinary SELECT statement is that the keyword END has been used; this would be a syntax error in SQL.

6.3.4 FORMAT section

To be consistent with the other sections, the FORMAT section is described briefly here, but in truth, the rest of this chapter is all about the FORMAT section. The FORMAT section consists of the keyword FORMAT followed by a format specification and the keyword END. The default format consists of the words EVERY ROW; if the default format is required, these are the only words allowed in the FORMAT section.

6.4 Basic report formatting

Within the FORMAT section, it is possible to specify control blocks which will govern the actions taken when each row of data is retrieved. The default control block is:

- EVERY ROW − the default layout.

This control block must appear on its own, and none of the other control blocks may be used, nor may any of the PRINT or other report control keywords be used. EVERY ROW must be the only thing in the FORMAT section. This means that it is seldom used once the report is retrieving the correct data, which is almost immediately if the alternative method of generating the report is used.

Instead of EVERY ROW, any combination of the following control blocks may be used to format the report. These all allow the report writer to format the layout in any way that is required. None of the control blocks is mandatory, but at least one of them must be present.

- ON EVERY ROW − for every row retrieved.
- PAGE HEADER − at the top of each page.
- PAGE TRAILER − at the bottom of each page.
- FIRST PAGE HEADER − at the top of the first page.
- ON LAST ROW − after all rows are processed.
- BEFORE GROUP OF − when a new key value starts.
- AFTER GROUP OF − when a key value changes.

Of these, ON EVERY ROW is by far the most important and will be considered first; the PAGE HEADER and PAGE TRAILER sections will be discussed briefly in this chapter; the other control blocks will be discussed in Chapter 9.

6.4.1 The difference between EVERY ROW and ON EVERY ROW

Although the point has been made before, it cannot be emphasized enough: it is very important to recognize the major differences between the keywords ON EVERY ROW and EVERY ROW. The ON EVERY ROW control block is followed by the specification of what should be printed for every row of data retrieved by the SELECT section, whereas the EVERY ROW control block indicates that the data should be printed in the default format and is only followed by the keyword END.

6.5 Basic actions for ON EVERY ROW

The basic statements for formatting the output are PRINT, SKIP *n* LINES and NEED *n* LINES. Only these three statements will be discussed in this chapter, and some aspects of the PRINT statement will be left until Chapter 9.

6.5.1 The PRINT statement – basics

The PRINT statement is used to generate one line of output. It is followed by a list of character strings and selected column names to be printed out on one line. There are a number of control features that allow the format to be specified very thoroughly, and they are almost all straightforward to use. The PRINT statement is very similar to the PRINT statement used in most micro-computer versions of BASIC; there are many constructs which are easily recognizable if you have used BASIC (and they are not difficult to learn, even if you haven't used BASIC). The simplest use of PRINT is illustrated by:

```
PRINT Salut, Firstname, Surname
```

This will print out the corresponding columns from the database table, using just enough space for each of the columns. The comma does not imply that any space should be inserted between the columns; if a salutation is five characters long (Messr) and a first name (or initial) was supplied, the `Salut` and `Firstname` fields will run into each other. Each different type of data has a default format in which it will be printed. The default for character columns is as many output spaces as there are characters in the column. However, the value in the `Firstname` field will probably not be as long as the space allowed in the database, so the PRINT statement shown above will produce an ugly format with lots of space between some items and no space between others. The keyword CLIPPED truncates each of the columns after the last non-blank character in the field, and the keyword SPACE inserts a space between the separate fields. The keyword SPACES can be used as a synonym for SPACE, and any number of spaces could be specified. A better version of this line would read:

```
PRINT Salut CLIPPED, 1 SPACE, Firstname CLIPPED, 1 SPACE, Surname CLIPPED
```

Literal text is enclosed in quotes, so an alternative way of printing one space is:

```
PRINT Salut CLIPPED, " ", Firstname CLIPPED, " ", Surname CLIPPED
```

As in BASIC, it is possible to suppress the newline after a PRINT statement by appending a semicolon to the end of the statement. This means that the previous statement could be written as:

```
PRINT Salut CLIPPED;
PRINT " ";
PRINT Firstname CLIPPED;
PRINT " ";
PRINT Surname CLIPPED
```

This technique is not a good idea, if only because it makes it unnecessarily difficult to count the number of lines that will be printed in the control block. There are occasions when it is necessary to use the semicolon, but this is not one of them. Since the FORMAT section of a report is free format, the PRINT statements can be spread over several lines, and it is better to use several lines with one PRINT statement than to use the semicolon unnecessarily.

The keyword COLUMN indicates that the first character of the next output field is to be printed in the specified column. If the output is already beyond the specified column (eg if the second number in the example below was 20 instead of 40), the data which follows will be added immediately after what is already on the line with no intervening spaces.

```
PRINT COLUMN 7, "Estimated spending power: ", COLUMN 40, Maxmoney
```

6.5.2 The SKIP statement

The SKIP *n* LINES statement is used to leave *n* blank lines. It is a shorthand for writing a PRINT statement *n* times in a row without any arguments. LINES and LINE are synonyms.

```
SKIP 1 LINE
```

6.5.3 The NEED statement

It is often helpful if a collection of related lines all appear on the same page, rather than being split with some on one page and the rest on the next. In the absence of instructions to the contrary, ACE will put as many lines as possible on to one page, output the page footer and the page header for the next page, and then continue printing.

```
NEED 6 LINES
```

The NEED *n* LINES statement is used to indicate that the next *n* lines of output should be kept together on one page: if there is not enough room left, the output should go at the top of the next page. There is no need to say NEED 1 LINE although that would be legal. The keywords LINES and LINE are still synonymous.

6.5.4 An example ON EVERY ROW control block

Putting these ideas together produces the following format section for the **Customers** report.

```
FORMAT

ON EVERY ROW
     SKIP 1 LINE
     NEED 6 LINES
     PRINT Salut CLIPPED, 1 SPACE, Firstname CLIPPED, 1 SPACE, Surname CLIPPED
     PRINT Address1 CLIPPED
     PRINT Address2 CLIPPED
     PRINT Address3 CLIPPED, 5 SPACES, Postcode
     PRINT COLUMN 7, "Estimated spending power: ", Maxmoney
     PRINT COLUMN 7, "Last model: ", Coname CLIPPED,
               1 SPACE, Modelname CLIPPED, 1 SPACE, Details CLIPPED
END
```

The only mildly unsatisfactory thing about this is that it does not use all the data that is returned by the SELECT section: it does not matter, but it is marginally less efficient and slightly untidy.

One detail to note is the order of the SKIP and NEED keywords. Given the order as shown (SKIP and then NEED), when the current line is, say, five lines from the bottom of the page, one line will be skipped and four lines will be left. The NEED statement then causes the remaining lines to be skipped, the PAGE TRAILER is printed, followed by the PAGE HEADER of the next page, and then the PRINT statements after the NEED are executed. If the order of the SKIP and NEED lines was reversed, and the number of lines needed was changed to seven (which would be consistent, since the skipped line is now part of the block controlled by the NEED statement), the result would be slightly different. There are still only five lines left to the bottom of the page, so those lines are skipped, the PAGE TRAILER is printed, followed by the PAGE HEADER of the next page, and then the SKIP statement is executed, skipping a line at the top of the page, which is presumably unnecessary since the PAGE HEADER will have been set up to leave the correct space. This order wastes one line on each page of the report when the previous page had some blank lines left at the bottom because of a NEED statement.

6.6 Page layout

The format for ON EVERY ROW allows the layout of each row to be specified, but most reports benefit from having information printed at the top and bottom of each page. This is controlled by the control blocks PAGE HEADER and PAGE TRAILER.

There are some restrictions on the printing statements that can follow the keyword PAGE HEADER, but the only relevant one at the moment is that it is not possible to use the NEED statement. Typically, the printing statements will output a suitable title and the page number, and possibly column headings for the ON EVERY ROW control block. Similarly, the keyword PAGE TRAILER can be followed by a group of printing statements. The number of lines needed for the page header and trailer is automatically taken into account by the NEED statement.

Among the items that can be printed are TODAY (representing today's date), TIME (representing the current time) and PAGENO (representing the current page number). The default representation for a date is controlled by the DBDATE environment variable. If DBDATE is not set explicitly, the default format is 'mm/dd/yy' – the American style of date. An alternative way for printing today's date is DATE, which gives a date such as 'Fri Jan 04 1991'. The following control block is suitable for use with the **Customers** report:

```
PAGE HEADER
    PRINT "List of customers", COLUMN 25, TODAY, COLUMN 40, "Page ", PAGENO
    SKIP 1 LINE

PAGE TRAILER
    SKIP 1 LINE
    PRINT "Company Confidential - Do Not Disclose"
```

```
{
    @(#)custom1.ace      5.2 90/12/29
    Example report: Customers list
}

DATABASE Cars END

SELECT Companies.Company, Models.Modelname, Models.Details, Customers.*
    FROM     Companies, Models, Customers
    WHERE    Customers.Lastmodel = Models.Model
      AND    Models.Maker = Companies.Maker
    ORDER BY Company, Modelname, Details, Surname, Firstname
END

FORMAT

ON EVERY ROW
    SKIP 1 LINE
    NEED 6 LINES
    PRINT Salut CLIPPED, 1 SPACE, Firstname CLIPPED, 1 SPACE, Surname CLIPPED
    PRINT Address1 CLIPPED
    PRINT Address2 CLIPPED
    PRINT Address3 CLIPPED, 5 SPACES, Postcode
    PRINT COLUMN 7, "Estimated spending power: ", Maxmoney
    PRINT COLUMN 7, "Last model: ", Coname CLIPPED,
            1 SPACE, Modelname CLIPPED, 1 SPACE, Details CLIPPED

PAGE HEADER
    PRINT "List of customers", COLUMN 25, TODAY, COLUMN 40, "Page ", PAGENO
    SKIP 1 LINE

PAGE TRAILER
    SKIP 1 LINE
    PRINT "Company Confidential - Do Not Disclose"

END
```

Figure 6.3 The complete **Customers** report

6.7 Putting it all together

All the example code shown in this chapter is used to create the complete **Customers** report shown in Figure 6.3. The first page of output from this report is illustrated in Figure 6.4. The default layout for a report has 66 lines per page, with the top three and bottom three left blank. The text of the report is indented by 5 spaces. This is ideal for reports where the output goes to a printer, but not entirely satisfactory for reports which go to the screen. Altering the page dimensions will be discussed in Chapter 9. The top and bottom margins have been removed from Figure 6.4.

```
List of customers        09/02/1991     Page      1

Mr I.G. Pye
20-22 Southampton St
Eastleigh
SOUTHAMPTON
        Estimated spending power:     £7500
        Last model: Audi Model 80 80 Turbo Diesel


Mr J. Goueralor
Security Centre
CWMBRAN
Gwent
        Estimated spending power:     £7500
        Last model: Audi Model 80 80CL


Mr Jose Vanterpool
87 London St
READING
Berkshire
        Estimated spending power:     £7500
        Last model: Audi Model 80 Coupe GT


Dr T.K. Metcalf
20 Queens Rd
St James
LONDON     SW1Y 6AP
        Estimated spending power:     £7500
        Last model: Austin-Rover Ambassador 2.0HLS


Mr D.I. Calderwood
8 Springfield
East Finchley
LONDON     N2 9NF
        Estimated spending power:     £7500
        Last model: Austin-Rover Metro Vanden Plas


Ms H. Murphy
58 Clapham Common Nth
LONDON     SW4
        Estimated spending power:     £7500
        Last model: BMW Series 3 323i


Mr T.F. Saint
Anzani House
EGHAM
Surrey     TW20 9DP
        Estimated spending power:     £7500
        Last model: BMW Series 7 735i


Mr Richard Plumb
14-15 Lemon Street
PAISLEY
Renfrewshire     PA1 2BE
        Estimated spending power:     £7500
        Last model: Citroen 2CV6 Club

Company Confidential - Do Not Disclose
```

Figure 6.4 The first page of output from the **Customers** report

6.8 Summary

This chapter has described what a report is and shown two methods for generating a report. It also described the six sections in a report and looked in detail at the most important one, the FORMAT section. The FORMAT section has a number of different control blocks which can be used to control the printing of the report; this chapter only described three of them in any detail – ON EVERY ROW, PAGE HEADER and PAGE TRAILER. It also pointed out the crucial difference between the default control block EVERY ROW and the control block used to print each row of data, ON EVERY ROW.

Exercises

1. Produce a report which lists all the cars in stock. Make sure that you list the maker's name, the model name and details, the price when new, as well as all the details from the **Stock** table.

2. Write a report listing the details of cars sold; we need to know the make, model and details, registration, the amount it was bought for, the amount it was sold for and the profit made.

## Part III

Intermediate INFORMIX-SQL

7
Multi-table forms

Chapter 4 introduced the basic ideas about how to build and use forms, but all the forms there only referenced one table. The majority of useful forms actually need to use more than one table at a time. For example, the form developed in Chapter 4 would be improved if the full name of the car model was displayed, rather than forcing the user to guess the correct model number.

This chapter covers some of the features of forms which were not covered in Chapter 4; the others are covered in Chapter 11. It first describes the extra attributes not covered in Chapter 4. It then describes how to build multi-table forms, use joining conditions for both display and verification of data, use the QUERYCLEAR and LOOKUP attributes, and use the **Screen**, **Table**, **Master**, **Detail** and **Current** options in the menu of PERFORM.

7.1 More attributes

The most frequently used attributes were described in Chapter 4. This section describes the remaining attributes except QUERYCLEAR and LOOKUP which are only applicable to multi-table forms and will therefore be covered later in this chapter.

7.1.1 Input attributes

NOUPDATE
The NOUPDATE attribute is essentially the same as NOENTRY, except it prohibits changes being made when the **Update** option is being used, rather than when the **Add** option is being used. It is not possible to update SERIAL columns regardless of whether this attribute is specified or not.

PICTURE
The PICTURE attribute is superficially similar to the FORMAT attribute, but it applies to character fields and it is an *input* attribute, not a display attribute. The symbols in Table 7.1 are recognized by PICTURE. Any other characters are regarded as literals. When the field is used for input, any literal characters will be shown in the display field to help remind the user of the required format. The user will be constrained to

Symbol	Interpretation
A	Any letter
#	Any digit
X	Any character

Table 7.1 Symbols for PICTURE

type digits where '#' occurs, alphabetic characters where 'A' occurs and may type anything where 'X' occurs. The literal characters are automatically skipped over.

This can be illustrated by the following example, which attempts to format British postcodes:

```
f007 = customers.postcode, UPSHIFT, PICTURE = "AXXX #AA";
```

This handles the postcodes in London such as WC1R 2HB, as well as Birmingham postcodes such as B7 8BJ or B15 2EN and provincial postcodes such as RG1 3PY or GL50 9TL. It does not give the operator any help.

To verify that the PICTURE attribute is not a display attribute, use a form without a PICTURE attribute to enter data into a field in a format that the PICTURE attribute would not allow. When this value is displayed via an enquiry, the value will not be changed to conform to the PICTURE specification. If, on the other hand, the user chooses to update the row and modifies any character in the PICTURE-validated field, the user will be made to modify the data to match the picture.

VERIFY

The VERIFY attribute is used when a particular entry is very important. The user is made to re-enter the data in this field and it must be re-entered identically, character for character. Thus, in a numeric field, 1 and 1.00 evaluate to the same value, but are different entries for verification.

RIGHT

The RIGHT attribute is used to right-justify the data in the corresponding field. Once the data has been entered, it will be shifted right unless it already extends to the end of the display field.

7.1.2 Display attributes

ZEROFILL

The ZEROFILL attribute can be applied to any field type but is most useful with numeric fields. The field is automatically right-justified and padded with leading zeros.

7.1.3 The WORDWRAP and COMPRESS attributes

Version 4.00. There are two variants of the WORDWRAP attribute, namely WORDWRAP and WORDWRAP COMPRESS. Both are used in conjunction with long

```
{
    @(#)longflds.sql    5.4 90/12/29
    @(#)Table for demonstrating WORDWRAP and COMPRESS
}

CREATE TABLE Long_fields
(
    Field00     SERIAL(1000) NOT NULL,
    Field01     CHAR(255)    NOT NULL,
    Field02     CHAR(255)    NOT NULL
);
CREATE UNIQUE INDEX Pk_long_fields ON Long_fields(Field00);
```

Figure 7.1 Table used to illustrate WORDWRAP and COMPRESS

character fields. The design of the **Cars** database deliberately avoids any very long fields because they are not handled very conveniently in older versions of INFORMIX-SQL. To illustrate WORDWRAP, a form will be created on the table **Long_fields** shown in Figure 7.1. A simple form based on this table is shown in Figure 7.2. This form shows that the two long database columns are treated as five independent form fields. They can, in fact, each be given different attributes. In particular, unless all the form fields are given the AUTONEXT attribute, the user will have to split the input manually, hitting the RETURN key at the end of each line and ensuring that words are not split.

With version 4.00, the form can be modified as shown in Figure 7.3. Looking at the long fields, you will observe that the first five long fields all have the same field tag, as do the second set of five. In the ATTRIBUTES section, there is only one entry for either **Long_fields.Field01** or **Long_fields.Field02**, and these both include the attribute WORDWRAP COMPRESS. (The significance of the UPSHIFT and DOWNSHIFT attributes will be made apparent in Chapter 9 where the use of WORDWRAP in reports is discussed.) When the user starts typing in **Field01**, the words will appear exactly as before, until the end of the first line. At the end of the first line, the built-in editor will automatically carry over any part-word on to the second line and let the user continue typing there, and so on for the third, fourth and fifth lines. The same obviously applies for **Field02**, except that everything will be converted to upper-case letters instead of lower case.

The difference between WORDWRAP and WORDWRAP COMPRESS becomes apparent when the data is saved in the database. If the attribute is simply WORDWRAP, any spaces inserted by the editor are retained in the database. This means that if the data is ever extracted, it must be shown in lines of the same length as on the form that was used to enter the data; otherwise, the words will not break cleanly and will have unwanted spaces between them where the original ends of the lines were. On the other hand, if the attribute WORDWRAP COMPRESS is used, the editor carefully notes which spaces it inserted and which were inserted by the user, and when the data is saved, it will remove the spaces it inserted (thus shortening the string, hence COMPRESS). This string can then be printed without unsightly extra spaces. One interesting consequence of the COMPRESS facility is that it would be possible to provide some extra space on the form to allow for the average space left at the end of each line where the words are wrapped. If words contain an average of

```
(
    @(#)longfdef.per    5.3 90/08/31
    Form showing how long character fields are handled
)

DATABASE Cars

SCREEN
(
Field00              [f000        ]
Field01              [f001                                                 ]
                     [f002                                                 ]
                     [f003                                                 ]
                     [f004                                                 ]
                     [f005                                                 ]
Field02              [f006                                                 ]
                     [f007                                                 ]
                     [f008                                                 ]
                     [f009                                                 ]
                     [f010                                                 ]
)
END

TABLES
Long_fields

ATTRIBUTES
f000 = Long_fields.Field00;
f001 = Long_fields.Field01[1,51];
f002 = Long_fields.Field01[52,102];
f003 = Long_fields.Field01[103,153];
f004 = Long_fields.Field01[154,204];
f005 = Long_fields.Field01[205,255];
f006 = Long_fields.Field02[1,51];
f007 = Long_fields.Field02[52,102];
f008 = Long_fields.Field02[103,153];
f009 = Long_fields.Field02[154,204];
f010 = Long_fields.Field02[205,255];
END
```

Figure 7.2 Simple form for table **Long_fields**

six characters each, then with five lines of data something like 15 extra characters could be entered.

Why is WORDWRAP alone useful? Because it allows you to subdivide the output knowing exactly where to break each line. If you look ahead to Section 9.12, you will see that if the data was entered using just WORDWRAP, it would be possible to print several long columns in parallel down the page, whereas if it was entered using WORDWRAP_COMPRESS, this is not feasible.

Within a multi-line field, some keys change their meaning slightly. For example, the up-arrow key will move the cursor up one line within the same multi-line field. If the cursor is already in the top line, it will jump to the start of the previous field, which is what it would normally do. Similarly, the down-arrow key will move down one line of a multi-line field, unless it is already in the bottom line in which case it moves on to the start of the next field. The RETURN key always moves on to the next field. The TAB key no longer moves you into the next field; if you are in typeover mode (as you are, by default), the TAB key moves you on to the tabstop

```
(
    a(#)longflds.per    5.3 90/08/31
    Form demonstrating WORDWRAP and COMPRESS
)

DATABASE Cars

SCREEN SIZE 24 BY 80
(
Field00            [f000]
Field01            [f001                                    ]
                   [f001                                    ]
                   [f001                                    ]
                   [f001                                    ]
                   [f001                                    ]
Field02            [f006                                    ]
                   [f006                                    ]
                   [f006                                    ]
                   [f006                                    ]
                   [f006                                    ]
)
END

TABLES
Long_fields

ATTRIBUTES
f000 = Long_fields.Field00;
f001 = Long_fields.Field01, WORDWRAP COMPRESS, DOWNSHIFT;
f006 = Long_fields.Field02, WORDWRAP COMPRESS, UPSHIFT;
END
```

Figure 7.3 Form using WORDWRAP

(multiple of eight characters) where there is a real character (as opposed to an editor-inserted blank). If you are in insert mode, the TAB inserts a TAB character. The CONTROL-N key also becomes significant; it inserts a newline character which means that the cursor will move to the following line of the same multi-line field. It will also move any text after the cursor down to the new line, possibly shunting some text off the end of the field (and thereby losing it).

7.1.4 The COLOR attribute

Version 4.00. The COLOR attribute (well, it is an American product, isn't it) is a useful addition to the attributes. It is, however, more complex than any other attribute, and is affected both by the terminal you are using and by whether you are using **termcap** or **terminfo** to describe your terminal to Informix. The basic use of COLOR is simple enough:

```
f001 = Companies.Company, COLOR = RED;
```

The accepted colours are WHITE, YELLOW, MAGENTA, RED, CYAN, GREEN, BLUE and BLACK. You can also specify one or more of the effects BLINK, UNDERLINE, REVERSE and LEFT, or you could specify one of the effects instead of a colour. What actually happens at run-time depends on the terminal, but with a sufficiently powerful terminal, you could have a green, blinking, underlined, reverse-video field with the number in it right-justified (instead of being left-justified as normal). On the other hand, if the terminal description that Informix uses only tells it how to do reverse video, you will only get reverse video.

The other useful facility with COLOR is that you can specify different colours depending on certain conditions. For example, the customer number could be colour coded depending on how recently the last contact was made with the customer.

```
f000 = Customers.Number,
        COLOR = RED   WHERE f011 <  (TODAY - 180),
        COLOR = BLUE  WHERE f011 >= (TODAY - 180)
                        AND f011 <= (TODAY - 31),
        COLOR = GREEN WHERE f011 <  (TODAY - 31);
```

This would show customers not contacted in the last six months or so in red, those contacted within the last month in green, and the remainder in blue. Field f011 is assumed to be the tag for **Customers.Contactdate**. There is one irritating feature to this; the field tag f011 must already have been defined when the COLOR specification for field tag f000 is defined. With the **Customers** form, this is not too severe, because the user does not normally enter anything in the field, but it could be a nuisance elsewhere. Note that if the colour only depends on the contents of the current field, there is no problem.

Colour (in the sense of red, blue, green) is not available if Informix is using **terminfo**; it requires non-standard capabilities in **termcap** which are well documented in one of the appendices in the reference manual or user guide (depending on which version of INFORMIX-SQL you are using). The BLINK, UNDERLINE, REVERSE and LEFT colour attributes are available with both systems.

7.2 Simple multi-table forms

Simple multi-table forms do not make any connections between the different tables listed; they offer little extra power over single-table forms from Chapter 4, but they are the basis for using the more powerful facilities described in the subsequent sections of this chapter.

7.2.1 Generating a simple multi-table form

The simplest way to generate a multi-table form is to use the **Generate** option in the **Form** menu, just as in Chapter 4. After you have chosen the first table, it will prompt you with the options **Table-selection-complete** or **Select-more-tables**. To generate a multi-table form, choose the second option and select another table, and repeat this until you have chosen all the tables which the form will use. It is worth choosing the tables in the order you will want to use them, although you can, of course, change the order later. The form that is generated will have one screen layout for each of the tables you specified (or, if any of the tables is so big that it will not fit on to one screen, the table will have several screen layouts, just as it would in a single-table form) and the ATTRIBUTES section will list all the columns in all the tables.

7.2.2 Customizing a simple multi-table form

Each screen on the generated multi-table form can be customized as before, but there is no requirement that the data for each table be kept on a separate screen. If it seems convenient, the fields from several tables can be included on one screen. This is often easier for users, since they do not have to worry about handling multiple screens. Also, any field can appear on several different screens. The display field should have the same tag and be the same length wherever it occurs.

7.3 Joining fields

The generated form does not make any connections between the different tables; the data in each table of the multi-table form is completely independent of the other tables. However, one of the most important features of PERFORM is that it allows fields from several tables to be joined together so that the user can see the values from both tables at once. It is also possible to verify that the data entered in a field corresponds to the value in the table to which the field is joined.

7.3.1 Simply joined fields

The form shown in Figure 7.4 is a customized version of a form generated on the three tables **Stock**, **Models** and **Companies**. In this form, a join has been declared between **Stock.Model** and **Models.Model**, and another join has been declared between **Models.Maker** and **Companies.Maker**. The basic way of joining two fields is:

```
f001 = Stock.Model = Models.Model;
f011 = Models.Maker = Companies.Maker;
```

Now the purpose of the field with tag f001 depends on which table is active: if the **Models** table is active, the value is the model number for the row of data on display from the current set of rows in the **Models** table; if the **Stock** table is active, the field shows the model number of the current row from the **Stock** table. The original field tag for **Models.Model** has to be changed; the field tag on the second screen would also be f001, and a similar change applies for field f011.

7.3.2 QUERYCLEAR

Suppose that you use the form to enquire for all the models in stock. If you need to see the details of what the current model is, you can use the **Screen** option, which

```
(
    a(#)stock3a.per      5.2 91/03/07
    Multi-table forms -- example
)

DATABASE Cars

SCREEN
(
        Stock List
        ==========

Registration  [f000   ]
Model         [f001] [f011]
              [f021           ]
              [f012                    ] [f013              ]
Colour        [f002  ]
Condition     [a]
Date Bought   [f003    ]
Bought For    [f004      ]
Mileage       [f005     ]
Notes
[f006                                          ]
[f008                                          ]
)

SCREEN
(
        Model List
        ==========

Model         [f001]
Maker         [f011]
              [f021           ]
Modelname     [f012            ]
Details       [f013            ]
Price         [f014   ]
Maxspeed      [f015    ]
Accel         [f016 ]
Tanksize      [f017 ]
Urban         [f018   ]
Mpgat56       [f019   ]
)

SCREEN
(
        Company Details
        ===============
```

Figure 7.4 Multi-table form with joined fields

will change the screen and show the data for the model which is currently on show in the **Stock** screen. Change the screen again and the details for the company are also visible. Notice that only the model number field on the **Models** screen has square brackets around it, and that none of the fields on the **Company** screen has brackets around it. Only the fields that correspond directly to the current table (**Stock**) have brackets around them.

```
Company Number  [f011]
Company Name    [f021          ]
Address         [f022                    ]
                [f023                    ]
                [f024                    ]
Postcode        [f025     ]
Phone           [f026         ]

Notes
[f028                                    ]
[f030                                    ]
}
END


TABLES
Stock
Models
Companies


ATTRIBUTES
f000 = Stock.Registration;
f001 = Stock.Model = Models.Model, QUERYCLEAR;
f002 = Stock.Colour;
a = Stock.Condition;
f003 = Stock.Datebought;
f004 = Stock.Boughtfor;
f005 = Stock.Mileage;
f006 = Stock.Notes1;
f008 = Stock.Notes2;

f011 = Models.Maker = Companies.Maker, QUERYCLEAR;
f012 = Models.Modelname;
f013 = Models.Details;
f014 = Models.Price;
f015 = Models.Maxspeed;
f016 = Models.Accel;
f017 = Models.Tanksize;
f018 = Models.Urban;
f019 = Models.Mpgat56;

f021 = Companies.Company;
f022 = Companies.Address1;
f023 = Companies.Address2;
f024 = Companies.Address3;
f025 = Companies.Postcode;
f026 = Companies.Phone;
f028 = Companies.Notes1;
f030 = Companies.Notes2;
END
```

Figure 7.4 (*cont.*)

If you change the current (or active) table to **Models**, the screen will automatically change to the **Models** screen, and the data for the model previously on show in the **Stock** screen will be shown. If you then do a query, notice that the model number field is not cleared; this is not a bug but a feature that makes it easier to do certain types of enquiries. If you want the field to be cleared on any enquiry, you can use the attribute QUERYCLEAR to force it to be cleared.

As an example of an enquiry that would be easier because the join field is not cleared unless the QUERYCLEAR attribute is used, consider selecting a set of companies first, then changing to the **Models** table. The company number field would already be set to the current company, so it would be very easy to select all the models made by that manufacturer.

7.4 Using a multi-table form

Using the form in Figure 7.4 is similar to using a single-table form as in Chapter 4, except that if you need to look up values in any of the other tables, you can do so without exiting from PERFORM. There is always a current (or active) table in PERFORM, and its name is shown at the right-hand end of the second line of the screen. You can use the **Table** option to change the current table; you can also type 2T to move to table 2 (the **Models** table in the example form), regardless of which table is the current table. Each table has a current list associated with it – that is, the rows from the current table which have been enquired – so you can make a separate enquiry for each table.

Notice that when you change table, the screen layout changes to the one showing the active table. You can always go back to another screen by using the **Screen** option, and you can also use 2S to move to screen 2. Sometimes a table is so big that not all the data can be fitted on to one screen; when that happens, you can use the **Screen** option to change between screens. Also notice that as you change screens, information is normally shown on each screen, and the information is deduced by selecting data that matches the current row of data from the current table using any joining conditions that are defined. The joining conditions may be of the type where table A joins to table B, table B joins to table C, and table C joins to table D. If table A is the current table and you switch to the screen displaying table D, the data displayed will be chosen using these three joins. If there are no appropriate joining conditions between the current table and the data that would be displayed on the screen, nothing will be displayed.

If you are adding data for a table with data shown on multiple screens, PERFORM will automatically switch screens so that all the data can be entered. You may need to change the screen after adding to such a table.

7.4.1 The Current option

The **Current** option is also relevant with multi-table forms. When there are several tables, there is an active list for each table, as mentioned above. Also, when the current table is changed, the data on display remains unchanged, except that the set of fields with brackets around them changes; this too was mentioned earlier. One consequence of this is that if you have an active list of models and an active list of companies, when you search through the list of models to find an answer to a question and then switch back to the companies screen, the data on show is probably not that of the current row in the companies list – it would only be the current row if the model looked at last was made by that manufacturer. To see the data in the current row of the companies list, use the **Current** option. This goes to the database and reselects the data for the current row of the current table and displays it.

This facility is also useful if you suspect that someone else may have changed the data recently; because it goes back to the database to fetch the current row again, the data which is shown is always the most recent available. Note that even in single-table forms, the **Current** option selects the data again.

Also, when you select the **Update** option, the row of data is fetched again and the row in the database is locked so that no one else can change it while you are doing so. This is important if more than one person could be changing the database at the same time; otherwise, one person could fetch the row to make the changes, and then a second person; both would edit the record, probably in different ways, and one person would write a set of amendments back, and then the other, and the first set of amendments would be lost completely. The automatic locking procedure prevents this happening.

7.5 Verify joins

Although the previous form was quite useful, there are several improvements that can be made. For example, the primary purpose of this form is to look through the **Stock** table; it would be useful if the information about model name and maker was on the same screen as the other stock information. Also, if the form is to be used for looking at the **Stock** table, there is no need to be able to change the **Models** and **Companies** tables. When the user adds a model to the **Stock** table, it would be helpful if the user was only allowed to enter a valid model number. Finally, there are a number of minor details that improve the usability of the form; in particular, the registration number should be in upper case and the user should not need to press RETURN after entering the seventh character in the registration number.

The next version of the form is shown in Figure 7.5. Notice that all the fields are on the one screen. This form cannot be used for entering **Models** or **Companies** data any longer; the NOENTRY and NOUPDATE attributes ensure that the user cannot enter data in the **Models** and **Companies** tables. However, the user can still delete a record from either of these tables – see Chapter 11 for details of how to prevent the user from deleting rows from a table, and another way of preventing the user from adding or updating rows in a table. (If the NOENTRY and NOUPDATE attributes were not present, the user could actually enter a new model or a new company because all the columns in those tables which do not accept null values are on display. When PERFORM inserts a record into the database, any columns which are not visible on the form are given a null value. Because all the columns which must have a non-null value are on display, an insert into either the **Models** or the **Companies** table would succeed. This form is not intended to be used for maintaining the **Models** and **Companies** tables, and the presence of the NOENTRY and NOUPDATE attributes prevents it from being used to maintain those tables.)

```
{
    @(#)stock4.per        5.5 91/02/24
    Multi-table forms -- verify join
}

DATABASE Cars

SCREEN
{

        Stock List
        ==========

Registration   [f000   ]
Model Number   [f001] [f011]
Description    [f021            ]
               [f012                  ][f013              ]
Colour         [f002   ]
Condition      [a]
Date Bought    [f003     ]
Bought For     [f004       ]
Mileage        [f005      ]
Notes
[f006                                       ]
[f008                                       ]
}
END


TABLES
Stock
Models
Companies

ATTRIBUTES
f000 = Stock.Registration, UPSHIFT, AUTONEXT, PICTURE = "AXXXXXA";
f001 = Stock.Model, QUERYCLEAR;
     =*Models.Model, QUERYCLEAR, NOENTRY, NOUPDATE;
f002 = Stock.Colour;
a    = Stock.Condition, AUTONEXT, UPSHIFT,
         INCLUDE = ('X', 'V', 'G', 'A', 'P'),
         COMMENTS = "Xcellent, Very good, Good, Average, Poor";
f003 = Stock.Datebought;
f004 = Stock.Boughtfor;
f005 = Stock.Mileage;
f006 = Stock.Notes1;
f008 = Stock.Notes2;

f011 = Models.Maker = Companies.Maker, QUERYCLEAR, NOENTRY, NOUPDATE;
f012 = Models.Modelname, NOENTRY, NOUPDATE;
f013 = Models.Details, NOENTRY, NOUPDATE;

f021 = Companies.Company, NOENTRY, NOUPDATE;
END
```

Figure 7.5 Multi-table form with verify joins

There are several important differences between the example attributes used previously and the ones in this form, quite apart from the extensive use of both NOENTRY and NOUPDATE.

First of all, the asterisk '*' in the join for f001 means that the join is a *verify* join. When the current table is Stock and the user is entering a new row, the model number entered is verified against the **Models** table to ensure that there is an entry in that table for the model number just entered; the user will be told if there is no such value in the **Models** table.

```
f001 = Stock.Model, QUERYCLEAR;
       =*Models.Model, QUERYCLEAR, NOENTRY, NOUPDATE;

f011 = Models.Maker = Companies.Maker, QUERYCLEAR, NOENTRY, NOUPDATE;
```

Secondly, different sets of attributes apply to field `f001` depending on whether the active table is **Stock** or **Models**. When **Stock** is the active table, the field is cleared whenever an enquiry is made, but the only other constraint is that imposed by the join. When **Models** is the active table, the field is cleared on query, but the user cannot alter the data in the **Models** table by adding a new row or by changing an existing row. (The user can still delete a row, though; the way of preventing that is described later.)

The way of specifying different attributes depending on which table is active uses the extra semicolon to indicate that the attribute list for the first table is complete (possibly empty) and that the second table then follows.

Notice that the user can still make enquiries on either the **Models** or the **Companies** tables; this means that the user can find out which model number is correct without having to remember it, without having to look at a paper list of models and without having to run another form.

7.6 Referential integrity with PERFORM

Verify joins can also be given another use. When you try to delete a row from a table, call it A, which is marked with an asterisk, PERFORM checks whether there are any rows which join with the row to be deleted in any of the tables listed as joining with table A. If any of the other tables does contain a matching row, PERFORM issues a suitable message saying that it cannot delete the row.

It would be possible, and probably sensible, to exploit this feature in a form such as the **Companies** form from Chapter 4 by adding the **Models** table to the list of tables, and making **Companies.Maker** the controlling column of a verify join with **Models.Maker**. Then, if the user ever tries to delete a record from the **Companies** table, PERFORM will check whether there are any rows in the **Models** table which join with it, and if so, the delete will be rejected. A similar precaution should be built into any form which maintains the **Models** table, except that the joining tables should be **Customers, Sales, Stock** and **Prices**.

7.7 Using LOOKUP attributes

The only attribute which has not been discussed now is the LOOKUP attribute. This can be used instead of (or as well as) joined fields. It is used to select data from a table other than the current one and to display the results in a particular field. It is

```
(
    @(#)stock5.per      5.5 91/02/24
    Multi-table forms -- lookup
)

DATABASE Cars

SCREEN
(

        Stock List
        ==========

Registration   [f000  ]
Model Number   [f001] [f011]
Description    [f021          ]
               [f012              ] [f013          ]
Colour         [f002  ]
Condition      [a]
Date Bought    [f003    ]
Bought For     [f004      ]
Mileage        [f005      ]
Notes
[f006                                          ]
[f008                                          ]
)
END


TABLES
Stock
Models
Companies


ATTRIBUTES
f000 = Stock.Registration, UPSHIFT, AUTONEXT, PICTURE = "AXXXXXA";
f001 = Stock.Model, QUERYCLEAR;
     =*Models.Model, QUERYCLEAR, NOENTRY, NOUPDATE;
f002 = Stock.Colour;
a    = Stock.Condition, AUTONEXT, UPSHIFT,
         INCLUDE = ('X', 'V', 'G', 'A', 'P'),
         COMMENTS = "Xcellent, Very good, Good, Average, Poor";
f003 = Stock.Datebought;
f004 = Stock.Boughtfor;
f005 = Stock.Mileage;
f006 = Stock.Notes1;
f008 = Stock.Notes2;

f011 = Models.Maker, QUERYCLEAR, NOENTRY, NOUPDATE,
         LOOKUP   f021 = Companies.Company
         JOINING Companies.Maker;
f012 = Models.Modelname, NOENTRY, NOUPDATE;
f013 = Models.Details, NOENTRY, NOUPDATE;

END
```

Figure 7.6 Multi-table form with look-up

also used to prevent data from being entered into the current table if the value does
not exist in another table.

For example, it would be possible to use a look-up to find the company name
for a given model, as shown in Figure 7.6. The main difference between this and the

previous form is in the specification used for field tags f011 and f021. Previously, the specification for f021 was as for an ordinary field. Now, it is the subject of a LOOKUP clause:

```
f011 = Models.Maker, QUERYCLEAR, NOENTRY, NOUPDATE,
       LOOKUP   f021 = Companies.Company JOINING Companies.Maker;
```

Note, too, that field f011 is not equated to **Companies.Maker** as it would be in an ordinary joined field. What happens now is that when a value is displayed in the **Models.Maker** field, that value is used to look up the corresponding company by joining the **Models.Maker** column with the **Companies.Maker** column. The selected value for **Companies.Company** is then displayed in the field with tag f021. This field (f021) cannot be used for input; indeed, the **Companies** table cannot now be made the current table at all.

Since this form cannot be used to add rows to the **Models** table, it is not critical whether the look-up is made into a *verify* look-up or not; the example is not a verify look-up. However, if data could be added to the **Models** table using this form, it would be important for the table to be kept consistent with the **Companies** table, and this could be done by making it into a verify join, thus:

```
f011 = Models.Maker, QUERYCLEAR, NOENTRY, NOUPDATE,
       LOOKUP   f021 = Companies.Company
       JOINING *Companies.Maker;
```

The asterisk '*' is crucial; it converts the look-up into a verify look-up, and the user could not now enter an invalid value for **Models.Maker**. In fact, the look-up need not actually display anything. This would be indicated by omitting the display tag and the column name:

```
f011 = Models.Maker, QUERYCLEAR, NOENTRY, NOUPDATE,
       LOOKUP JOINING *Companies.Maker;
```

Although the asterisk is theoretically optional, if there is no display and no verify look-up, there is no point in having the look-up at all.

Although it has not been illustrated here, a single look-up could be used to fetch several values at once, so that, for example, the company address could be shown as well as the name:

```
f011 = Models.Maker, QUERYCLEAR, NOENTRY, NOUPDATE,
       LOOKUP   f021 = Companies.Company,
                f022 = Companies.Address1,
                f023 = Companies.Address2,
                f024 = Companies.Address3,
                f025 = Companies.Postcode
       JOINING *Companies.Maker;
```

7.8 Master/detail relationships

When one row of a table in a database is associated with several rows of another table, it is useful to set up a master/detail relationship between the two tables. This can be achieved by adding a suitable instruction to the INSTRUCTIONS section of the

```
{
   a(#)masdet1a.per    5.1 91/03/07
   Master/Detail Form Example
}

DATABASE Cars

SCREEN
{

                    Add New Manufacturer

Company Number[f000]
Company Name  [f001          ]
Address       [f002               ]
                         [f003              ]
                         [f004              ]
                         [f005   ]


Notes:
[f007                                      ]
[f008                                      ]
}

SCREEN
{

                 Models Made by New Manufacturer

Model Number  [f009     ]
Maker         [f000][f001          ]
Model Name    [f010             ]
Model Details [f011             ]

Price         [f012   ]
Maximum Speed [f13]mph
Acceleration  [f014]seconds
Tank Size     [f015]gallons

Fuel consumption
Urban Cycle   [f016]mpg
At 56 mph     [f017]mpg

                    Guide prices
Year [g001] Low [g002    ] High [g003    ]
}
END

TABLES
Companies
Models
```

Figure 7.7 Multi-table form showing master/detail relationships

form. For example, there are many models associated with any manufacturer, so it would be useful to add the instruction:

```
Companies MASTER OF Models
```

This means that when a row of data is entered into the **Companies** table, the user can select the **Detail** option and some of the information from **Companies** can be

```
Prices

ATTRIBUTES

f000 =*Companies.Maker = Models.Maker,
         NOENTRY, NOUPDATE, QUERYCLEAR;
f001 = Companies.Company, QUERYCLEAR;
f002 = Companies.Address1;
f003 = Companies.Address2;
f004 = Companies.Address3;
f005 = Companies.Postcode,
         PICTURE = "AXXX #AA", UPSHIFT, AUTONEXT;
f007 = Companies.Notes1;
f008 = Companies.Notes2;

f009 =*Models.Model, QUERYCLEAR;
     = Prices.Model, NOENTRY, NOUPDATE, QUERYCLEAR;
f010 = Models.Modelname,
         COMMENTS =
         "Enter basic name of model (eg Escort)";
f011 = Models.Details,
         COMMENTS =
         "Enter all details (eg 1.4GL 4-door)";
f012 = Models.Price,
         INCLUDE = (1000 TO 100000);
f13  = Models.Maxspeed,
         INCLUDE = (30 TO 200);
f014 = Models.Accel,
         FORMAT = "##.#",
         INCLUDE = (1 TO 50),
         COMMENTS = "Time for 0 - 60 mph";
f015 = Models.Tanksize,
         FORMAT = "##.#",
         INCLUDE = (5 TO 50);
f016 = Models.Urban,
         INCLUDE = (1 TO 100);
f017 = Models.Mpgat56,
         INCLUDE = (1 TO 100);

g001 = Prices.Year_made,
         COMMENTS = "Enter a year between 1960 and now",
         INCLUDE = (1960 TO 1999);
g002 = Prices.Lo_price;
g003 = Prices.Hi_price;
END

INSTRUCTIONS
Companies MASTER OF Models
Models MASTER OF Prices
END
```

Figure 7.7 *(cont.)*

carried over to **Models,** providing the ATTRIBUTES section allows this. There must be a join between the two tables for there to be a master/detail relationship between them. The information carried over in the **Companies/Models** example would be **Companies.Maker,** which becomes **Models.Maker** when the **Models** table is active. Suppose that the value displayed in the field containing **Companies.Maker** was 18. When the **Detail** option was selected, PERFORM would automatically execute a query to find all the rows in the **Models** table (the detail table) which have the value 18 stored in the **Models.Maker** column and display the first such row. When you had finished working with the list of models for maker number 18, you would use the **Master** option to resume operations on the list of companies.

Suppose we have a form for entering new manufacturers. When a manufacturer is added, we will also want to add the models made by the manufacturer and the prices of those models. We do this by creating a form with two screens. We specify the three tables **Companies**, **Models** and **Prices**, and a master/detail relationship between **Companies** and **Models**, and another between **Models** and **Prices**. The form shown in Figure 7.7 illustrates this.

When the details for a manufacturer have been added (or enquired or updated), the **Models** table can be used by selecting the **Detail** option. This makes the **Models** table into the current table, and also makes PERFORM enquire all the models corresponding to the current maker and display the first of these on the second screen. (Of course, if it was a new manufacturer, there would not be any models yet, and PERFORM would display the message 'There are no rows satisfying the conditions'.) It is then possible to work on the **Models** table using the same mechanism as before. Because of the way the NOENTRY and NOUPDATE conditions have been set up, the user cannot add any new models except for the current manufacturer. When all the models have been entered, selecting the **Master** option allows another manufacturer to be dealt with.

There is an important difference between using a master/detail relationship and using the **Table** option, and this is what happens when you switch from the **Companies** table to the **Models** table. If you use the **Table** option, the current company number is transferred to the **Models** screen and one row of data from the **Models** table is displayed. It is now possible to use the **Models** table in any way that is required. If, instead, you use the **Detail** option, PERFORM automatically runs a query for all the rows in the **Models** table made by the current manufacturer, and these rows can be viewed using **Next** and **Previous** as usual. If there are no models, you will be told.

As the example shows, it is possible to have multiple master/detail relationships on one form. To use this properly in the example, the user either adds a new company or enquires a list of old ones and chooses one of them to work with. Using the **Detail** option to make the **Models** table current, the user can then add or change the models associated with the manufacturer. For any model, the user can use the **Detail** option again to make the **Prices** table current and edit the prices associated with the current model. When the prices are correct, the user would use the **Master** option to make the **Models** table current again and move on to another model, changing the prices for that in the same way as before. When all the models for the manufacturer are complete, the user would use the **Master** option again to make the **Companies** table current again.

If necessary, one table can be the master of several others; in the **Cars** database, the obvious candidate is the **Models** table which every other table joins with. If this is used, choosing the **Master** option uses the first master/detail relationship specified; to choose one of the other detail tables, the form '2D' or '3D' must be used to select the second or third detail table. You should only expect an experienced and well-informed user to use such a form.

PERFORM also allows a form to have two master/detail relationships between two tables; for example, there could be a master/detail relationship between **Models** and **Prices** and a second between **Prices** and **Models**. In the **Cars** database, this would not serve any useful purpose, but with some databases it could be useful. For example, consider a database much used by database textbook authors, a register of students and courses. Students take courses, so there would be a sensible master/detail relationship between the **Students** and **Courses** table so that the user could easily list which courses a particular student was taking. In the same way, each course has students on it, so there is a useful master/detail relationship between the **Courses** and **Students** tables which would allow the user to find out which students are taking a particular course. Thus, there are useful master/detail relationships in both directions, so this facility could be useful on a form which worked with these tables. Any such form is in danger of confusing the user, so a two-way master/detail relationship should not be used without very good reason.

As an aside, many of these more complex forms would be made easier to use by using an INFORMIX-4GL program which imitated some of the functionality of PERFORM. A program like this does not need to use master/detail relationships; when the user enters the master data, it can automatically switch to the detail table, and when the detail data has been entered, it can switch back to the master table. The disadvantage of this is that it would take several days for a skilled INFORMIX-4GL programmer to produce such a program, whereas a PERFORM form for the same tables would take part of a day to produce.

7.9 Order of operations

If the user adds a row of data using a single-table form, the fields on the screen are entered in the order in which the field tags appear in the ATTRIBUTES section, starting at the top and working downwards. If the fields on the screen are dotted at random, the cursor will jump around to each field in turn and the form will be difficult to use. If the fields are in some logical order, the cursor will move predictably.

When the form has multiple tables, the order of the tables is determined by the order in which they appear in the ATTRIBUTES section. Thus, in the last form, the **Companies** table is table 1 because it appears first and the **Models** table is table 2 because it appears next (although it is on the same line). The **Prices** table is table 3; it would become table 1 if the first field tag associated with the **Prices** table (f009) came before field tag f000 in the ATTRIBUTES section, and if the attributes for **Prices.Model** came before those for **Models.Model**. Within one table, the order of the fields is also determined by the order of the field tags in the ATTRIBUTES section, starting with the first field tag for the table and moving down the list.

7.10 Summary

This chapter has shown that it is simple to generate a multi-table form and that by careful customization it can be made to do many useful things. It allows one form to be created for maintaining a collection of related tables. The data from several tables can be displayed on one screen and any one item can be displayed on several screens if that seems appropriate. The mechanisms of joining fields and looking up values have been illustrated in both verified and unverified versions. The master/detail mechanism has been introduced as a way of making it easier to search for data in two closely related tables, as in the **Companies** and **Models** tables in the **Cars** database.

Exercise

1. Modify the **Customers** form from Chapter 4 so that it shows the maker and model name. Make sure that the user can enquire about both companies and models.

8
Advanced SQL

Chapter 5 covered the basic elements of SQL; this chapter extends the material presented there. It covers the aggregate functions, which allow you to produce statistics from the database, date-manipulation functions and sub-queries (which allow you to embed a complete SELECT statement in the WHERE clause). There is then a small diversion to discuss the behaviour of null values in selection conditions. The remaining three clauses of the SELECT statement are covered next: the INTO TEMP clause, which selects data into temporary tables, the GROUP BY clause and the HAVING clause.

This completes the coverage of the features used regularly in SQL; the discussion then moves on to the three statements which change the data in the database, the INSERT, DELETE and UPDATE statements. It is left to Chapter 12 to discuss OUTER JOINS, table aliasing, self-joins and UNION statements.

8.1 SELECT statement – aggregates

So far, the SELECT statement has been used to retrieve data which already exists in the database. Using SQL, it is possible to derive data from the values stored in the database by using the aggregate functions. For example, it is possible to count the number of rows selected using the aggregate function COUNT(*). The following SELECT statement counts the number of customers whose surname starts with letters in the range M – Z:

```
SELECT COUNT(*) FROM Customers WHERE Surname MATCHES "[M-Z]*";
```

The other aggregate functions available are:

```
COUNT(DISTINCT x)
SUM([DISTINCT] x)
AVG([DISTINCT] x)
MAX(x)
MIN(x)
```

In each of the above, x represents a column name. The keyword DISTINCT means that only the different values in the named column are operated upon. That is, if there are duplicate values in the column, the value is only counted once. Because COUNT(DISTINCT x) returns the number of distinct values in the named column, this

119

enquiry counts the number of different car makers with models in the table **Models:**

```
SELECT COUNT(DISTINCT Maker) FROM Models;
```

AVG (or AVERAGE – the two words are synonyms) returns the average of all the values selected from the named column, and MAX and MIN return the maximum and minimum values found in the column. This enquiry finds the maximum, minimum and average cost of cars which do more than 50 mpg at 56 mph:

```
SELECT MAX(Price), MIN(Price), AVG(Price) FROM Models WHERE Mpgat56 > 50;
```

SUM returns the sum of all the values selected from the named column, so this enquiry returns the net cost of all the cars in stock which would have cost more than £8000 new:

```
SELECT SUM(Boughtfor)
    FROM   Stock, Models
    WHERE Stock.Model = Models.Model
    AND Models.Price > 8000;
```

The functions SUM, AVG, MAX and MIN may be used to evaluate an expression as well as a column name. Thus, to calculate the gross margin on the cars sold so far, the following SELECT statement could be used:

```
SELECT SUM(Soldfor - Boughtfor) FROM Sales;
```

8.2 SELECT statement – dates

SQL provides six functions to manipulate dates. The simplest one is DATE which takes an argument which can be converted into a DATE value. This could be a string such as '25/12/1991', or a simple number. If the date expression is a number, the number is the number of days since 31 December 1899; that is, day number 1 is 1 January 1900.

The function MDY takes three integer arguments which represent month, day and year respectively (hence MDY as the name). The year may not be abbreviated: 91 was in the first century AD.

The other four functions may be given a date expression and return the day of the month (DAY), day of the week (WEEKDAY, with Sunday = 0, Saturday = 6), month of the year (MONTH) and year (YEAR).

With the additional function TODAY, which returns today's date, these functions may be used in WHERE clauses and select lists. For example, this enquiry lists the customers who bought a car during the week (as opposed to the weekend):

```
SELECT Contactdate, Salut, Firstname, Surname,
       WEEKDAY(Contactdate), DAY(Contactdate), MONTH(Contactdate), YEAR(Contactdate)
    FROM    Customers
    WHERE   Enquiry = 'S'
       AND   WEEKDAY(Contactdate) BETWEEN 1 AND 5
    ORDER BY Contactdate;
```

The next enquiry lists two groups of customers: those who were contacted during the course of the last four weeks, and those who were contacted over a year ago.

DBDATE	Date		
	Day	Month	Year
y2md/	1	2	1903
y2dm/	2	1	1903
my2d/	1	3	1902
mdy2/	2	3	1901
dy2m/	3	1	1902
dmy2/	3	2	1901

Table 8.1 Interpretations of "03/02/01"

```
SELECT Contactdate, Salut, Firstname, Surname
    FROM    Customers
    WHERE   Contactdate >= TODAY - 28
      OR    Contactdate < MDY(MONTH(TODAY), DAY(TODAY), YEAR(TODAY)-1)
    ORDER BY Contactdate;
```

The final example using dates illustrates the DATE function and selects the list of cars sold between 1 January 1990 and 31 December 1990:

```
SELECT Company, Modelname, Details, Registration, Datesold
    FROM    Companies, Models, Sales
    WHERE   Companies.Maker = Models.Maker
    AND     Models.Model = Sales.Model
    AND     Datesold BETWEEN DATE("01/01/1990") AND DATE("31/12/1990")
    ORDER BY Datesold;
```

Note that the behaviour of the above example may be changed by altering the value of the DBDATE environment variable (see Chapter 16), as the strings passed to the function DATE will be interpreted differently. To show this, save the statement:

```
SELECT DAY(DATE("03/02/01")), MONTH(DATE("03/02/01")), YEAR(DATE("03/02/01"))
    FROM Systables WHERE Tabid = 1;
```

in a file called datetest.sql. On UNIX, running the following commands produces the results shown in Table 8.1:

```
DBDATE=y2md/ isql cars datetest
DBDATE=y2dm/ isql cars datetest
DBDATE=my2d/ isql cars datetest
DBDATE=mdy2/ isql cars datetest
DBDATE=dy2m/ isql cars datetest
DBDATE=dmy2/ isql cars datetest
```

There is another example making extensive use of the date-manipulation facilities in Section 8.9 at the end of this chapter.

8.3 SELECT statement – sub-queries

The syntax of the WHERE statement has been listed as:

```
WHERE condition
```

and the condition has so far been a set of simple Boolean expressions. The full syntax of the WHERE clause can be extended by using a SELECT statement in the WHERE clause, which is called a sub-query:

```
WHERE expr relop (ALL|[ANY|SOME]) (select_statement)
WHERE expr [NOT] IN (select_statement)
WHERE [NOT] EXISTS (select_statement)
```

The keyword NOT inverts the logical condition. A sub-query may return any number of values, but the *select-list* may only contain a single column or expression and the SELECT statement may not contain an ORDER BY clause.

8.3.1 Sub-queries using comparison operators

The first form of sub-query is normally used without the qualifying keywords ALL, ANY or SOME. The sub-query must return a single value; this can be guaranteed by selecting an aggregate or by doing a look-up for a specific value.

The first example selects those models which cost more than the average price, and the second lists all the models made by Ford using a sub-query instead of the more normal joining condition:

```
SELECT Companies.Company, Models.Modelname, Price
    FROM Models, Companies
    WHERE Models.Maker = Companies.Maker
      AND Price > (SELECT AVG(Price) FROM Models);

SELECT "Ford", Modelname, Price
    FROM Models
    WHERE Maker = (SELECT Company FROM Companies WHERE Company = "Ford");
```

If the sub-query may return more than one row of data, one of the qualifying keywords must be used. The keyword ALL means that the sub-query may return any number of rows (each of which may only contain one value) and that the search condition is true if the comparison is true for all the rows returned. If no rows are returned, the search condition is deemed to be true. This SELECT statement lists the customers who could afford to buy any of the Ford models. It shows how sub-queries may be nested. Note that it could be reformulated without the keyword ALL or the second sub-query as shown in the second SELECT statement.

```
SELECT Salut, Firstname, Surname
    FROM Customers
    WHERE Maxmoney >= ALL
        (SELECT Price FROM  Models
         WHERE Maker = (SELECT Company FROM Companies WHERE Company = "Ford")
        );

SELECT Salut, Firstname, Surname
    FROM Customers
    WHERE Maxmoney >= (SELECT MAX(Price) FROM Models, Companies
                       WHERE Models.Maker = Companies.Maker
                         AND Companies.Company = "Ford"
                      );
```

Operator	Equivalent
IN	= ANY
IN	= SOME
NOT IN	!= ALL

Table 8.2 IN/NOT IN operator equivalences

The keywords ANY and SOME are synonyms and mean that the search condition is true if any of the comparisons is true. If the sub-query returns no values, the search condition is false.

8.3.2 Sub-queries using the IN operator

The IN operator is used to check whether the expression on the left is among the list of values returned by the sub-query. For example, this SELECT statement selects the companies which have a model listed in the database:

```
SELECT Company FROM Companies WHERE Company IN (SELECT UNIQUE Maker FROM Models);
```

Both the IN and NOT IN operators are readable shorthands for the statements using the qualifying keywords ALL, ANY or SOME shown in Table 8.2. Note in particular that in spoken English, the equivalent of 'not in' would be 'does not equal any of', whereas in SQL, NOT IN is equivalent to '!= ALL'. Because of this, the NOT IN operator should always be used in preference to '!= ALL'.

8.3.3 Sub-queries using the EXISTS operator

The operator EXISTS returns true if the sub-query returns one or more rows of data, and false if it does not return any rows of data. The example selects those customers who bought a car which cost more than three-quarters as much as the most expensive car, provided there is at least one model in the model list which costs between £30 000 and £45 000.

```
SELECT Salut, Firstname, Surname
    FROM  Customers, Models
    WHERE Lastmodel = Models.Model
      AND Maxmoney > 0.75 * (SELECT MAX(Price) FROM Models)
      AND EXISTS (SELECT Model FROM Models WHERE Price BETWEEN 30000 AND 45000);
```

This example is very artificial, but there is an instance where the EXISTS operator is crucial in the last example of this chapter (in the section on the UPDATE statement).

8.4 Behaviour of nulls

The behaviour of nulls in arithmetic expressions and in the condition clauses of SELECT statements needs to be explained because it is not immediately obvious.

x	NOT x
T	F
U	U
F	T

AND	T	U	F
T	T	U	F
U	U	U	F
F	F	F	F

OR	T	U	F
T	T	T	T
U	T	U	U
F	T	U	F

Table 8.3 Three-state truth tables for NOT, AND and OR

In an arithmetic expression, if either (or both) of the operands is NULL, the result is also NULL. This much is easy, but the aggregate functions treat nulls in different ways. COUNT(*) counts all the rows regardless of any nulls. COUNT(DISTINCT x) ignores any rows in which the column being counted (x) contains NULL, and it returns zero if all the rows contain NULL. This means that one way of finding out how many nulls there are in a particular column of a table is:

```
SELECT COUNT(*) - COUNT(DISTINCT column_name)
    FROM table_name;
```

The other aggregate functions also ignore any nulls they encounter, and if all the values are NULL, the result is NULL too. One curious result of this is that the following SELECT statement could return different results from the two expressions if both columns allowed nulls to be stored:

```
SELECT SUM(Soldfor - Boughtfor) expression1,
       SUM(Soldfor) - SUM(Boughtfor) expression2
    FROM Sales;
```

This is because when the first expression is calculated, each row that contains a null in either **Soldfor** or **Boughtfor** will produce a null value from the subtraction and then be ignored by SUM, whereas the sums of the individual columns will ignore only those rows where the value is null in their respective columns. If any row contains a null value for **Boughtfor** but not for **Soldfor** (or vice versa), the two expressions will be different.

To explain the behaviour of nulls in comparisons, we need to consider a three-state logic (true, false and unknown) instead of the normal two-state (true, false) logic. In an arithmetic or string comparison between two quantities, if either quantity is NULL, the result of the comparison is 'unknown'. Table 8.3 shows the behaviour of the NOT operator (which inverts the result of a single comparison), and the AND operator and the OR operator (which combine the results of two comparisons). In the table, 'T' stands for *true*, 'F' stands for *false* and 'U' stands for *unknown*.

In the WHERE clause of a SELECT statement, any row for which the condition evaluates to unknown is not selected (or updated, or deleted). Suppose the **Boughtfor** column allowed nulls and consider the following SELECT statement:

```
SELECT Registration, Boughtfor
    FROM  Sales
    WHERE Boughtfor > 0
      OR Boughtfor < 0
      OR Boughtfor = 0;
```

The SELECT statement would not select all the rows, because the rows containing nulls would give unknown results to each of the three conditions, and the combination of three unknowns is also unknown. If you want the rows which contain nulls, then they must be selected explicitly using IS NULL:

```
SELECT Registration, Boughtfor
    FROM  Sales
    WHERE Boughtfor > 0
       OR Boughtfor < 0
       OR Boughtfor = 0
       OR Boughtfor IS NULL;
```

In an ORDER BY clause, all NULL values are treated as smaller than any non-NULL value, so any null rows will appear first if the order is ascending, and last if the order is descending. One more peculiarity of ANSI standard SQL and Informix SQL is that you cannot treat NULL as a constant in the *select-list*. That is, the following statement is syntactically incorrect:

```
SELECT Registration, NULL    ( Syntax error )
    FROM Sales;
```

If you have reached the conclusion that nulls are more trouble than they are worth, you are somewhat justified. Certainly, if a database does not allow nulls anywhere, it will generally be easier to manipulate – there will be fewer surprises caused by the behaviour of nulls. Nevertheless, most databases need to allow nulls in a few fields, but it is imperative that you avoid nulls in primary keys. Consequently, most foreign keys should also not allow nulls. Some foreign keys do not always have to match a value; these keys should either contain a valid value from the cross-referencing table or should be completely null. For example, if a customer has never bought a model from ABC Cars Ltd, the **Lastmodel** column may be null; however, if it contains a value, it must match a value in the **Models** table. If the foreign key is itself composite, then every component of the key should be null.

8.5 SELECT statement – INTO TEMP

The INTO TEMP clause is used to save the results of a SELECT statement into a temporary table in the database. The name of the temporary table must be distinct from the name of every other table in the database, including other temporary tables created by the user. However, a temporary table is private to one user – another user may create a temporary table with the same name, but there would be two distinct temporary tables. (More precisely, a temporary table has to be unique to one database engine. If you were logged in twice, you could create a temporary table with the same name at each terminal, but they would be distinct tables because there would be a different database agent for each login.) The temporary table continues to exist as a normal database table until the program terminates or the table is explicitly dropped using DROP TABLE. A temporary table has no indexes on it by default; indexes may be added to temporary tables in the same way as for a normal table – they will be dropped at the same time as the table is.

A temporary table allows you to check the intermediate results of a complicated SELECT statement, or to use the selected output over and over again without having to rerun the original SELECT statement. It is often helpful to name (or rename) the columns of the temporary table using display labels, which were introduced with the ORDER BY clause. If two columns from different tables which have the same name are included in the *select-list* of the SELECT statement which creates the temporary table, at least one of those columns *must* have a display label. If one of the columns is an aggregate function or other expression, that column must be given a display label.

The following SELECT statement sets up a temporary table of manufacturer and model names and calls it **Model_list**:

```
SELECT Model Number, Company Manufacturer, Modelname, Details
    FROM     Models, Companies
    WHERE    Models.Maker = Companies.Maker
    INTO TEMP Model_list;
```

The columns in the temporary table are **Number**, **Manufacturer**, **Modelname** and **Details**. These names can be used in subsequent SELECT statements using the temporary table **Model_list**:

```
SELECT Manufacturer, Modelname, Number
    FROM     Model_list
    ORDER BY Manufacturer, Number;
```

SELECT INTO TEMP statements are often used in a report to accumulate intermediate data in a convenient form ready for use in the final SELECT statement (or other SELECT INTO TEMP statements before the final SELECT statement).

8.6 SELECT statement – GROUP BY

As a reminder, the full syntax of the SELECT statement is:

```
SELECT select-list
    FROM table-list
    [WHERE condition]
    [GROUP BY group-list]
    [HAVING condition]
    [ORDER BY column-list]
    [INTO TEMP table-name]
```

The GROUP BY and HAVING clauses work together, and both are associated with aggregate functions. So far, the SELECT statements with aggregates have only contained aggregate functions in the *select-list*, and the SELECT statement has only produced one row of data. There has not been a mixture of ordinary column names and aggregates in the *select-list*. The GROUP BY statement is used when there *is* a mixture of both ordinary columns and aggregate values in the *select-list* of a SELECT statement. When there is such a mixture, the data is sorted so that all the rows with the same values in the columns are grouped together, and the aggregate functions are applied to each group in turn.

As an example, suppose you need to list the different types of model produced by each manufacturer, count the number of different models in each type and also list the price of the most expensive type of each model. That is, you have to produce a SELECT statement which counts the number of different types of Ford Escort and the number of types of Vauxhall Cavalier, and also lists the price of the most expensive Ford Escort and the price of the most expensive Vauxhall Cavalier. The SELECT statement shown below will do what is required. The GROUP BY clause produces a single row of results for each group of rows which cannot be distinguished uniquely from the columns listed in the *group-list*.

```
SELECT Company, Modelname, COUNT(*), MAX(Price)
    FROM      Companies, Models
    WHERE     Companies.Maker = Models.Maker
    GROUP BY Company, Modelname
    ORDER BY Company, Modelname;
```

The *group-list* is a list of one or more column names, separated by commas, which governs the rows in a group. When a GROUP BY clause is used, the *select-list* in the SELECT statement is restricted to the columns named in the *group-list*, or to aggregates of any columns. Every column named in the *group-list* must also appear in the *select-list*, and every column named in the *select-list* which is not part of an aggregate must also appear in the *group-list*. If a column only appears in an aggregate in the *select-list*, the column may not appear in the *group-list*. The example below returns the average price of vehicle produced by each manufacturer:

```
SELECT Company, AVG(Price) Aveprice
    FROM      Companies, Models
    WHERE     Companies.Maker = Models.Maker
    GROUP BY Company
    ORDER BY Aveprice DESC;
```

8.7 SELECT statement – HAVING

The HAVING clause is a qualifier applied to the GROUP BY statement. It performs a similar function to the WHERE clause. The condition must relate one aggregate property of the group with either another aggregate property or with a constant. Thus, the previous query could be qualified with a HAVING clause to select the manufacturers with more than one model listed, or to select the manufacturers with a range of models such that the most expensive model is more than twice as expensive as the cheapest:

```
SELECT Company, AVG(Price) Aveprice
    FROM      Companies, Models
    WHERE     Companies.Maker = Models.Maker
    GROUP BY Company
    HAVING   COUNT(*) > 1
    ORDER BY Aveprice DESC;
```

```
SELECT Company, AVG(Price) Aveprice
   FROM     Companies, Models
   WHERE    Companies.Maker = Models.Maker
   GROUP BY Company
   HAVING   MAX(Price) > 2 * MIN(Price)
   ORDER BY Aveprice DESC;
```

It is possible to use a HAVING clause without a GROUP BY clause. However, it does not often make sense to do this.

8.8 INSERT, DELETE and UPDATE

Having dealt with the SELECT statement which retrieves data from the database, we now move on to consider the SQL statements which change the data in the database. There are three of these statements: INSERT to add new records, UPDATE to change values already in the database and DELETE to remove data from the database. There were two main reasons for deferring the discussion of these:

1. They are not often used in INFORMIX-SQL by the user – they are more generally useful to programmers writing in INFORMIX-4GL or ESQL/C.
2. They all use syntactic constructs which are part of the SELECT statement.

This means that it was not sensible to consider these constructs until after the SELECT statement had been discussed fully. It is worth knowing that PERFORM uses these statements internally to alter the database; indeed, these statements are the only way of changing the data in the database, so *all* programs which change the data in the database use one or more of these three statements.

8.8.1 INSERT

The INSERT statement is used to insert rows of data into a table. The full syntax of the INSERT statement is:

```
INSERT INTO table-name [(column-list)]
   〈VALUES 〈value-list〉|select-statement〉
```

The *table-name* is the name of the table to be updated. The *column-list* allows the user to specify the order of the columns in which the data is to be inserted; it also means that values do not have to be provided for every column, although since the value inserted in the unspecified columns is NULL, the missing columns must be able to accept null values. If the columns are not listed, the values will be inserted into the columns in the order listed in the **Syscolumns** table in the system catalogue.

The less useful form of the INSERT statement for the average user uses the keyword VALUES, as in the following example which inserts a new record into the **Stock** table:

```
INSERT INTO Stock(Registration, Model, Colour, Condition, Datebought, Boughtfor, Mileage)
   VALUES ("RXD193Y", 133, "Red", "G", "23/01/1991", 2100.0, 53419);
```

Only one row is inserted for each INSERT statement. This form is used extensively in programs, including PERFORM when it adds a row of data. The first value in the *value-list* will be inserted into the first column in the *column-list*. The values inserted must be convertible to the type of the corresponding column. Date and character values must be enclosed within quotation marks.

When a SELECT statement is used, one row is inserted for each row selected. This is useful for transferring data from one table to another, or for adding data to a temporary table. The SELECT statement can be as complicated as necessary, but it cannot retrieve data from the table into which the data is to be inserted, nor can the SELECT statement use INTO TEMP or ORDER BY clauses.

When entering a value in a SERIAL column, the key value zero (0) indicates that the inserted record is to be given the next available serial number. Of course, an explicit value (which may be greater than zero or less than zero, but may not be equal to zero) can be inserted provided there is not already a row in the table with the same serial number. This assumes that there is a unique index on the serial column, which there certainly should be. When an explicit number is inserted, if the previous highest value was less than the new value, the next available serial number after the insertion is one greater than the value which was inserted.

This example first creates a list of all the cars currently in stock and then inserts all the sales records for cars which have been sold previously back into the stock list. The temporary table is necessary since it is not possible to reference the table which is having data inserted into it in the SELECT statement which is generating the data to be inserted. The sub-select would have to reference the **Stock** table if the temporary table was not created.

```
SELECT Registration FROM Stock INTO TEMP Currentcars;

INSERT INTO Stock
        (Registration, Model, Colour, Condition, Datebought, Boughtfor,
            Mileage, Notes1, Notes2)
     SELECT Registration, Model, Colour, Condition, Datebought, Boughtfor,
            Mileage, Notes1, Notes2
        FROM   Sales
        WHERE Registration NOT IN (SELECT Registration FROM Currentcars);
```

8.8.2 DELETE

The DELETE statement deletes rows from the named table. The full syntax of this statement is:

```
DELETE FROM table-name [WHERE condition]
```

If the condition is omitted, all the rows in the table are deleted. If the script is run from the **Query-Language** option of ISQL, you will be prompted to verify that this is what you meant to do; if it is run from the UNIX command line, there is no reprieve.

The WHERE clause is the same as for a SELECT statement: only those rows that satisfy the condition will be deleted. If the WHERE clause selects all the rows, there is no warning that all the rows will be deleted, even when the condition is always true, as in:

```
DELETE FROM Customers WHERE 1 = 1;
```

The first of the examples below deletes customers who have not been given any spending power, and the second deletes any records in the **Stock** table which have been transferred to the **Sales** table but not deleted from the **Stock** table:

```
DELETE FROM Customers WHERE Maxmoney IS NULL;

SELECT Stock.Registration
    FROM      Stock, Sales
    WHERE     Sales.Registration = Stock.Registration
      AND     Sales.Datebought = Stock.Datebought
    INTO TEMP Del_stock;

DELETE FROM Stock WHERE Registration IN (Select * FROM Del_stock);
```

When writing a DELETE statement, it is recommended that you test it first by replacing the keyword DELETE with the keywords 'SELECT *': this will show the rows that would be deleted.

8.8.3 UPDATE

The UPDATE statement updates (changes) the rows in the named table by setting the named columns to the value of the expressions. The full syntax of this statement is:

```
UPDATE table-name SET column-name = expr[, ...]
    [WHERE condition]
```

If the expression is a SELECT statement, it must be enclosed in parentheses and obey the rules for sub-queries, and it may not select data from the table being updated.

The WHERE clause defines which rows will be updated. The next example sets the **Maxmoney** column to £7500 for all those customers who had a value of less than £1000 set. Note that it does not affect the customers for whom the **Maxmoney** value was set to NULL; to change them as well, the extra condition 'OR Maxmoney IS NULL' would have to be added.

```
UPDATE Customers
    SET    Maxmoney = 7500
    WHERE Maxmoney < 1000;
```

The following example amends the **Models** table: the new price of each model is increased by £100 plus 3% of the maximum price of the model in the table **Prices** − not a plausible formula, but useful as an example:

```
UPDATE Models
    SET Price = Price + 100 +
            0.03 * (SELECT MAX(Hi_price) FROM Prices WHERE Prices.Model = Models.Model);
```

Note that the column **Models.Model** is used in the sub-query despite the fact that the table **Models** is not listed in the FROM clause of the sub-query. This is a *correlated sub-query*. The UPDATE statement allows this to happen, and it means that for every row in the **Models** table, the sub-query is run with the current value of

Models.Model. Similarly, the SELECT statement can also use a correlated sub-query; the UPDATE statement above can be adapted to produce:

```
SELECT  Models.Model, Models.Modelname, Models.Details,
        Models.Price,
        MAX(Prices.Hi_price)
    FROM    Models, Prices
    WHERE   Prices.Model = Models.Model
    AND     Models.Price >
            (SELECT MAX(Prices.Hi_price) FROM Prices WHERE Prices.Model = Models.Model)
    GROUP BY 1, 2, 3, 4;
```

As it stands, the UPDATE statement has a serious defect: it nullifies the price of any models without prices listed in the **Prices** table. To prevent this from happening, an extra clause must be inserted as shown below, using the EXISTS operator:

```
UPDATE Models
    SET Price = Price + 100 + 0.03 *
        (SELECT MAX(Hi_price) FROM Prices
            WHERE Prices.Model = Models.Model
                AND EXISTS (SELECT * FROM Prices WHERE Prices.Model = Models.Model)
        );
```

8.9 Using the date functions

The powerful date-handling facilities can be very useful in practice. One case in point was in a system where the dates were stored in CHAR(8) fields in the format "dd/mm/yy"; when the year field was less than 50, the year was actually in the range 2000 .. 2049, and otherwise was in the range 1950 .. 1999. These fields needed to be converted into real dates. This was done in a two-stage operation: the first stage converted all the dates into the range 1900 .. 1999; the second stage added a century to all those dates in the range 1900 .. 1949. There were two tables called **Old_format** and **New_format** which had the same set of column names, but the type of **Eff_date** in **Old_format** was CHAR(8), and in **New_format** it was a DATE. The statements used to transfer the data were:

```
INSERT INTO New_format
    SELECT ...,
        MDY(Eff_date[4,5], Eff_date[1,2], Eff_date[7,8] + 1900),
        ....
    FROM Old_format;

UPDATE New_format
    SET Eff_date = MDY(MONTH(Eff_date), DAY(Eff_date), YEAR(Eff_date) + 100)
    WHERE YEAR(Eff_date) < 1950;
```

The square brackets denote sub-strings on CHAR fields. The first number is the index of the first character in the sub-string and the second number (which is optional) is the index of the last character in the sub-string. Thus, Eff_date[4,5] refers to characters 4 and 5 of **Eff_date**, which corresponds to the month. Note that Informix automatically converts the string into an integer before passing the value to the MDY function; if the value is not a number, Informix detects an error. To prevent this happening, the data had to be checked first using a SELECT statement like the one below (**Pkey** was the unique identifier for the table):

```
SELECT Pkey, Eff_date FROM Old_format
    WHERE Eff_date NOT MATCHES "[0-9][0-9]/[0-9][0-9]/[0-9][0-9]";
```

8.10 Summary

This chapter has covered some more complex aspects of the SELECT statement, notably the use of aggregate functions for producing statistics from the database, the use of sub-queries to build up a complex enquiry from several smaller enquiries and the behaviour of nulls. The remaining major clauses of the SELECT statement were discussed next, the INTO TEMP, GROUP BY and HAVING clauses. Finally, the chapter discussed the three related statements, the INSERT, UPDATE and DELETE statements, which are the only statements which change the data in the database.

Exercises

1. List the details of the most expensive model.

2. Find the minimum, maximum and average cost of the models made by those manufacturers whose name begins with one of the letters **A–M** and which also contains the letter **r**.

3. Calculate the average range of all models on one tank of fuel at 56 mph.

4. Delete all customers last contacted before 1 June 1990 who did not make a purchase.

5. Delete all manufacturers for which no model is listed.

6. Some customers have no maximum spending power specified. Change their spending power to £7500.

7. List the average range of all models for each manufacturer. The output should consist of one row for each manufacturer, and each row should consist of the manufacturer's name and the average range for that manufacturer.

8. Use SQL to insert a customer record for yourself.

9. Produce a list of manufacturers who have more than two models listed. List the name, the number of models and the price range.

10. Ensure that the spending power of anybody who bought a car is at least as much as the cost of the car they bought.

11. List the different models bought by customers in the past. Order them by the total value of the sales for each model, with the model which has sold most listed first.

9

Report formats and statistics

Just as the previous two chapters have taken what was covered in Part II and extended it, so this chapter takes what was covered in Chapter 6 and extends it. The new material covered here includes the USING clause of the PRINT statement, which gives precise control over how the results will be presented, a discussion of the FORMAT control blocks which have not already been covered (especially the BEFORE GROUP OF and AFTER GROUP OF control blocks), the aggregate and group aggregate functions, and the OUTPUT section.

As with the previous chapter on reports, the examples build up to a complete report which is presented at the end of the chapter. The report developed in this chapter concentrates on formatting the data and on producing statistics from the data. It actually lists the profit or loss made on each sale; the statistics it produces include the average profit and the total profit on each model and on each manufacturer, as well as the overall profit.

9.1 The SELECT section again

In many reports, particularly on large databases with many tables connected in complicated ways, it is not possible to write a single SELECT statement which will generate the data for a report. The SELECT section of a report often consists of several SELECT statements, all but the last of which must store their results into temporary tables (using INTO TEMP). The last SELECT statement must be followed by the keyword END, and the intermediate ones must be separated by semicolons.

The selected columns from the last (or only) SELECT statement are the only columns that can be printed in the report. The selected columns may have to be given display labels. The names used to identify the columns when printing the report will be the display labels, if they were defined, or the column names if not.

If an ORDER BY clause is used in a SELECT statement, the sorted column name cannot have a table prefix (that is, the notation *table.column* is not permitted). If a column is not unique, define a display label and use that in the ORDER BY clause and in the FORMAT section of the report.

9.1.1 Creating the SELECT statement

As usual, the first step in producing a report is to ensure that the correct data is being selected. For development purposes, we shall use a simple SELECT statement with no restrictions on either the range of dates reported or the set of manufacturers. In a production report, we would probably want to be able to specify both constraints, but to do so involves features not covered until the next chapter on reports. The SELECT statement we need is:

```
SELECT Companies.Company,
       Models.Modelname, Models.Details,
       Sales.Boughtfor,  Sales.Soldfor,
       Sales.Datebought, Sales.Datesold
   FROM    Companies, Models, Sales
   WHERE   Models.Model = Sales.Model
   AND     Models.Maker = Companies.Maker
   ORDER BY Company, Modelname, Details, Datesold;
```

9.2 PRINT USING

When formatting the report, we want to have precise control over how the money figures and dates are formatted. In general, we want to have precise control over all the formatting, but just printing the column names gives us a default format, which is not always satisfactory. To get the precise control, we can specify the format of any numeric type by following the column name (or expression) with the keyword USING and a format string:

expr USING *format-string*

The USING keyword allows you to specify the format of date or numeric expressions in great detail, and it is particularly valuable for handling money quantities. It is normally used as an element of a PRINT statement, but it could also be used on the right-hand side of an assignment statement (see Chapter 13). The only limitation, if it is a limitation, is that the strings that USING produces are always of a fixed length.

9.2.1 PRINT USING – numeric formats

The characters that can be used for formatting numeric expressions are listed in Table 9.1. The simplest format is probably a string of hashes '#' which will print the number right-justified with leading blanks as necessary. Both negative and positive numbers will be printed without a sign, and zero will be printed as an all-blank string. To ensure that at least one digit is printed, the rightmost character should be an ampersand '&'. If negative numbers should be printed with a minus sign, use minus signs '–' in place of the hashes. If only one minus sign is used at the left of a string of hashes, the minus sign will be printed in that column and the number will be right-justified and blank-padded as before. If both positive and negative numbers should be given a sign, use plus signs '+' in place of the minus signs.

Format Character	Floats	Affected by DBMONEY	Interpretation
#	No	No	Print digit or blank
&	No	No	Print digit (zero if necessary)
*	No	No	Print digit or asterisk
<	No	No	Left-justify numbers in field
,	No	Yes	Print numeric separator or blank
.	No	Yes	Print decimal indicator or blank
−	Yes	No	Print sign when value is negative
+	Yes	No	Print sign even when value is positive
(	Yes	No	Literal open parenthesis if negative
)	No	No	Literal close parenthesis if negative
$	Yes	Yes	Print currency symbol

Table 9.1 Numeric formatting symbols for USING

If a number such as a page number is to be printed left-justified, use a string of less-than signs '<'. If the report is printing cheques or other documents which require that there are no blanks in the number even when there are no significant digits in the printing position, then you should either use ampersands (which will zero-pad the number) or asterisks '*' in place of the hashes. If the report is an accounting report (like the one we are developing), negative values may need to be placed in parentheses. An open parenthesis '(' behaves rather like a minus sign; it only appears when the value is negative, and it will float rightwards if there are several adjacent floating characters. Every close parenthesis ')' in the format string will appear when the number is negative.

9.2.2 The influence of DBMONEY

The remaining symbols are all affected by the value of the environment variable DBMONEY, which also affects the behaviour of PERFORM. Since INFORMIX-SQL is an American product, the default currency units are dollars '$', and the default decimal indicator is the decimal point '.'; this is indicated by the default value of DBMONEY:

```
DBMONEY="$."; export DBMONEY
```

If you do not work in dollars, you can set the environment variable DBMONEY to specify the currency units and decimal indicator. The only alternative decimal indicator is the comma ',', but almost any string can be used as the currency symbol, and the currency symbol can come either before or after the decimal indicator (or, indeed, there could be one symbol before and a different one after the decimal indicator). If you were working in Germany, you would probably want to set DBMONEY as:

```
DBMONEY=",DM"; export DBMONEY
```

This indicates that the currency symbol is 'DM' for Deutschmarks, the decimal indicator is ',', and the currency symbol comes after the numeric value. In PERFORM, a value of 12 000 Deutschmarks would be printed on the screen as:

```
12000,00DM
```

In the UK, the normal setting is shown below, together with the appearance of £12 000 in PERFORM:

```
DBMONEY="£."; export DBMONEY
£12000.00
```

In theory, the same principles apply with ACE; in practice, the currency symbol must precede the decimal indicator. This means that the Germans either have to do without any currency symbols in their reports, or they have to embed them as literals in the report (neither of which is really satisfactory), or they would redefine DBMONEY as:

```
DBMONEY="DM,"; export DBMONEY
```

This would display the currency symbol before the amount, rather than after it, but at least it would be shown.

Returning to the USING formats, the symbol represented as '$' in the format string is printed using the value of the currency symbol defined before the decimal indicator in DBMONEY. In other respects, the currency symbol behaves rather like a hash; it will be left blank if the column does not need either a digit or part of the currency symbol printed in it, and if it occurs at the right-hand end of the format string, it behaves exactly as a hash would. The symbol represented as '.' in the format string is the value of the decimal indicator as defined by DBMONEY, defaulting to '.' if no value is defined by DBMONEY. Conversely, the symbol represented as ',' in the format string is the opposite value to the one specified as the decimal indicator defined by DBMONEY, and it defaults to ',' if no value is defined by DBMONEY.

9.2.3 Examples of numeric formatting

The report we are going to produce will need the following formats (at least):

```
PRINT Boughtfor USING "$###,##&.&&"
PRINT Soldfor - Boughtfor USING "($###,##&.&&)"
PRINT PAGENO USING "<<<<"
```

To illustrate some of the other formats, it is hard to avoid showing a list of formats, numbers and the resulting output. In Appendix B, you will find some table definitions and the report used to produce the raw version of the list shown in Figure 9.1. The output shown is a heavily edited version of what the report produced. The DBMONEY environment variable was set for UK use. Note that where extra decimal places appear in the formatted output compared with the default output (eg with the format '########.####'), it is because the data was stored with a number of extra digits of accuracy, but the default format used to print the middle column only shows two decimal places. Notice that numbers are not rounded but are truncated. If you

Format string	Decimal value	Formatted value
#######	0.00	
#######	491.51	492
#######	-123.46	123
#######.####	0.00	.0000
#######.####	10.31	10.3124
#######.####	-0.67	.6700
#######.####	-123.46	123.4568
######&.####	0.00	0.0000
-######.##	-0.67	- .670
-######.##	-123.46	- 123.457
+######.##	0.00	+ .000
+######.##	-12345.67	- 12345.670
$######.##	-123.46	£ 123.457
$(,(((,((&.&&)	0.00	£ 0.00
$(,(((,((&.&&)	1023.45	£ 1,023.45
$(,(((,((&.&&)	-0.67	£ (0.67)
$(,(((,((&.&&)	-12345.67	£ (12,345.67)
$$$ $$$ $$&.&&	0.00	£0.00
$$$ $$$ $$&.&&	-23547684.24	£23 547 684.24
($$$ $$$ $$&.&&)	-12345.67	(£12 345.67)
($$$ $$$ $$&.&&)	-23547684.24	(£23 547 684.24)
((((((($$&.&&)	2.31	£2.31
((((((($$&.&&)	-0.67	(£0.67)
((((((($$&.&&)	-23547684.24	(£23 547 684.24)
(((($$$ $$&.&&)	-0.67	(£0.67)
(((($$$ $$&.&&)	-12345.67	(£12 345.67)
(((((((($&.&&)	1023.45	£1 023.45
(((((((($&.&&)	-0.67	(£0.67)
(((((((($&.&&)	-12345.67	(£12 345.67)

Figure 9.1 Examples of formatting decimal numbers

want to find out what other format specifications do, you should experiment with the data used to derive this report.

9.2.4 PRINT USING – date formats

The set of format items which can be used to print dates are listed in Table 9.2. Note that there are some date-manipulation functions which can also be used. The two formats which will be used in this report are:

```
PRINT TODAY USING "ddd dd mmm yyyy"
PRINT Datesold USING "dd mmm yyyy"
```

9.3 Date-manipulation functions

There are six date-manipulation functions. One of these functions is MDY, which converts three integers into a DATE type. The first integer is the month (0 .. 12), the second is the day of the month (1 .. 31) and the third is the year (eg 1991).

The other functions all accept one argument which can be converted to the DATE type. Any of the following quantities could be used as the argument to one of

Format Characters	Interpretation
dd	Day of month: two digits 01 .. 31
ddd	Day of week: three-letter abbreviation Sun .. Sat
mm	Month of year: two digits 01 .. 12
mmm	Month of year: three-letter abbreviation Jan .. Dec
yy	Year: two-digit number 00 .. 99 (representing 1900 .. 1999)
yyyy	Year: four-digit number 0001 .. 9999

Table 9.2 Date formatting symbols for USING

these functions:

```
"31/12/1991"
TODAY
MDY(12,31,1991)
1850
```

All date strings are interpreted using the environment variable DBDATE. The second two are self-explanatory (if you remember the MDY function from the previous chapter), and the last one is the number of days since day number 1 (which was 1 January 1900) and corresponds to 24 January 1905. Note that ISQL as a whole is quite happy with dates prior to 1 January 1900, but it does not understand about the switch between the Julian and Gregorian calendars in September 1752. These functions are called using parentheses '( )' to enclose the argument. The functions available for manipulating dates are:

- DATE – returns a value of type DATE.
- DAY – returns the day of the month.
- MONTH – returns the month.
- WEEKDAY – returns the day of the week.
- YEAR – returns the year.

It is important to note that there are three meanings for the word DATE, depending on the context in which it appears. In CREATE TABLE statements, it is the name of a type. In a report, there is the form DATE("31/12/1991") which converts the string into a DATE value, and there is also the form DATE which prints today's date (eg 'Mon 11 Mar 1991'). This is analogous to the keyword TODAY which is printed in the format determined by DBDATE unless it is qualified by a USING clause.

9.4 PAUSE

The PAGE TRAILER control block was introduced in Chapter 6, but if you have watched a report go scrolling past on the screen at high speed, you will have wanted something to make the report stop at the end of each page. There is a very useful statement, PAUSE, which does precisely that. Whenever it is called (which need not be in a PAGE TRAILER block, although that is the place where it is most frequently used), it suspends the report printing until the user hits the RETURN key. It is normally a good idea to use PAUSE in the form:

```
PAGE TRAILER
    PAUSE "Hit RETURN to continue"
```

This prints the message and causes the output to stop and wait for the RETURN key to be pressed before the next page of the report is produced. If there is no string after PAUSE, no message will be produced; the terminal will be locked until the user hits the RETURN key. If the report is going to a file, or to the printer or another program, the PAUSE statement has no effect. On UNIX, it only has an effect when the report is being sent to a teletype device (/dev/tty*xx*).

If an audible reminder is required, the special function ASCII could be used to print the BEL (^G) character, which has the decimal value 7:

```
PAGE TRAILER
    PAUSE ASCII(7)
```

It is worth remembering that if the report is run often, the noise of the report beeping on every page will quickly annoy most people (it will annoy the user's colleagues, even if it does not annoy the user).

The ASCII function can be used to print any ASCII character. The most frequent use for it is to print double quotes '"'. The only way of producing these in the output from a report is to use:

```
PRINT ASCII(34)
```

If the report is always going to a particular printer, the ASCII function could be used to introduce control codes to turn special modes on and off, such as bold or enlarged fonts, but beware, any report containing such control codes is inherently non-portable. This is doubly true if the report is sent to the screen and contains control codes for a particular terminal; as soon as you connect a different terminal in its place, the report is no use.

9.5 PRINT FILE

ACE provides facilities which can be used, among other things, for producing standard letters. So far, the only way of producing a standard letter would be to use a separate PRINT statement for each line of text. Apart from being horribly tedious to produce, if the letter was of any reasonable length, it would overflow the amount of space that ACE allocates for strings. Fortunately, there is a way around this problem, namely the PRINT FILE statement. This is used to include the text from a file into a report verbatim. Each line of text from the file is printed starting at the left margin and using as much space as there are characters in the line. If the text flows past the end of a page, the PAGE TRAILER and PAGE HEADER control blocks are activated at the appropriate points.

It may be useful to know that you can specify the name of the file with a variable; this could be a file name selected from the database, or it could be from a parameter to the report, or a variable which the user was prompted to enter. (For

```
DATABASE Cars END

SELECT * FROM Customers END

FORMAT

    ON EVERY ROW
        SKIP TO TOP OF PAGE
        PRINT address and salutation
        SKIP 1 LINE
        PRINT FILE "prepared_text"

END
```

Figure 9.2 Skeleton report for personalized letters

details of how to use parameters and variables, see Chapter 13.)

Another statement which is useful, particularly in this context, is SKIP TO TOP OF PAGE. This does precisely what its name implies, and would often be used with standard letters to ensure that each new letter started on a new page. The general structure of reports for producing personalized letters is shown in Figure 9.2.

9.6 FIRST PAGE HEADER

The control block FIRST PAGE HEADER is used to control the layout of the first page. This control block is executed instead of the PAGE HEADER block before the report starts. It is a good place to do the initialization of variables, if you have any (see Chapter 13). However, if you initialize some variables but otherwise want the standard printing at the top of the first page, you have to copy the PRINT statements from the PAGE HEADER control block into the FIRST PAGE HEADER block.

There is a restriction on what can be done inside a FIRST PAGE HEADER, PAGE HEADER or PAGE TRAILER block; the amount of text printed must be fixed and determinable in advance. This is not much of a problem, but it does mean that you cannot use the PRINT FILE statement in any of these control blocks because ACE cannot tell how many lines are needed to print the file. Also, you cannot use SKIP TO TOP OF PAGE in any of these control blocks. This is perfectly reasonable for the PAGE HEADER and PAGE TRAILER blocks, because when they are at work, the report is already going to the top of the next page. Both these restrictions are potentially annoying in the FIRST PAGE HEADER block where it might well be useful to have a cover page which is completely different from the main body of the report; furthermore, there is no obvious reason why this flexibility cannot be provided.

9.7 ON LAST ROW

This control block is executed last of all (except for the final PAGE TRAILER). It is therefore the place to print the final totals and any other suitable statistics. In all other respects, it is an orthodox control block without any petty restrictions, as there are on, say, the FIRST PAGE HEADER.

In the report being developed for this chapter, we shall need to use the ON LAST ROW block to print out the net profit or loss made on all the transactions. However, before that can happen, it is necessary to know how to print aggregate values (eg the sum of the profits or losses).

9.8 Aggregates

ACE provides three related facilities to produce statistics from reports, namely aggregates, groups and group aggregates. The aggregate functions are extensions of the MAX, MIN, SUM and AVG functions provided in SQL. Groups are a mechanism which allows the rows of data to be split up into groups; in each group, certain key variables will be the same for each row in the group. Every row can belong to several groups simultaneously. Group aggregates apply aggregate functions to the data in a group. The syntax of the aggregate functions in ACE is illustrated by:

```
COUNT WHERE Maxmoney > 7500
PERCENT WHERE Maxmoney > 7500
TOTAL OF Maxmoney * 0.85 WHERE Maxmoney > 7500
AVERAGE OF Maxmoney WHERE Maxmoney > 7500
MAX OF Maxmoney
MIN OF Maxmoney
```

The WHERE clause is always optional and is typically absent. COUNT counts the number of rows satisfying the WHERE condition. PERCENT calculates the number of rows satisfying the WHERE condition as a percentage of the total number of rows selected. TOTAL accumulates the total value of the expression, AVERAGE the average value, MIN the minimum value and MAX the maximum value. The keyword AVG is a synonym for AVERAGE.

The value of an aggregate is calculated by operating on all the rows of data. If an aggregate appears anywhere other than the ON LAST ROW control block, its value will be calculated before any printing is done; even if used in the ON EVERY ROW control block, the value printed is always the same. This is important: the aggregate functions described are the grand total aggregates – eminently suitable for printing in the ON LAST ROW control block. If you wish to print the grand total in the FIRST PAGE HEADER, you may do so, but none of your report will appear until all the data has been processed, so that the aggregates can be calculated and printed on the first page. If you want running or cumulative totals, or other statistics which cannot be derived using these functions, you will have to program them yourself using variables and assignment statements, which will be covered in Chapter 13.

9.9 Groups

The control blocks BEFORE GROUP OF and AFTER GROUP OF are used to control what happens when a group is started or finished. A group of rows is a sequence of

```
DATABASE Cars END

SELECT Coname, Modelname, Details, Year_made, Hi_price, Lo_price
    FROM     Companies, Models, Prices
    WHERE    ...
    ORDER BY Coname, Modelname, Details, Year_made
END

FORMAT
    FIRST PAGE HEADER
        ...
    BEFORE GROUP OF Coname
        ...
        BEFORE GROUP OF Modelname
            ...
            BEFORE GROUP OF Details
                ...
                ON EVERY ROW
                ...
            AFTER GROUP OF Details
            ...
        AFTER GROUP OF Modelname
        ...
    AFTER GROUP OF Coname
    ...
    ON LAST ROW
    ...
END
```

Figure 9.3 Skeleton report showing groups

rows, all of which have the same value in one column, which allows a report to be divided into sub-sections. For groups to be effective, the SELECT statement must include an ORDER BY clause on the columns to be grouped.

It is possible to have nested group control blocks if the ORDER BY clause lists more than one column. In this case, the outer level of grouping will be the first column listed in the ORDER BY clause, the second level the second column and so on. In fact, the ORDER BY clause frequently lists at least one more column than there are groups of data; the first groups subdivide the output and the extra columns are used to sort the items within the innermost group. The report outline shown in Figure 9.3 shows an outline report where the prices of cars are printed, with the data grouped by manufacturer, model, details and year.

The idea behind the indentation is to show that after the FIRST PAGE HEADER block is executed, the report starts a loop. When it gets the first row of data, it will execute all three BEFORE GROUP OF blocks, and then the ON EVERY ROW block. Each subsequent row with the same value of Coname, Modelname and Details is part of the same group and will only activate the ON EVERY ROW block. When the Details value changes, it will execute the AFTER GROUP OF Details block with the old value of Details and then the BEFORE GROUP OF Details block with the new value, and then it will execute the ON EVERY ROW. When either the Modelname or Coname value changes, ACE executes the appropriate set of AFTER GROUP OF blocks in the order Details, Modelname, Coname (all with the old values of the group column) and then executes the set of BEFORE GROUP OF

```
DATABASE Cars END

SELECT Coname, Modelname, Details, Year_made, Hi_price, Lo_price
    FROM      Companies, Models, Prices
    WHERE     ...
    ORDER BY Coname, Modelname, Details, Year_made
END

FORMAT
    FIRST PAGE HEADER
        ...
    BEFORE GROUP OF Coname
        ...
    AFTER GROUP OF Coname
        ...
    BEFORE GROUP OF Details
        ...
    ON EVERY ROW
        ...
    ON LAST ROW
        ...
END
```

Figure 9.4 Skeleton report showing that the order of groups is unimportant

blocks in the opposite order. Note that `Year_made` is used to present the results in a logical order within the group of `Details`.

ACE will interpret the report as if it had the nested structure shown in Figure 9.3, even if the control blocks were in a completely different order, and if one or two of them were missing. In fact, it is not recommended to format the report as shown in the figure; normally, each control block is at the same level of indentation as each of the others, as shown in Figure 9.4.

9.10 Group aggregates

Group aggregates are somewhat similar to the aggregates introduced earlier, but there are two vital differences. First, they can only appear in AFTER GROUP OF blocks, and second, the value printed by a group aggregate depends on the context in which it appears. Also, different values will be produced by the same group aggregate at different times in the report. A group aggregate in the AFTER GROUP OF `Details` block in the outline report shown in Figure 9.3 operates on all the rows related to one particular model, say Ford Escort 1.4 L:

```
AFTER GROUP OF Details
    PRINT "Number of years listed  = ", GROUP COUNT USING "&<<<"
    PRINT "Average price for model = ",
        GROUP AVERAGE OF (Lo_price + Hi_price) / 2 USING "$$$ $$&.&&"
```

The GROUP COUNT will be the number of rows printed (the number of years for which there is price data), and the GROUP AVERAGE calculates the average price. When the model changes from Ford Escort 1.4 L to Ford Escort XR3i, the group aggregates will be reset and a new set of figures for the new model will be produced.

When the model changes from Ford Escort to Ford Granada, say, the AFTER GROUP OF `Modelname` block will be activated after the AFTER GROUP OF `Details` block and the group aggregates will be printed for all the Ford Escorts. Even though the expression that is used to define the group aggregate is the same as in the AFTER GROUP OF `Details`, the value that is produced is, in general, different. However, any group may only contain one sub-group, in which case the totals for the sub-group and the group are obviously identical.

```
AFTER GROUP OF Modelname
    PRINT "Average cost of any type of ", Coname CLIPPED, " ", Modelname CLIPPED, " = ",
        GROUP AVERAGE OF (Lo_price + Hi_price) / 2 USING "$$$ $$&.&&"
```

One thing which, curiously, it is not possible to do without using variables (see Chapter 13) is to count the number of sub-groups. That is, there is no way of saying how many different types of Ford Escort were listed. It is possible to count the total number of prices printed for Ford Escorts — that is what GROUP COUNT does — but it is not possible to count (with an aggregate function) the number of distinct types of Ford Escort.

9.11 The OUTPUT section

The OUTPUT section has two purposes: it is used to specify where the report should go to (the screen, a file, the printer, etc), and to control the dimensions of the pages of the report. It consists of the keyword OUTPUT followed by some attributes followed by the keyword END. The full set of options is illustrated below. Each of the fields is optional. Only one of the three REPORT TO options may be used, and if none is given, the report will go to the screen.

```
OUTPUT
    TOP MARGIN     3
    LEFT MARGIN    5
    RIGHT MARGIN   132
    BOTTOM MARGIN  3
    PAGE LENGTH    66
    REPORT TO PRINTER
    { REPORT TO "filename"      }
    { REPORT TO PIPE "program" }
END
```

9.11.1 Controlling the layout of the report

The remaining statements in the OUTPUT section control the size of the page. The values given in the example are the default values. The way these figures are used is illustrated in Figure 9.5. The top, bottom and left margins are always left blank. The TOP MARGIN is a white space left before the PAGE HEADER, the BOTTOM MARGIN is a white space left after the PAGE TRAILER and the LEFT MARGIN is the number of columns printed as blanks at the left edge of the paper. Column 1 for the print statements is the first column after the left margin.

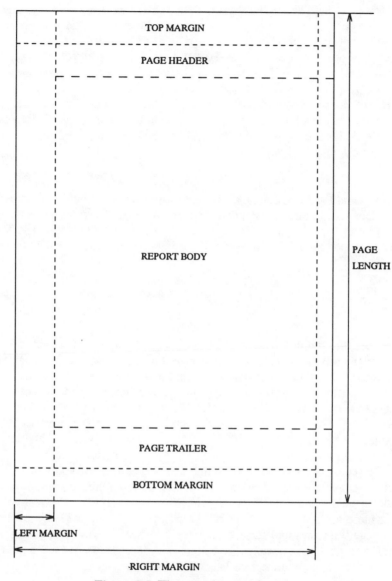

Figure 9.5 The page layout of a report

Version 2.10 and earlier. The RIGHT MARGIN is only effective when the FORMAT section is 'FORMAT EVERY ROW END' and dictates how long the output lines may be. If the FORMAT section contains any of the other control blocks, the RIGHT MARGIN is ignored completely and the length of each line of output is as long as the printing commands say it should be – the onus is on the person who writes the report to get the sums correct.

Version 4.00. The RIGHT MARGIN is sometimes used when the FORMAT section just specifies the default layout, but it also has an effect when using the WORDWRAP option to print long character fields (and if you are using INFORMIX-ONLINE, when printing VARCHAR and TEXT fields with WORDWRAP − see Section 14.1 for more details about these types, and Section 9.12 for more information about WORDWRAP).

Notice that the PAGE HEADER and PAGE TRAILER are always a fixed number of lines long in any given report. (Even when conditions and loops are introduced in Chapter 13, the header and trailer must be a fixed length.) The number of lines available for printing the body of the report on is:

report body = page length - top margin - page header - page trailer - bottom margin

There must be at least one line on each page for printing the body of the report. The default values are set up for a standard printer; the RIGHT MARGIN assumes a wide-carriage printer, but this should not matter for production reports. The following OUTPUT section is suitable for a report that is intended for a standard 24-line screen:

```
OUTPUT
    PAGE LENGTH    23
    TOP MARGIN      0
    BOTTOM MARGIN 0
    LEFT MARGIN     0
END
```

The TOP MARGIN and BOTTOM MARGIN are reset because most screens are 24 lines long, and if the top and bottom margins are left at three lines each, a quarter of the screen is wasted as white space, let alone what is used in the page header or trailer. The LEFT MARGIN is set to 0 as it gives a little more space, but that is not so crucial. The PAGE LENGTH is set to 23 so that the PAUSE statement can be used in the PAGE TRAILER. If the PAGE LENGTH is 24, the top line of each page vanishes off the top of the screen, which is irritating, but setting the page length to one line less means that all the data *and* the prompt from the PAUSE statement are visible.

The report is always an exact number of pages long. If you wish to simulate continuous text, the PAGE LENGTH can be set to 1, but there cannot be a PAGE HEADER or PAGE TRAILER. If the page length is 1, the NEED statement will always find that there are not enough lines on the current page, and will skip to the top of the next page (one line) and start printing there. There is no way of configuring the shape of a report dynamically. It cannot be done using variables and INPUT statements. This is a nuisance, but that is the way it goes.

9.11.2 Controlling the destination of the report

The report may be sent to the screen, to a printer, to a file or, on UNIX, it may be piped to another program. If there is no OUTPUT section, or if the OUTPUT section only sets the page sizes, the report will go to the screen.

The REPORT TO PRINTER option will send the report to the printer spooler nominated by the environment variable DBPRINT, which defaults to **lp** on UNIX

```
{
    @(#)longflds.ace 5.6 91/03/11
    @(#)Report demonstrating WORDWRAP
}

DATABASE dummy END

OUTPUT
    REPORT TO "longflds.out"
    TOP MARGIN    0
    BOTTOM MARGIN 0
    LEFT MARGIN   0
    PAGE LENGTH   23
END

SELECT field00, field01, field02 FROM long_fields END

FORMAT

    ON EVERY ROW
        SKIP 1 LINE
        NEED 10 LINES
        PRINT
            COLUMN  1, field00 USING "###&",
            COLUMN  6, field01 CLIPPED WORDWRAP RIGHT MARGIN 30,
            COLUMN 32, field02 CLIPPED WORDWRAP RIGHT MARGIN 56

    PAGE TRAILER
        PAUSE "Hit return to continue"

END
```

Figure 9.6 Report using WORDWRAP

systems. The default option is usually '-s' which means that the spooler does not report the job number when the report is spooled. This can, of course, be changed; for example, if the system had several printers, and the one to be used for printing reports was called 'delta', the DBPRINT environment variable should be set to:

```
DBPRINT="lp -ddelta -s"
```

REPORT TO PIPE only works on UNIX and sends the output to the specified program (which may have arguments given to it inside the quoted string) instead of to the screen. The report fails if it cannot run the program. This can be used to send the report to someone by e-mail, to send the report to a formatter such as **troff** or to send the report as a telex (assuming the telex software is *in situ*).

The other form of REPORT TO sends the output to the specified file. If the file already exists, it is overwritten; if it cannot be overwritten, the report fails.

9.12 WORDWRAP

Version 4.00. The WORDWRAP facility is used to print long character fields over several lines, if necessary, with the field being split into sections at a break between words. By default, the text is wrapped from the current column up to the current value of the RIGHT MARGIN, which is the only time in a formatted report that the

```
1000 this text, all in lower
     case, was entered in
     field01 of this table.
     the form has wordwrap
     compress defined on this
     field (as well as
     downshift), and is
     entered on five lines of
     51 characters each.
                          THIS TEXT, ALL IN UPPER
                          CASE, WAS ENTERED IN
                          FIELD02 OF THIS TABLE.
                          THE FORM DEFINITION FOR
                          THIS FIELD IS VERY
                          SIMILAR TO THAT FOR
                          FIELD01, EXCEPT THAT THE
                          DOWNSHIFT IS REPLACED BY
                          UPSHIFT.
```

Figure 9.7 Output from report using WORDWRAP

value of the RIGHT MARGIN is significant. However, it is frequently desirable to be able to wordwrap at some other margin, and this is allowed by using the qualifier RIGHT MARGIN and a number which is the effective value of the RIGHT MARGIN. Indeed, it is recommended that every report which uses WORDWRAP should explicitly specify the relevant RIGHT MARGIN every time.

The use of WORDWRAP is illustrated by the report shown in Figure 9.6, which uses the same database and table as was used to illustrate the handling of long fields in forms (see Section 7.1.3). The first page of output from the report (which is shown in Figure 9.7) shows an unfortunate oversight on the part of Informix, namely that a report cannot have two columns wordwrapped in parallel. Nevertheless, WORDWRAP is a very useful facility.

9.13 The profit-and-loss report

The report shown in Figure 9.8 is the profit-and-loss report described at the beginning of the chapter. For each transaction recorded in the **Sales** table, it prints out a number of the vital (and not so vital) statistics.

This report makes use of calculations on aggregates, a topic which has not been covered formally but which any experienced programmer should understand from knowing other programming languages. Chapter 13 covers this in detail, and also the use of variables, which would make it easier to format the report code readably, particularly in the ON LAST ROW block.

There are several points to notice about the layout of the report. It is somewhat compressed in width to ensure that it can be printed in this book, but it clearly shows the use of one PRINT statement for each line of output. This is

```
{
    a(#)report2a.pt1      5.3 91/03/08
    Example report illustrating PRINT USING and Aggregates
}

DATABASE Cars END

OUTPUT
    PAGE LENGTH    23
    TOP MARGIN      0
    BOTTOM MARGIN  0
    LEFT MARGIN     0
END

SELECT Companies.Company, Models.Modelname, Models.Details,
       Sales.Boughtfor,  Sales.Soldfor, Sales.Datebought, Sales.Datesold
    FROM       Companies, Models, Sales
    WHERE      Models.Model = Sales.Model
      AND      Models.Maker = Companies.Maker
    ORDER BY Company, Modelname, Details, Datesold
END

FORMAT

    PAGE HEADER
        PRINT "Analysis of profit-and-loss on Sales", COLUMN 50, "Page ", PAGENO USING "<<<"
        PRINT "Manufacturer: ", Company CLIPPED
        SKIP 1 LINE

    PAGE TRAILER
        PAUSE "Hit return to continue"

    BEFORE GROUP OF Company
        SKIP TO TOP OF PAGE
        PRINT
            COLUMN  1, "Bought",
            COLUMN 13, "Sold",
            COLUMN 26, "Bought for",
            COLUMN 38, "Sold for",
            COLUMN 50, "Profit(Loss)",
            COLUMN 64, "Days on books"

    AFTER GROUP OF Company
        SKIP 1 LINE
        PRINT "Number of cars made by ", Company CLIPPED, GROUP COUNT USING " = <<<<"
        PRINT "Number of sales on which a loss was made = ",
            GROUP COUNT WHERE Soldfor < Boughtfor USING "&<<<"
        PRINT "Total profit (loss) on this brand = ",
            GROUP TOTAL OF Soldfor - Boughtfor USING "(((( ((( ($&.&&)"

    BEFORE GROUP OF Modelname
        SKIP 1 LINE

    AFTER GROUP OF Modelname
        SKIP 1 LINE
        PRINT "Number of ", Company CLIPPED, " ", Modelname CLIPPED, GROUP COUNT USING " = <<<<"
```

Figure 9.8 The profit-and-loss report

```
BEFORE GROUP OF Details
    PRINT Company clipped, " ", Modelname clipped, " ", Details

AFTER GROUP OF Details
    SKIP 1 LINE
    PRINT "Number of ", Company CLIPPED, " ", Modelname CLIPPED,
          " ", Details CLIPPED, GROUP COUNT USING " = <<<<"

ON EVERY ROW
    PRINT
        COLUMN  1, Datebought USING "dd mmm yyyy",
        COLUMN 13, Datesold USING "dd mmm yyyy",
        COLUMN 26, Boughtfor USING "$$$ $$&.&&",
        COLUMN 38, Soldfor   USING "$$$ $$&.&&",
        COLUMN 50, Soldfor - Boughtfor USING "(((( ($&.&&)",
        COLUMN 64, Datesold - Datebought USING "##&"

ON LAST ROW
    SKIP TO TOP OF PAGE
    { Print general statistics }
    PRINT "Number of cars sold  = ", COLUMN 25, COUNT USING "<<<<"
    PRINT "First car bought on ", MIN OF Datebought USING "dd mmm yyyy"
    PRINT "Last  car bought on ", MAX OF Datebought USING "dd mmm yyyy"
    PRINT "First car sold  on ", MIN OF Datesold   USING "dd mmm yyyy"
    PRINT "Last  car sold  on ", MAX OF Datesold   USING "dd mmm yyyy"
    SKIP 1 LINE

    { Print financial statistics }
    PRINT "Total cost of cars   = ", COLUMN 25, TOTAL OF Boughtfor USING " $$$ $$$ $$&.&&"
    PRINT "Total value of sales = ", COLUMN 25, TOTAL OF Soldfor USING " $$$ $$$ $$&.&&"
    PRINT COLUMN 25, "---------------"
    PRINT "Gross profit         = ", COLUMN 25,
        TOTAL OF (Soldfor - Boughtfor) USING "(((( ((( ($&.&&)"
    PRINT "Employment costs   , = ", COLUMN 25, { Rated at #950 per 28-day month }
        ((950.00 / 28) * ((MAX OF Datebought) - (MIN OF Datebought)))
                    USING " $$$ $$$ $$&.&&"
    PRINT COLUMN 25, "================"
    PRINT COLUMN 25,
        (TOTAL OF Soldfor - Boughtfor) -
        ((1000.00 / 28) * ((MAX OF Datebought) - (MIN OF Datebought)))
        USING "(((( ((( ($&.&&)"

END
```

Figure 9.8 *(cont.)*

preferable to using multiple PRINT statements ending with semicolons to print parts of a line when the things that describe what should be printed are too long to fit conveniently on one line of the report code. It also shows how to use the COLUMN keyword to ensure that headings and the material printed under the headings align correctly. Even if the headings needed to be right-justified, it would be worth using the same column numbers in both the place where the headings are printed and where the data is printed. The layout of a report always changes sooner or later (usually sooner), and it is much simpler to realign the columns if all the items in the sixth output column can be identified because they all start at column 57. The alternative, in which the column numbers are all carefully calculated to include the leading spaces needed to get the column heading correctly right-justified, is more difficult to change because one of the items starts in column 57, another in column

60, and the heading is actually in column 61, and these three numbers must all have the same amount added, instead of simply changing 57 to 63 globally.

When working with expressions involving two aggregate functions the brackets around the aggregates are necessary to indicate the end of the expression which the aggregate is calculating, thus:

```
(MAX OF Datesold) - (MIN OF Datebought)
```

If the brackets are omitted, ACE assumes that you are trying to use an aggregate of an aggregate; the bracketing it assumes is indicated by the brackets below:

```
MAX OF (Datesold - MIN OF Datebought)
```

ACE rejects this as a semantic error and the report does not compile.

9.14 Summary

This chapter has discussed a number of important features of ACE. The PRINT USING statement is crucial for obtaining well formatted reports, and is a very powerful tool. It also showed how to use the WORDWRAP facility available with version 4.00. All the remaining control blocks have been discussed, with considerable emphasis being placed on the use of the BEFORE GROUP OF and AFTER GROUP OF control blocks. The aggregate functions were described in two forms; the global aggregates which are applied to all the data printed in the report, and the group aggregates which can only be used in the AFTER GROUP OF block. Group aggregates apply the same set of aggregate functions as the global aggregates, but they only operate on the set of rows in the group of the AFTER GROUP OF block they appear in. The chapter also described the method of configuring the dimensions of the report.

Exercises

1. Create a report on the models which customers enquired about between 1 June 1990 and 31 December 1990. Group the models by manufacturer. List the customer name and phone number, the maker name, the model, the date of the enquiry and the full price of the model. For each manufacturer, report on the number of cars sold and the value of the sales. At the end of the report, give the total number of cars sold and the total value of the sales.

2. Write a personalized letter to each customer who bought a Ford describing a mythical new Ford car.

10
User menus

This chapter describes how to build a customized application using the user-menu facility provided with INFORMIX-SQL, which provides a simple method of building a complete application without having to write any programs. It also discusses the methods of giving a user a completely controlled login which automatically runs the INFORMIX-SQL application developed using user menus, including the method of preventing the user executing commands from the shell escape facility provided in the interactive INFORMIX-SQL programs such as PERFORM.

10.1 What is a user menu?

A user menu allows an application developer to construct a complete application without having to resort to a programming language to construct the menu system which guides the user around the application.

The user-menu system allows arbitrary menu hierarchies to be built. Each menu has a name and a title and some options associated with it. Each menu option has a sequence number, a title and a specification of what should happen when the user selects the option. The basic options are to move to a new level in the menu hierarchy or to run a program specified by the developer. With INFORMIX-SQL versions 1.10 and 2.00, the only action was to run another program; with version 2.10 and later, the menu provides actions to run a form, a report, an ordinary program, an SQL script or a *script menu*, which is a simple (unconditional) sequence of operations from the choices listed above.

A user menu is a connected series of menus. The menus are of the list-down-the-page variety, rather than the ring menus used throughout the rest of INFORMIX-SQL. Each menu has a title, which appears at the top of the page, and a sequence of options which the user can select by using the cursor keys or by typing an option number.

There is one default menu for each database, but it is possible to build several different menu systems in one database, and there are several ways of specifying which one should be used.

All the menus for a database are stored in two tables called **Sysmenus** and **Sysmenuitems**. These are created automatically when you use the menu system;

```
┌─────────────────────────────────────────────────────────────────────┐
│  USER-MENU:  [Run] Modify  Exit                                      │
│  Run the user-menu for the current database.                         │
│                                                                      │
│  --------------------- cars ----------------- Press CTRL-W for Help --------  │
│                                                                      │
```

Figure 10.1 User-Menu menu in ISQL

they are not created when the database is created. The **Sysmenus** table contains the names of the menus and the text that should be used as the title. The **Sysmenuitems** table contains the description of each option for each menu, which includes the name of the menu in which the option appears, the text used to describe the option, the type of action to be performed and the text defining exactly what should be done.

10.2 How is a user menu created?

The first step in creating a user menu is to design it on paper. The design should list the menu names, titles, options and what action is to be performed when each option is chosen. This sounds trite but is necessary, especially with versions 1.10 and 2.00 because then you *must* define the names of the menus before you can cross-reference them. With the design on hand, select the **User-Menu** option from the ISQL main menu, which allows the user the choice of options shown in Figure 10.1.

The **Run** option would be used to run the menu system. If the DBMENU variable is set, its value is the name of the first menu the user will see; otherwise, the menu that is run will be called main. If this menu does not exist and DBMENU is not set, the program will not run any menu. The **Modify** option is used both to create and modify a user menu. When it is chosen, ISQL runs PERFORM with the special form shown in Figure 10.2 which is used to alter the menu system.

The special form has a master/detail relationship between the **Sysmenus** and **Sysmenuitems** tables. The names of the menus and the title lines are entered in the **Sysmenus** table, and the details of the options are entered in the **Sysmenuitems** table. The normal sequence of operations to create the user menu is:

1. Add menu main – this must be the top-level menu.
2. Add each of the sub-menus and their titles.
3. Use the **Query** option to enquire all the menu names.
4. For each menu or sub-menu:
5. Select the **Detail** option. If you are creating a new menu, not modifying it, PERFORM will give the standard message 'There are no rows satisfying the conditions'.
6. Add rows describing the menu options for the current menu and specify what should be done when that option is chosen.
7. Select the **Master** table again.
8. Choose the next sub-menu and fill in its details as in steps 5–8.
9. When the menu system is complete, exit PERFORM.

```
PERFORM:   [Query] Next  Previous  Add  Update  Remove  Table  Screen  ...
Searches the active database table.                ** 1: sysmenus table**

==========================MENU ENTRY FORM===================================

Menu Name:  [main              ]

Menu Title: [ABC Cars Ltd                                            ]

----------------------SELECTION SECTION----------------------------------

Selection Number:   1                 Selection Type:   F

Selection
Text:       Sales

Selection
Action:     sales
```

Figure 10.2 User-menu form

This sequence is strictly necessary with versions 1.10 and 2.00; the form has verify joins in it. With version 2.10 and later, the form does not include verify joins, so you can refer to menus which do not exist yet.

You should now be able to select the **Run** option from the **User-Menu** menu and check that it works as you intended. You can actually have options which run forms and reports where the form or report is not yet available; when you select the option, INFORMIX-SQL will complain that it cannot find the form or report and leave you in the menu where you chose the option.

Although the documentation suggests that there can only be one user menu in a database, this is not really true. There will certainly only be one default user menu (which will be called main), but there is nothing to stop you creating another menu system which has a different name. This new menu will be the starting point for a different menu hierarchy, and it may have a completely disjoint set of sub-menus, although there is no reason why the second menu system should not use some of the sub-menus designed for the main menu. This new menu can be accessed if the environment variable DBMENU is set to the new menu name, or if the menus are run from the command line and the menu name is specified.

Incidentally, there is no reason why one of the sub-menus of the main menu should not be specified as the starting point for a user; the only special feature of the main menu is that it is the menu that ISQL runs in the absence of instructions to the contrary. Similarly, it would be possible to set up a separate top-level menu for each user (or a number of different top-level menus, each of which could be used by a group of users), and each of these menu systems could use some of the sub-menus under the main menu as standard options. Indeed, the same sub-menu could be used in several different places in any one menu hierarchy.

10.3 What are the actions?

The actions, as mentioned earlier, depend on the version of INFORMIX-SQL. With versions 1.10 and 2.00, there are just two options:

P – run the program specified.
M – go into the next level of the menu hierarchy.

If the 'P' option is specified, the action specified will be a program to run – typically **sacego** or **sperform** – together with any arguments that are required. There is nothing to stop you running any executable program or shell script that does the job you need doing. The 'M' option indicates that the user should be presented with the next menu down the hierarchy of menus.

With version 2.10 and later, these types of action are augmented by:

F – run the named form.
R – run the named report (no arguments).
Q – run the named SQL script.
S – run the named script menu.

Running a form or a report is simple, but a report cannot take any parameters when used like this (see Chapter 13). The third new option, 'Q', runs an SQL script. For the forms and the reports, the manual says it is not necessary to add the extension; it should state 'it is necessary not to add the extension' because an extension will cause an error.

A script menu needs some explanation. It is a menu that is not treated as a menu but as a rudimentary shell script. Basically, the actions for each 'menu option' are executed in turn, ranging from the smallest sequence number to the largest. Thus, without using the shell, the programmer can run a form, and then automatically run a report and a query (update perhaps). This is very useful if you are not confident in writing shell scripts, but you may prefer to run a real shell script. If you ever invoke a script menu via DBMENU, it will appear as an ordinary menu with actions that can be selected individually in any sequence. A script menu is only special when invoked as an option from some other menu.

The menu designer does not have to supply an exit option; it is supplied automatically, and the user can invoke it by typing 'e' or 'E'.

One point worth noting is that with version 2.10 and later, when a form, report, query or script action is used, INFORMIX-SQL does not start any new processes. Instead, it changes its mode of operation internally, executes the appropriate action and then reverts to the menu. This means that there is still just one copy of INFORMIX-SQL and one copy of the database engine running for the user. By contrast, if the program option is used to run a program which manipulates the database, there will be one copy of INFORMIX-SQL and its database engine, plus a shell, the new program and its database engine. This means that there is a smaller load on the machine. (When the program is running, INFORMIX-SQL and its database engine are both completely passive, so the extra load comes from having to start three new processes.)

10.4 Running a user menu

There are two ways of running a user menu. The first is by running ISQL and choosing the **User-Menu** and **Run** options. This, however, also allows the user access to all the facilities available from ISQL – everything! Often, it is desirable to restrict the use to just the facilities available from the user menu, and this can be done by using the alternative method of starting a user menu, namely running it direct from the UNIX command line (or inside a user's profile, of which more will be said later).

Unfortunately, the arguments used to drive ISQL have also changed with different versions of ISQL. With version 1.10 and version 2.00, the following syntaxes could be used:

```
$ isql -u database [menu]
$ isql database -u [menu]
```

Both these would immediately run either the named user menu or the menu specified by the environment variable DBMENU, or the default menu, main, and the user could not gain access to any of the other facilities offered by ISQL. The optional argument *menu* overrides the default menu; if it is omitted, the menu specified by DBMENU will be run, and if no menu is specified by DBMENU, the menu called main will be run.

The equivalent method in version 2.10 and later would be:

```
$ isql database -ur [menu]
```

If the 'r' was omitted, the user would be given the choice of running the user menu or modifying it – probably not a good idea. (See Chapter 16 for a discussion of the command-line arguments to the INFORMIX-SQL programs.)

10.5 Using the menu

Using a user menu is very simple; the options are presented in a list down the screen as shown in Figure 10.3, and the user can either use the arrow keys to choose an option or enter the number of an option, and then hit RETURN to select the option. (The options will be displayed in two columns if there are sufficient options to need it and the text strings are short enough to allow the choices to be shown side by side). If the option leads to another menu, that menu is shown; if the option invokes a program, the program is run, and when it exits, the user is left in the menu from which the program was chosen. When the **Exit** option is invoked, the system returns up one level of the menu hierarchy; if the top is reached, the user menu terminates and what happens next depends on how it was invoked. If it was run automatically from a login, the user will probably be logged off (it depends on how the program was started). If it was run from the ISQL menu system, the user will be returned to that level.

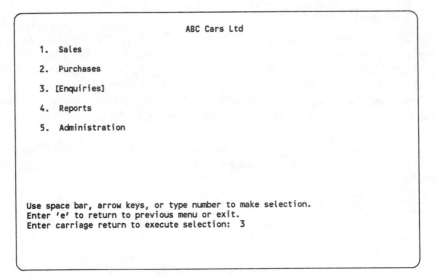

Figure 10.3 An example of a user menu

10.6 Creating a customized application

Clearly, the second method of running a user menu is of great use when it comes to producing a customized application. This allows a special login to be set up which will have access to the database, and which will always start ISQL when the user logs in. The method of setting up a fully customized application is:

1. Create a database administrator login, with new user and group numbers. This user should be given a password and a standard login shell.
2. Login as this user and create the database, the forms and the reports. Ensure that only the database administrator can change the reports, forms, SQL scripts and the user menus. To stop unauthorized users modifying the user menu, you will need to use the GRANT and REVOKE statements discussed in Chapter 14.
3. Create a database user login, with another new user number but with the same group number as the database administrator login.
4. Create a profile for the database user which sets up the environment correctly and as the last step includes the line:

        exec isql *database* -ur

This sequence of operations means that the ordinary user login can be used by anyone who knows the password, but they can only do those things which the database administrator has authorized them to do and for which a command has been provided.

10.6.1 Containing a user inside INFORMIX-SQL

There is just one problem with this system: both the user-menu system and PERFORM have a shell escape built in. This allows any user to run any command at any time as if it had been typed at the UNIX command line. It is used by typing '!' as the menu option chosen, which produces an exclamation mark at the bottom of the screen, after which a UNIX command can be typed. One such UNIX command is '**sh**', the Bourne shell. This allows the user to do almost anything.

It is difficult to prevent the user from getting a shell escape. To make matters worse, a different strategy is required for INFORMIX-SQL versions 1.10 and 2.00 from the one that works with version 2.10 and later.

All the programs executed by a user menu ('P' type options) are executed by the 'shell' indicated by the environment variable SHELL. With INFORMIX-SQL version 2.10 and later, the user menu could be invoked as:

```
$ SHELL="" isql cars -ur
```

This notation invokes the program **isql** with the environment variable SHELL set to an empty string. When the user tries to use the menu system to invoke a shell to run the command, the user can type the command but it is never executed. However, this trick is only acceptable if none of the menu options are 'P' options, since they are also invoked using the shell. With versions 1.10 and 2.00, even this trick was no help: there were no 'F', 'R' or 'Q' options, so the user always used 'P' options.

The only solution to this problem is to use a C program which allows a restricted list of commands to be executed in the ordinary way (programs such as **sperform**, **sacego** and possibly **date** or **ls**), but anything not in the list would not be executed. The commands should be run using their full path name to minimize the possibility of Trojan horses. It could be tuned to detect which user was using it and to execute different lists of commands for different users. When the user menu was run, this program would be specified as the shell; if its name was **isqlsh**, the syntax for invoking the command in .profile would be:

```
SHELL=/usr/informix/bin/isqlsh exec isql cars -ur
```

The code for one such program is given in Appendix C. The program given there stops casual users of UNIX but cannot be guaranteed to stop an experienced UNIX hacker from escaping to the system. (If you let users have access to **vi**, even indirectly through the e-mail system, for example, they can, if they know what they are doing, get at a useful shell.)

10.7 Organizing a database project

In addition to the database, a working INFORMIX-SQL application will have a collection of screen forms, reports, SQL scripts and maintenance tools which are used to manipulate the database. On very small projects, it is often convenient to have all

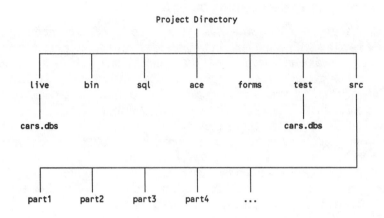

Figure 10.4 Example project organization

these files in one directory, and to have the database as a sub-directory of that directory. It is the technique used by many novices, as well as a good few people who should know better. The grave disadvantage of this system is that as the project grows, so does the number of files in the directory, and sooner (rather than later), the directory listing will not all fit on to one screen, even when listed with multiple columns (using 'ls -C'). At this point, the users normally cease cleaning up this directory and it just fills up with rubbish.

If the application is large, or is likely to become large, then it is better to put the compiled forms in one directory, the compiled reports in another directory, SQL scripts in a third directory and any tools in yet another directory, roughly as shown in Figure 10.4. The project manager should choose an environment variable which will be set to represent the project directory (eg PROJECT). The source code for the forms and reports lives in directories under the project source directory (eg $PROJECT/src/part1). Related sets of forms and reports will be kept together in different sub-directories of $PROJECT/src. When a form is recompiled, the new compiled form is moved or (preferably) linked to the project forms directory ($PROJECT/forms), and similarly for forms.

Those people who use the database will only run scripts from $PROJECT/bin, and those scripts will all ensure that the complete environment is set correctly. This will involve ensuring that $PROJECT/bin is included in $PATH, and that $PROJECT/ace and $PROJECT/forms are both components of $DBPATH. Those people using the live version of the system will also include $PROJECT/live on their $DBPATH, but those developing the system will include $PROJECT/test on their $DBPATH to ensure that they do not damage any operational data by accident.

If the database has a user menu which non-development staff should use to obtain access to the database, you can write a simple script such as the one in Figure 10.5 to set the environment correctly and run the user menu. This can be added to

```
:        "a(#)run_it.sh   5.1 90/08/19"
#
#        Run correct user menu for PROJECT

PROJECT=${PROJECT:-/usr/project}
export PROJECT

INFORMIXDIR=${INFORMIXDIR:-/usr/informix}
export INFORMIXDIR

PATH=$PROJECT/bin:$INFORMIXDIR/bin:$PATH
export PATH

dbase=$PROJECT/${PROJECT_DATABASE:-live/cars}
dpath=`basename $dbase`

DBPATH=$dpath:$PROJECT/forms:$PROJECT/ace:$DBPATH
export DBPATH

DBDATE=dmy4/
export DBDATE

DBMENU=${PROJECT_MENU:-main}
export DBMENU

# -- Could set SHELL
# SHELL=/usr/lbin/isqlsh; export SHELL
# -- Could set DBPRINT
# DBPRINT="lp -dproject -onobanner -s"; export DBPRINT
# -- Could set DBEDIT
# DBEDIT="wordprocessor"; export DBEDIT

exec isql $dbase -ur
```

Figure 10.5 Example program to control access to a database

one of the standard directories already on everybody's PATH, such as /usr/lbin. If required, different menus can be run for different people by setting DBMENU.

Of course, if a project gets very large, it may turn out to be sensible to introduce another level of directory into the source directory hierarchy, so that $PROJECT/src/part1 itself has a collection of sub-directories, probably one for each program which makes up that part of the project. Some of these programs are likely to be written in INFORMIX-4GL if the project is big enough to need this extra level of sub-division. Also, the project directory normally acquires some extra administrative directories (such as $PROJECT/etc and $PROJECT/doc). One important point to emphasize is that a directory either contains source files or object files or other directories, but not a mixture of these. Thus, $PROJECT/bin only contains shell scripts and programs, $PROJECT/forms only contains compiled form files, $PROJECT/src/part1 only contains source and object files, and $PROJECT/src only contains directories. If you use a change control system (eg SCCS), the files normally live in a sub-directory below the directory where the source lives, so $PROJECT/src/part1 would probably contain a sub-directory SCCS, but these sub-directories (and only these sub-directories) are allowed.

10.8 Summary

This chapter outlined the facilities provided by user menus for creating applications and described how to set up users so that when they log in, the application is run automatically. It also warned you about a security loophole and outlined a solution to the problem; the C code needed is given in Appendix C. It also showed you one method of organizing a complete database project.

Exercises

No answers have been provided for these exercises.

1. Create a menu system for the reports and forms you have generated. Allow the user access to ISQL as one of the options.

2. Set up a thoroughly controlled user who can only use the database to make purchases (add to **Stock**) or sales (transfer from **Stock** to **Sales**). You will need to use database permissions (see Chapter 14) and also set up a suitable `.profile` and a suitable user menu.

3. (*An advanced exercise in forms*) Try reverse engineering the form used to create user menus. Notice that the two tables **Sysmenus** and **Sysmenuitems** are ordinary user tables, despite the names given to them.

Part IV
Advanced INFORMIX-SQL

11
Advanced forms

Chapter 4 showed the basic techniques for building and using forms and Chapter 7 described multi-table forms. This chapter completes the coverage of forms. So far, the INSTRUCTIONS section of a form has only had either the DELIMITERS or the MASTER OF instructions, but there are many other things that can be done in this section, and this chapter describes what they are. It also includes a description of COMPOSITES, and a couple of the tables from the **Cars** database are slightly modified to allow this to be illustrated.

11.1 Control blocks

The INSTRUCTIONS section specifies DELIMITERS (discussed in Chapter 4), creates master/detail relationships (discussed in Chapter 7), establishes *composite joins* (to be discussed in Section 11.4) and defines *control blocks*.

One of the problems when explaining control blocks is that there are both conditions and actions to be described, and neither the conditions nor the actions can be illustrated properly until the other has also been discussed. The conditions are discussed first, so if part of the discussion assumes a knowledge of an action which has not been described yet, please be patient; all will be explained in due course.

11.1.1 What are control blocks for?

Control blocks are used to control the behaviour of PERFORM while it is running the form. Control blocks can be used to:

- Control the cursor movement when rows are added or updated.
- Validate data entered against specific criteria, or against data which has already been entered.
- Modify data in fields after standard options such as **Add, Update, Query** and **Remove** have been used.
- Perform calculations on field values and enter the results in another field.
- Display aggregate information such as totals, counts and averages on rows in the current list of selected records.

The basic actions of PERFORM as seen so far are useful for many purposes, but sometimes extra validation is necessary. For example, consider the master/detail form used in Chapter 7. When the user enters a high guide price, the value should be at least as large as the low guide price. There is no way of specifying that this should be the case using the mechanisms presented so far.

Another thing that is sometimes required is to prevent the user from deleting rows from one of the tables; although this could be achieved by setting database permissions (see Chapter 14), it is quite probable that the user should be allowed to edit the data in the table, but not using the current form because the current form does not display all the relevant data.

The way that these sorts of control are implemented is by creating control blocks in the INSTRUCTIONS section of the form.

11.1.2 Conditions

A control block is always introduced by one of the keywords BEFORE or AFTER, followed by one or more keywords defining when the control block is to be activated, and then followed by one or more actions.

The control blocks recognize seven conditions – ADD, UPDATE, QUERY, REMOVE, DISPLAY, EDITADD and EDITUPDATE – some of which can be used with the BEFORE keyword, all of which can be used with the AFTER keyword. The ADD, UPDATE, REMOVE, QUERY and DISPLAY actions always apply when the action occurs to a table, whereas the EDITADD and EDITUPDATE actions can be applied when an individual column in a table is changed or when the table as a whole is changed.

The ADD condition is executed after a row of data has been added to the table; it cannot follow the keyword BEFORE. The UPDATE condition is executed after a row of data has been updated in the table; it cannot follow the keyword BEFORE either. The QUERY condition is another one that can only come after the AFTER keyword – it is executed after the user makes an enquiry – and the DISPLAY condition applies whenever an operation causes data to be displayed on the screen; this could be after an enquiry or when some data is displayed as the result of a joining condition.

The REMOVE condition behaves differently in different versions of INFORMIX-SQL.

Version 2.00 and earlier. REMOVE could only occur after the AFTER keyword, which meant that it could be used to do things such as to comment 'You should not have done that'.

Version 2.10 and later. The condition BEFORE REMOVE is also valid, and this, combined with the ABORT action (see the next section), allows the form designer to prevent the user from deleting data.

The EDITADD and EDITUPDATE conditions can be applied with either the BEFORE or AFTER keywords, and apply when the user changes a field while doing either an **Add** or an **Update** operation. If a table name follows, then the actions are either the very first thing that happens, or the very last thing that happens, when the table is the active table and the user adds or updates a row of data. If a column name follows the keyword, then the action will be performed either before or after the cursor enters that field. This is used for detailed validation of the value in a column.

One point to watch for is that lists of conditions and lists of tables and columns are separated by spaces only, not commas. This is inconsistent with almost everything else, but that is the way the system works.

11.1.3 Actions

Having looked at the different times when actions can be applied, it is time to look at what actions can be performed. The examples of how they are used will then be more comprehensible. The basic actions available are LET, NEXTFIELD, COMMENTS, ABORT and IF/THEN/ELSE.

The LET action allows a value to be displayed in a field. This value could be a constant (possibly TODAY), or it could be the result of a calculation based on the values in any of the fields on the screen. The destination field could be a DISPLAYONLY field or an ordinary field where the user might enter a value; it can be used to insert a value into a NOENTRY field where the value must be calculated. The fields are all identified by the field tag.

The NEXTFIELD action allows the form to specify which field the cursor should go into next. It can be used to send the user back to a field if the data is incorrect, normally in conjunction with the IF/THEN/ELSE action. The NEXTFIELD field is specified by a field tag. There is a special value of EXITNOW, which is equivalent to the user hitting the ESC key; it will initiate any tidying up and then add, update or remove the row as appropriate.

Version 2.10 and later. The keyword ABORT, which was not available in the earlier versions, is used to terminate the user's action as if the user had hit the INTERRUPT key. This prevents the add, remove, update from succeeding. It is an invaluable addition to PERFORM, even if the syntax is inconsistent with the EXITNOW keyword.

As mentioned earlier, it is possible to write comments on the screen by using the COMMENTS keyword. This may be followed by a string which will be displayed on the comment line of the form, overwriting any comments which would appear there otherwise. The keywords BELL and REVERSE may precede the string to indicate that the terminal should beep to tell the user what is happening or display the text in reverse video, or both. The only thing to be aware of is that if the next action is ABORT, the message does not stay visible for very long at all, and there is no SLEEP command to indicate that the terminal should wait for a couple of seconds before continuing.

The final action is IF/THEN/ELSE; this allows the form to test the values in fields against other fields or against constants, and to do different sets of actions based on the results of the test. The conditions can be more or less arbitrary combinations of the basic relational operators ($<$, $>=$, $=$, etc), the Boolean operators (AND, OR or NOT) and the IS NULL operator. Character fields can be compared using the MATCHES operator, just as in the SELECT statement (see Chapter 5). To invert the IS NULL or MATCHES operator, the condition must be inverted by prefixing it with the NOT operator, not by embedding the NOT operator in the middle as in SQL. A single action can follow the IF clause or the ELSE clause, but if several actions are required, they can be enclosed between the keywords BEGIN and END and are then treated as one statement. The ELSE clause is optional.

11.1.4 Examples using control blocks

Now that the ground work has been done, the way these actions are used can be illustrated. To take the first of the problems, that of validating the low and high guide prices in the form in Figure 11.1, the following control blocks could be used:

```
AFTER EDITADD EDITUPDATE OF Hi_price
    IF g002 > g003 THEN
    BEGIN
        COMMENTS BELL "High price is less than Low price"
        NEXTFIELD = g002
    END

AFTER EDITADD EDITUPDATE OF Prices
    IF g002 > g003 THEN
    BEGIN
        COMMENTS BELL "High price is less than Low price"
        NEXTFIELD = g002
    END
```

The logic behind this is that if the high price is too small, the user should be sent back to the *low* price field, where either value can be adjusted. The second condition is necessary to ensure that if the user hits the ESC key while in the low price field, PERFORM does not add the data, or update it, until it is consistent.

Because the actions are in fact identical, these two conditions can be combined into one control block:

```
AFTER EDITADD EDITUPDATE OF Prices Hi_price
    IF g002 > g003 THEN
    BEGIN
        COMMENTS BELL "High price is less than Low price"
        NEXTFIELD = g002
    END
```

The second problem, that of preventing the user from using the **Stock** adjustment form in Figure 11.2 to modify the **Models** or **Companies** tables, is unsolvable with version 2.00 and earlier, and trivially solvable with version 2.10 and later.

```
BEFORE REMOVE OF Models Company
    COMMENTS BELL REVERSE "You cannot change this table with this form"
    ABORT

BEFORE EDITADD EDITUPDATE OF Models Company
    ABORT
```

Why the two control blocks? PERFORM does not allow the EDITADD and EDITUPDATE options to be combined with REMOVE. Why does the BEFORE REMOVE block have a message and not the other one? PERFORM recognizes the second case and automatically produces a message:

```
Permission not granted to allow add of "models"
Permission not granted to allow add of "companies"
```

depending on which table is active. It produces this message instead of the COMMENTS message, even when the COMMENTS action is included. With the BEFORE REMOVE block, it does not recognize the ABORT, so the message has to be included as well. As mentioned in the discussion earlier, the only snag here is that the message flashes up on the screen and then vanishes rather too quickly, and there is nothing that can be done to stop that. Changing the order of the COMMENTS and ABORT actions makes no difference whatsoever.

11.2 DISPLAYONLY fields

A DISPLAYONLY field is a field that does not correspond to a column in the database. It is manipulated from the INSTRUCTIONS section of the form. A DISPLAYONLY field must have its type specified, which may be any valid database type except SERIAL. If the field is a DECIMAL or MONEY field, the precision need not be specified, but if it is, the display field must be big enough for the precision. DISPLAYONLY fields can be used for any purpose required, but one of the most common is to display aggregate values. A DISPLAYONLY field may be given display attributes such as REVERSE, FORMAT or PICTURE if required.

```
gavg  = DISPLAYONLY TYPE MONEY;
```

A DISPLAYONLY field can be declared ALLOWING INPUT in which case the user can enter data in it; presumably, there is an AFTER EDITADD EDITUPDATE control block which uses the value and changes the value in one of the ordinary DISPLAYONLY fields.

```
goff  = DISPLAYONLY ALLOWING INPUT TYPE INTEGER,
          DEFAULT = 0, INCLUDE = (-31 TO 7),
          COMMENTS = "Enter offset in range -31..+7";
```

Each DISPLAYONLY ALLOWING INPUT field is treated as a column of a pseudo-table called **Displaytable**. This is not a real database table, although PERFORM treats the fields as if they were part of such a table. The names of the columns in **Displaytable** are the names of the field tags of the fields on the screen section. When PERFORM is used, **Displaytable** can be made into the current table, and data could be added or changed. The **Displaytable** is always the last table in the list of tables, even if the first field in the ATTRIBUTES section is a DISPLAYONLY ALLOWING INPUT field.

Aggregates are the subject of the next section, and the example in the next section shows the use of DISPLAYONLY fields. There is no example of a DISPLAYONLY ALLOWING INPUT field, simply because there is no need for one in the **Cars** database – not even in a contrived example.

11.3 Aggregates

The LET statement does not only allow calculations based on the values on display in other fields on the form, it also allows aggregate values to be displayed based on the values in the current list of the current table. For example, the basic statistics about the prices listed in the **Prices** table for one model are the minimum, maximum and average prices, and these can be shown in DISPLAYONLY fields on the form:

```
AFTER DISPLAY ADD UPDATE REMOVE QUERY OF Prices
    LET gmin = MIN OF g002
    LET gmax = MAX OF g003
    LET gavg = (AVG OF g002 + AVG OF g003) / 2
```

(Actually, there is no requirement that the fields to which the values are displayed are DISPLAYONLY fields, but it would be very unusual if they were not DISPLAYONLY fields.) There are two other aggregates: COUNT and TOTAL which display the number of rows in the current list and the sum of the values in a column in the current list.

The example form in Figure 11.1 contains the control block shown above. It is a form which works with the **Companies**, **Models**, **Prices** and **Stock** tables, and there are few restrictions on what the user can do.

It is not a form for novice users; there are two detail tables specified for the **Models** table. If the user selects a company and chooses the **Detail** option, the current table changes to **Models**, as would be expected. If the user selects **Detail** again, the current table is changed to **Stock**. To change to the **Prices** table, it is necessary to type 3D, which selects the third table, which is **Prices**. It is possible to select the **Stock** table by typing 4D, too.

What is happening is that the D key chooses a default detail table (apparently the last named detail table for the current table in the list of MASTER OF specifications), but it is possible to dynamically make any table a detail of the current table by typing the number of the new table followed by D (eg by typing 3D), provided the two tables are joined.

11.4 Composite joins

Composite joins are joins between tables where the values of more than one column must be specified to identify a row uniquely. The composite join must be entered in the INSTRUCTIONS section to enable it to be made. The joins on each table (which must be individually indexed and also jointly indexed by the use of a composite index) are entered within angle brackets '<>' as shown here:

```
COMPOSITES <table1.col1, table1.col2, ...>
       [*] <table2.col1, table2.col2, ...>
```

COMPOSITES is the keyword indicating that the following entries in angle brackets are composite columns which are joined together. The entries within the angle brackets may contain as many columns as are necessary to establish the composite join. The optional '*' character indicates that the join is a verify join; as with every

```
<
    @(#)aggr1a.per       5.1 91/02/25
    Form using displayonly and aggregates
>

DATABASE Cars

SCREEN
<

          Add New Manufacturer

Company Number[f000]
Company Name   [f001          ]
Address        [f002                    ]
               [f003                    ]
               [f004                    ]
               [f005   ]

Notes:
[f007                                        ]
[f008                                        ]
>

SCREEN
<

          Models Made by New Manufacturer

Model Number    [f009]
Maker           [f000][f001        ]
Model Name      [f010              ]
Model Details   [f011              ]

Price           [f012  ]
Maximum Speed   [f13]mph
Acceleration    [f014]seconds
Tank Size       [f015]gallons

Fuel consumption
Urban Cycle     [f016]mpg
At 56 mph       [f017]mpg
>

SCREEN
<

          Guide prices

Model Number    [f009]
Maker           [f000][f001        ]
Model Name      [f010              ]
Model Details   [f011              ]

Year [g001] Low [g002    ] High [g003   ]

Average [gavg    ]
Minimum [gmin    ]
Maximum [gmax    ]
>
```

Figure 11.1 Form using aggregates

```
SCREEN
(

        Stock List
        ==========

Registration    [s000   ]
Model Number    [f009] [f000]
Description     [f001          ]
                [f010                   ][f011                   ]
Colour          [s002   ]
Condition       [s]
Date Bought     [s003      ]
Bought For      [s004        ]
Mileage         [s005        ]
Notes
[s006                                                    ]
[s008                                                    ]
)
END


TABLES
Companies
Models
Prices
Stock

ATTRIBUTES

f000 =*Companies.Maker = Models.Maker, NOENTRY, NOUPDATE, QUERYCLEAR;
f001 = Companies.Company, QUERYCLEAR;
f002 = Companies.Address1;
f003 = Companies.Address2;
f004 = Companies.Address3;
f005 = Companies.Postcode, PICTURE = "AXXX #AA", UPSHIFT, AUTONEXT;
f007 = Companies.Notes1;
f008 = Companies.Notes2;

f009 =*Models.Model, QUERYCLEAR;
     = Prices.Model
     = Stock.Model, NOENTRY, NOUPDATE, QUERYCLEAR;
f010 = Models.Modelname,
       COMMENTS = "Enter basic name of model (eg Escort)";
f011 = Models.Details,
       COMMENTS = "Enter all details (eg 1.4GL 4-door)";
f012 = Models.Price, INCLUDE = (1000 TO 100000);
f13  = Models.Maxspeed, INCLUDE = (30 TO 200);
f014 = Models.Accel,
       FORMAT = "##.#", INCLUDE = (1 TO 50),
       COMMENTS = "Time for 0 - 60 mph";
f015 = Models.Tanksize,
       FORMAT = "##.#", INCLUDE = (5 TO 50);
f016 = Models.Urban, INCLUDE = (1 TO 100);
f017 = Models.Mpgat56, INCLUDE = (1 TO 100);

g001 = Prices.Year_made,
        COMMENTS = "Enter a year between 1960 and now",
        INCLUDE = (1960 TO 1999);
g002 = Prices.Lo_price;
g003 = Prices.Hi_price;
```

Figure 11.1 (*cont.*)

```
gmin = DISPLAYONLY TYPE MONEY;
gmax = DISPLAYONLY TYPE MONEY;
gavg = DISPLAYONLY TYPE MONEY;

s000 = Stock.Registration, UPSHIFT, AUTONEXT, PICTURE = "AXXXXXA";
s002 = Stock.Colour;
s    = Stock.Condition, AUTONEXT, UPSHIFT,
         INCLUDE = ('X', 'V', 'G', 'A', 'P'),
         COMMENTS = "Xcellent, Very good, Good, Average, Poor";
s003 = Stock.Datebought, DEFAULT = TODAY, QUERYCLEAR;
s004 = Stock.Boughtfor;
s005 = Stock.Mileage;
s006 = Stock.Notes1;
s008 = Stock.Notes2;

END

INSTRUCTIONS
Companies MASTER OF Models
Models MASTER OF Prices
Models MASTER OF Stock

AFTER EDITADD EDITUPDATE OF Datebought
     IF s003 > TODAY THEN
     BEGIN
          COMMENTS "You can't have bought it yet!"
          NEXTFIELD = s003
     END
     ELSE IF s003 < TODAY - 14 THEN
     BEGIN
          COMMENTS "You must have bought it since then!"
          NEXTFIELD = s003
     END

AFTER DISPLAY ADD UPDATE REMOVE QUERY OF Prices
     LET gmin = MIN OF g002
     LET gmax = MAX OF g003
     LET gavg = (AVG OF g002 + AVG OF g003) / 2

AFTER EDITADD EDITUPDATE OF Prices Hi_price
     IF g002 > g003 THEN
     BEGIN
          COMMENTS BELL
          "High price is smaller than Low price"
          NEXTFIELD = g002

END
```

Figure 11.1 (*cont.*)

other verify join, the values of the composite columns in *table1* must exist in *table2* for the *table1* entry to be written.

In the standard **Cars** database, there are no composite keys which can be joined like this, so to illustrate the use of composites, it is necessary to modify the definition of the model numbers on the **Models** table, and to modify the schemas of the tables (other than **Companies**) which join with **Models**. The model number is redefined so that it is not unique; that is, there is (or could be) a model number 1 for each company. The primary key for the **Models** table is now the combination

```
{
    a(#)compos1.per      5.5 91/02/24
    Form using composites
}

DATABASE Cars

SCREEN
{

        Stock List
        ==========

Registration   [f000   ]
Model Number   [f001] [f011]
Description    [f021            ]
               [f012                    ] [f013              ]
Colour         [f002  ]
Condition      [a]
Date Bought    [f003    ]
Bought For     [f004     ]
Mileage        [f005    ]
Notes
[f006                                              ]
[f008                                              ]
}
END


TABLES
Stock2
Models2
Companies

ATTRIBUTES
f000 = Stock2.Registration, UPSHIFT, AUTONEXT, PICTURE = "AXXXXXA";
f001 = Stock2.Model, QUERYCLEAR;
     =*Models2.Model, QUERYCLEAR, NOENTRY, NOUPDATE;
f011 = Stock2.Maker, QUERYCLEAR,
        LOOKUP  f021 = Companies.Company
        JOINING *Companies.Maker;
     = Models2.Maker, QUERYCLEAR, NOENTRY, NOUPDATE;
f002 = Stock2.Colour;
a    = Stock2.Condition, AUTONEXT, UPSHIFT,
        INCLUDE = ('X', 'V', 'G', 'A', 'P'),
        COMMENTS = "Xcellent, Very good, Good, Average, Poor";
f003 = Stock2.Datebought;
f004 = Stock2.Boughtfor;
f005 = Stock2.Mileage;
f006 = Stock2.Notes1;
f008 = Stock2.Notes2;

f012 = Models2.Modelname, NOENTRY, NOUPDATE;
f013 = Models2.Details, NOENTRY, NOUPDATE;

END

INSTRUCTIONS
COMPOSITES <Stock2.Maker, Stock2.Model> *<Models2.Maker, Models2.Model>
END
```

Figure 11.2 Multi-table form showing use of composites

Models.Model and **Models.Maker**. The tables **Models2, Stock2** and **Prices2** implement the revised schema. The change to the **Models** table is minimal; the SERIAL column becomes an INTEGER column and the indexing is altered. The other tables acquire a **Maker** column and the indexing changes. The form in Figure 11.2 is a simple adaptation of the form shown in Figure 7.3.

The form in Figure 7.3 needed a number of modifications (most of them obvious) to work with the revised schema:

1. Rename **Models** as **Models2** throughout.
2. Rename **Stock** as **Stock2** throughout.
3. Make f011 a join with **Stock2.Maker**.
4. Allow entry of **Stock2.Maker**.
5. Reorder attributes to allow **Stock2.Maker** to be entered after **Stock2.Model**.
6. Add INSTRUCTIONS section and COMPOSITES specification.

Interestingly, LOOKUP is executed whether the **Stock2** or the **Models2** table is active. Logically, it ought only to be executed when the **Stock2** table is active, because it is associated with the **Stock2.Maker** attribute, but (a) the table cannot have two LOOKUP specifications for field f021 and (b) LOOKUP is executed even when the active table is **Models2**.

This version of the database is less convenient to use because the user must know (or find out) the correct model number *and* the correct maker number for the model. During the data-entry process, the model number and maker number are validated both independently and jointly. This means that it is possible to enter a model number followed by a maker number, and if the model is made by that manufacturer, both the maker's name and the model name and details will be displayed. If the maker number is invalid – the maker does not exist – the verify look-up will tell the user. If the maker is valid but the maker does not make a model with the specified number, the name of the maker will be displayed but no model details. However, when the ESC key is hit to enter the data, the verify composite join checks whether the maker/model number combination is valid; it does not accept the data if it is not.

11.5 Screen size

Prior to version 4.00, PERFORM had a very fixed idea that every terminal had 80 columns and 24 lines in which to display the form. By the time four lines were used for the menu, error and comments, there were only 20 lines left for use in the screen layout section of the form.

Version 4.00. It is now possible to specify an alternative screen size by appending the details after the first SCREEN line in the form, thus:

```
DATABASE Cars

SCREEN SIZE 25 BY 80
{
    ...
```

11.6 Drawing boxes on forms

Version 4.00. Another new and powerful facility is the ability to draw boxes on the screen. The basic technique for drawing a box on the screen is illustrated by:

```
SCREEN
(
\gp------------q\g
\g|\g            \g|\g
\g|\g Number [f0] \g|\g
\g|\g            \g|\g
\gb------------d\g
)
```

Although this is fiendishly difficult to read, what it would do is draw a box around a field with the label 'Number' and the field tag f0. The control sequence '\g' is used to toggle in and out of graphics mode, and it does not appear on the screen. In graphics mode, the six characters 'bdpq-|' are specially interpreted by PERFORM:

  p Top left corner.
  q Top right corner.
  b Bottom left corner.
  d Bottom right corner.
  – Horizontal line.
  | Vertical line.

These are relatively easy to remember because the tail of each of the four letters forms the relevant corner. This facility requires support from both **termcap** and **terminfo** and is fully described in Appendix J in the version 4.00 manuals. Beware of the description of the **terminfo** entry for **acsc** in the chapter on FORMBUILD in the reference manual – it is misleading, but the appendix is correct and clear. If you are using **terminfo**, you should be able to get proper tee-shapes and the centre cross as well by using the characters:

  n Centre cross.
  t Left tee.
  u Right tee.
  v Upwards tee.
  w Downwards tee.

To generate a form with a box, you should expect to work in two stages. In stage 1, you should omit all the '\g' sequences, which means that the boxes will not look very tidy. When the layout is correct, you can insert the '\g' sequences into the form where necessary. As an example of what can be done, one of the forms for the **Stock** table has been modified to include a box, as shown in Figure 11.3.

11.7 Summary

This chapter has discussed what the control blocks do, and how they can be used to improve the behaviour of forms. In particular, it showed how they can be used to

```
{
    @(#)stock6.per   5.4 91/02/24
    Multi-table forms -- lookup
}

DATABASE Cars

SCREEN
{

        Stock List

\gp--------------------------------------------------------q\g
\g|\g   Registration   [f000  ]                            \g|\g
\g|\g------------------------------------------------------|\g
\g|\g   Model Number   [f001] [f011]                       \g|\g
\g|\g   Description     [f021            ]                  \g|\g
\g|\g                   [f012              ] [f013      ]   \g|\g
\g|\g------------------------------------------------------|\g
\g|\g   Colour         [f002  ]                            \g|\g
\g|\g   Condition      [a]                                 \g|\g
\g|\g   Date Bought    [f003    ]                          \g|\g
\g|\g   Bought For     [f004      ]                         \g|\g
\g|\g   Mileage        [f005     ]                          \g|\g
\g|\g   Notes                                              \g|\g
\g|\g   [f006                                      ]       \g|\g
\g|\g   [f008                                      ]       \g|\g
\gb--------------------------------------------------------d\g
}
END


TABLES
Stock
Models
Companies

ATTRIBUTES
f000 = Stock.Registration, UPSHIFT, AUTONEXT, PICTURE = "AXXXXXA";
f001 = Stock.Model, QUERYCLEAR;
     =*Models.Model, QUERYCLEAR, NOENTRY, NOUPDATE;
f002 = Stock.Colour;
a    = Stock.Condition, AUTONEXT, UPSHIFT,
       INCLUDE = ('X', 'V', 'G', 'A', 'P'),
       COMMENTS = "Xcellent, Very good, Good, Average, Poor";
f003 = Stock.Datebought;
f004 = Stock.Boughtfor;
f005 = Stock.Mileage;
f006 = Stock.Notes1;
f008 = Stock.Notes2;


f011 = Models.Maker, QUERYCLEAR, NOENTRY, NOUPDATE,
       LOOKUP  f021 = Companies.Company
       JOINING Companies.Maker;
f012 = Models.Modelname, NOENTRY, NOUPDATE;
f013 = Models.Details, NOENTRY, NOUPDATE;

END
```

Figure 11.3 Form showing box characters in use

prevent a form from being used for operations which the form was not designed to handle, such as updating or deleting rows from tables which should only be referenced by the form. It also showed how aggregates could be displayed on a form, so that, for example, if the database was recording the items which made up an order, the total value of the order could be displayed on the screen. Lastly, it showed how composite joins can be handled.

Exercise

The exercise below is demanding and makes use of many of the techniques described in the three chapters discussing forms. The answer in Appendix A has a substantial explanation and illustrates a couple of interesting points which have not been mentioned in the main text. It would be worth trying to answer the question, and then looking at the answer and the explanation.

1. (*Hard*) Create a form which can be used to record a sale as it occurs. It should include the following facilities:

    i.   The user should be given the **Stock** table as the default table so that the car which is about to be sold can be selected.
    ii. The user should be able to add sales records, but should not be able to delete or update them.
    iii. The manufacturer name, model name and model details should be shown wherever a model number is needed.
    iv. The user should be able to make enquiries on the **Customers, Models, Prices** and **Companies** tables.
    v.   The user should not be able to alter the **Models** table, the **Prices** table nor the **Companies** table, but should be able to work on the **Sales** table, the **Stock** table and the **Customers** table (since it may be a new customer, or perhaps the customer has moved since the record was last kept).
    vi. When the user adds a sales record, the sold car should be designated by the registration number. This will be used to transfer all the relevant details from the **Stock** record to the **Sales** record. The transferred details must not be amendable. The sensitive details (basically the cost of the car to ABC Cars Ltd, the condition and the date when it was bought) should be concealed on a second screen.
    vii. The date of the sale is the current date. It should not be editable.
    viii. The form should show the profit and the mark-up (as a percentage) on the form – this is sensitive information too.

    Hint: do not try to do all this at once; build it in stages. The answer was developed in stages.

Outer joins, unions and self-joins

Chapter 5 covered the basic elements of SQL and Chapter 8 covered most of the rest of the features of the SELECT statement, as well as the INSERT, DELETE and UPDATE statements. This chapter has three sections which cover some topics which are occasionally useful – outer joins, unions, aliasing and self-joins – but this chapter can certainly be omitted on first reading the book.

12.1 Outer joins

Version 2.00 and later. Outer joins are quite a complex subject, so they will be introduced using an example. A normal SELECT statement will only select rows which meet *all* the conditions of the WHERE clause, including the join conditions. Sometimes it is necessary to choose data from one table but only choose rows from the second table if there is a row which satisfies the join condition (otherwise returning null values for the columns from the second table). This is known as an *outer join* and the keyword OUTER is provided so that a SELECT statement can indeed return rows from a multi-table select where some of the rows in the first table do not have rows which join with the second table and yet every row in the first table satisfying the non-joining conditions is returned.

12.1.1 The data for the example

By way of a change, a set of tables from a database other than the **Cars** database will be used to explain outer joins. These tables are part of a data dictionary system used to describe libraries and the source files which have to be compiled and put into the libraries. When a source file is compiled, an object file is produced, and a number of object files are later collected together by a program called a linker to create an executable program. If some of the object files are used in a lot of programs, it is convenient to have some way of collecting these together so that the files that are needed can be selected automatically by the linker, and this is what a library does. A library is a single file which contains a number of object files in a format that the linker can understand.

Table: **Libraries**		Table: **Libfiles**		Table: **Files**	
Library	**Libid**	**Libid**	**Fileid**	**Fileid**	**File**
libgeneral.a	1000	1000	1000	1000	stdopt.4gl
libbunker.a	1001	1000	1002	1002	mktemp.c
libjl.a	1002	1000	1009	1005	stderr.c
		1000	1010	1006	setarg0.c
		1000	1011	1009	usertype.4gl
		1000	1012	1010	decformat.c
		1002	1025	1011	isfile.c
		1002	1034	1012	isdir.c
		1002	1005	1025	getpwd.c
		1002	1006		

Table 12.1 Tables used in outer join examples

For the data dictionary, the key information needed is a list of libraries, a list of the source files and a list which indicates which source files have to be compiled to produce the object files that go into each library. There are three tables to consider, and only the most essential columns from each of the three tables will be used. The table **Libraries** defines the names of the libraries known to the data dictionary, the table **Files** defines the source files known to the data dictionary and the table **Libfiles** is the glue between the other two tables (it indicates which file belongs to which library). The data in the tables is shown in Table 12.1.

Notice that the data in the tables is not fully consistent; the entry in **Libfiles** with a **Fileid** of 1034 does not match the **Fileid** of any file in the table **Files**, and the library libbunker.a does not have any member files defined. These inconsistencies are there to help demonstrate how outer joins work, and a working data dictionary would certainly eliminate the entry in **Libfiles**. The entry in **Libraries** could be a brand new library which has simply not yet been fully defined.

12.1.2 Why use an outer join?

The problem is to list all the libraries and all the files defined for each library, if there are any. The normal SELECT statement joining the three tables will only select the rows which satisfy *all* the conditions of the WHERE clause, including the joins.

```
SELECT Library, File
    FROM Libraries, Libfiles, Files
    WHERE Libraries.Libid = Libfiles.Libid
    AND Libfiles.Fileid = Files.Fileid;
```

The results of this enquiry are shown in Table 12.2. Clearly, this statement does not solve the problem because the library libbunker.a is not listed in the data. All the rows from the **Libraries** table should be printed, regardless of whether there are any rows which match it in the **Libfiles** table.

Library	File
libgeneral.a	stdopt.4gl
libgeneral.a	mktemp.c
libgeneral.a	usertype.4gl
libgeneral.a	decformat.c
libgeneral.a	isfile.c
libgeneral.a	isdir.c
libjl.a	getpwd.c
libjl.a	stderr.c
libjl.a	setarg0.c

Table 12.2 Results of standard SELECT statement

To actually solve the problem, we have to use an outer join. An outer join is indicated by using the keyword OUTER as an element in the FROM clause of the SELECT statement. There must always be at least one table which is not preceded by the keyword OUTER; such tables are called the *dominant* tables. The dominant tables are treated in exactly the same way as in an ordinary SELECT – an ordinary SELECT is simply one where all the tables are dominant. The tables which are marked by OUTER do not affect whether the rows from the dominant tables are selected or not. When there is a row in the subservient table which satisfies the join condition, the data from the subservient table will be used; otherwise, nulls will be used in place of values from the subservient table.

12.1.3 Outer join of two tables

The answer to the full question will require an outer join between the three tables, and there are a number of ways of making a three-way outer join (which is one of the reasons why outer joins are fairly difficult to understand). To simplify things a little, consider the example below, which is a simple two-way outer join which lists all the libraries, and if there are any files specified in **Libfiles** for that library, the file numbers are shown. The results of this enquiry are shown in Table 12.3. The library libbunker.a is listed now, even though there are no files defined as belonging in that library.

```
SELECT Library, Fileid
    FROM  Libraries, OUTER Libfiles
    WHERE Libraries.Libid = Libfiles.Libid;
```

12.1.4 Outer join of three tables

Extending outer joins to three tables is complicated because there are a total of five different sets of join conditions which can be specified, four of which use outer joins. The set of join conditions not using outer joins was shown as the first example.

Library	Fileid
libgeneral.a	1000
libgeneral.a	1002
libgeneral.a	1009
libgeneral.a	1010
libgeneral.a	1011
libgeneral.a	1012
libbunker.a	
libjl.a	1025
libjl.a	1034
libjl.a	1005
libjl.a	1006

Table 12.3 Results from two-table outer join

Suppose we want to extend the last example to show the file names as well as the file numbers. The **Libfiles** and **Files** tables should be joined in the normal way, and **Libraries** should be outer-joined with the results of the join of **Libfiles** and **Files**. This ordering is indicated by the syntax below, and the results of this enquiry are shown in Table 12.4. The library libbunker.a is selected and a null value printed as the file name because no files have been specified as belonging to that library.

```
SELECT Library, File
    FROM  Libraries, OUTER (Libfiles, Files)
    WHERE Libraries.Libid = Libfiles.Libid
    AND Libfiles.Fileid = Files.Fileid;
```

There is still one problem: at least one of the rows in **Libfiles** cross-references a non-existent file. To be able to notice this inconsistency, the SELECT statement is modified to choose the file number as well as the file name. Also, **Libfiles** is outer-joined to **Files** to make sure that all the file numbers listed in **Libfiles** are displayed, and **Libraries** is outer-joined with the results of the outer join of **Libfiles** and **Files**. This ordering is indicated by the syntax in the next example, and the results of this

Library	File
libgeneral.a	stdopt.4gl
libgeneral.a	mktemp.c
libgeneral.a	usertype.4gl
libgeneral.a	decformat.c
libgeneral.a	isfile.c
libgeneral.a	isdir.c
libbunker.a	
libjl.a	getpwd.c
libjl.a	stderr.c
libjl.a	setarg0.c

Table 12.4 Results from first three-table outer join

Library	Fileid	File
libgeneral.a	1000	stdopt.4gl
libgeneral.a	1002	mktemp.c
libgeneral.a	1009	usertype.4gl
libgeneral.a	1010	decformat.c
libgeneral.a	1011	isfile.c
libgeneral.a	1012	isdir.c
libbunker.a		
libj1.a	1025	getpwd.c
libj1.a	1034	
libj1.a	1005	stderr.c
libj1.a	1006	setarg0.c

Table 12.5 Results from second three-table outer join

enquiry are shown in Table 12.5. Note that the file number for which there is no name is now listed as a member of the library libj1.a.

```
SELECT Library, Libfiles.Fileid, File
    FROM  Libraries, OUTER (Libfiles, OUTER Files)
    WHERE Libraries.Libid = Libfiles.Libid
    AND Libfiles.Fileid = Files.Fileid;
```

There are still two possible variants of the SELECT statement which have not been shown; it is left as an exercise for the reader to find the other two statements and to interpret the results. There is a reasonable interpretation for one of the constructs, but the second produces meaningless results. In one of the appendices of the INFORMIX-SQL reference manual (the actual appendix depends on the version), there is a diagrammatic method of explaining outer joins. In Date (1986), there is an extended discussion of outer joins, using a different syntax altogether.

One feature of the way Informix has implemented outer joins is that if a filter condition is applied to a column in one of the outer-joined tables and the filter condition would reject one of the rows that would be produced if the filter condition was not present, then Informix still returns a row from the dominant tables, but the row is matched with null values from the outer table. This means that the two sequences below, both of which attempt to produce a list of the C source files (extension '.c') listed for each library, produce different answers. (You should determine, empirically or otherwise, how the answers differ, and try to understand whether the difference is significant.)

```
SELECT Library, File
    FROM  Libraries, OUTER (Libfiles, OUTER Files)
    WHERE Libraries.Libid = Libfiles.Libid
    AND Libfiles.Fileid = Files.Fileid
    AND File MATCHES "*.c";
```

```
SELECT Library, File
    FROM      Libraries, OUTER (Libfiles, OUTER Files)
    WHERE     Libraries.Libid = Libfiles.Libid
    AND       Libfiles.Fileid = Files.Fileid
    INTO TEMP Libfilenames;

SELECT *
    FROM  Libfilenames
    WHERE File MATCHES "*.c";
```

12.2 Unions

Sometimes the conditions to be applied to a SELECT statement are very complex and involve several distinct alternative sets of data, possibly even from different tables. This can result in uncomfortably large SELECT statements. There is, however, a method of joining otherwise separate SELECT statements together using the keyword UNION.

SELECT-statement-1
UNION [ALL]
SELECT-statement-2
[*ORDER-BY-clause*]

Logically, this executes each SELECT statement separately and combines the result. In practice, the database engine will optimize the enquiry and will often be able to execute the statements in parallel, especially if the data comes from the same tables in both parts of the union. By default, any duplicate rows of data are removed. To leave the duplicates, the ALL keyword is used.

The *select-list* from each SELECT statement must contain the same number of columns, and the columns must be of corresponding types. Note that CHAR(30) and CHAR(20) are not corresponding types for this purpose, nor does a DECIMAL(10,6) column correspond to a DECIMAL(16) column.

The column names or display labels are taken from the first SELECT statement only. If an ORDER BY clause is included in the query, it must follow the last SELECT statement, and the columns to be sorted must be specified by number, not by column name or display label.

In principle, any number of SELECT statements may be connected by a UNION clause, but there is an upper limit on the number which varies somewhat from system to system − it is normally more than six.

As an example of a union which cannot be handled by a complex WHERE statement in a single SELECT statement, solve the following problem:

> *List all the cars in stock, and all the cars which have ever been sold. Include the registration number, company name and model name. List each car only once.*

One way of answering this, not using a UNION clause, uses a temporary table:

```
SELECT Registration, Company, Modelname, Details
   FROM      Stock, Models, Companies
   WHERE     Stock.Model = Models.Model
    AND      Models.Maker = Companies.Maker
   INTO TEMP Tlist;

INSERT INTO Tlist
   SELECT Registration, Company, Modelname, Details
      FROM  Sales, Models, Companies
      WHERE Sales.Model = Models.Model
        AND Models.Maker = Companies.Maker;

SELECT DISTINCT * FROM Tlist;

DROP TABLE Tlist;
```

A neater way of achieving the same result is to use the UNION clause to join two otherwise disjoint SELECT statements:

```
SELECT DISTINCT Registration, Company, Modelname, Details
    FROM  Stock, Models, Companies
    WHERE Stock.Model = Models.Model
      AND Models.Maker = Companies.Maker
UNION
SELECT Registration, Company, Modelname, Details
    FROM  Sales, Models, Companies
    WHERE Sales.Model = Models.Model
      AND Models.Maker = Companies.Maker
    ORDER BY 2, 3, 4;
```

One place where the UNION formulation of this query is vital is inside a report. The SELECT section of a report cannot use the INSERT statement, so there is no way of writing one report to do this job without using the UNION clause.

12.3 Table aliasing and self-joins

In Chapter 5, display labels were introduced as a method of naming or renaming items in the *select-list* of a SELECT statement. A *table alias* is similar to a display label in that it introduces an alternative name for something in the SELECT statement. However, table aliases occur in the FROM clause and are used to give an alternative name to a table. In the simplest cases, it is simply a shorthand, as in the example below, where the **Models** table is aliased 'M' and the **Companies** table is aliased 'C'. As with a display label, a table alias is separated from the thing it names by a space instead of a comma.

```
SELECT C.Company, M.Modelname, M.Details
    FROM  Companies C, Models M
    WHERE C.Maker = M.Maker;
```

By itself, this does not confer any great advantage beyond saving some typing, but there is one type of operation which cannot work unless aliasing is used, and that is a *self-join*. A self-join occurs when the same table is used to provide two different values from the same column in one *select-list*. For example, suppose we wanted to list all pairs of models which cost the same as each other. We want to list Model 1 which costs £8000 and Model 2 which also costs £8000 on one row of the results. To do this, the **Models** table must be listed twice in the FROM clause and each name must have an alias, and the conditions and the *select-list* must use the aliases.

```
SELECT M1.Model, M2.Model, M1.Price, M2.Price
   FROM  Models M1, Models M2
   WHERE M1.Price = M2.Price;
```

As you might expect, this statement lists each model paired with itself, and it also lists each pair in the order AB and BA. To prevent this happening, an extra condition is needed; the simplest is to request that the second model number is larger than the first:

```
SELECT M1.Model, M2.Model, M1.Price, M2.Price
   FROM  Models M1, Models M2
   WHERE M1.Price = M2.Price
     AND M1.Model < M2.Model;
```

The output from this statement is not very informative; it really needs the maker's name and the model name and description too. Since we are (in general) going to select two different values from the **Companies** table, we need two names for the **Companies** table as well as the **Models** table, and we also need two joining conditions between **Models** and **Companies**.

```
SELECT C1.Company, M1.Modelname, M1.Details, C2.Company, M2.Modelname, M2.Details, M1.Price
   FROM     Models M1, Models M2, Companies C1, Companies C2
   WHERE    M1.Price = M2.Price
     AND    M1.Model < M2.Model
     AND    C1.Maker = M1.Maker
     AND    C2.Maker = M2.Maker
   ORDER BY M1.Price DESC;
```

Another example of a self-join would come from a table of companies somewhat different from the one in the Cars database. In many instances, one company is a subsidiary or affiliate of another, and the subsidiary can, in some cases, have subsidiaries of its own. There are several ways of recording this sort of information. One design would use the **Company** table shown below:

```
CREATE TABLE Company
(
      Number      SERIAL(1000) NOT NULL,
      Coname      CHAR(30)     NOT NULL,
      Parent      INTEGER,
      Etc         CHAR(30)
);
CREATE UNIQUE INDEX ix_co1 ON Company(Number);
CREATE INDEX ix_co2 ON Company(Parent);
```

A company which is not a subsidiary of any other would store a null value in the **Parent** column; any subsidiary would have the number of the parent company stored in the **Parent** column. To list the parent companies and their subsidiaries, a SELECT statement such as this would be used:

```
SELECT P.Coname, C.Coname
   FROM     Company P, Company C
   WHERE    P.Number = C.Parent
   ORDER BY P.Coname, C.Coname;
```

An alternative and more flexible system would use two extra tables. The **Company** table would not store any details of the relationships between companies, but the **Relationship** table would record the numbers of two companies that were related in any way, along with a code which defined the type of relationship. The **Relation** table simply defines the valid types of relation.

```
CREATE TABLE Company
(
    Number      SERIAL(1000) NOT NULL,
    Company     CHAR(30)     NOT NULL,
    Etc         CHAR(30)
);
CREATE UNIQUE INDEX ix_co1 ON Company(Number);

CREATE TABLE Relation
(
    Code        CHAR(1)  NOT NULL,
    Description CHAR(30) NOT NULL
);
CREATE UNIQUE INDEX ix_rel1 ON Relation(Code);

CREATE TABLE Relationship
(
    Company_A   INTEGER NOT NULL,
    Company_B   INTEGER NOT NULL,
    Relation    CHAR(1) NOT NULL
);
CREATE INDEX ix_relship1 ON Relationship(Company_A);
CREATE INDEX ix_relship2 ON Relationship(Company_B);
CREATE INDEX ix_relship3 ON Relationship(Relation);
CREATE UNIQUE INDEX ix_relship4 ON Relationship(Company_A, Company_B, Relation);
```

This system allows for more relationships than just the 'subsidiary of' one in the previous scheme. If the relation code 'P' describes the relation 'Company A is the parent of Company B', the appropriate SELECT statement would be written:

```
SELECT P.Company, C.Company
    FROM  Company P, Company C, Relationship
    WHERE P.Number = Relationship.Company_A
      AND C.Number = Relationship.Company_B
      AND Relationship.Relation = 'P';
```

OnLine. One other place where table aliases come in handy is when accessing tables in remote databases. Imagine that there are two machines, Osiris and Isis, both of which have been set up with INFORMIX-ONLINE and INFORMIX-STAR and are connected over a network. Furthermore, there is a database called `cars` in each system which contains a **Stock** table, and these tables are identical in structure. We can now write a single SELECT statement to list all the cars in stock on either site.

```
SELECT S1.Registration, M1.Price, C1.Manufacturer, M1.Modelname, M1.Details
    FROM cars@isis:abc.Stock S1, cars@isis:abc.Models M1, cars@isis:abc.Companies C1
    WHERE S1.Model = M1.Model
      AND M1.Maker = C1.Maker
UNION
SELECT S2.Registration, M2.Price, C2.Manufacturer, M2.Modelname, M2.Details
    FROM cars@osiris:abc.Stock S2, cars@osiris:abc.Models M2, cars@osiris:abc.Companies C2
    WHERE S2.Model = M2.Model
      AND M2.Maker = C2.Maker
ORDER BY 3, 4, 5;
```

This query can be run on either Osiris or Isis because it is written symmetrically. The notation *database@machine:owner.table* is used to identify the machine, database, table owner and table which is being referred to. For full details of this notation, you should refer to the INFORMIX-ONLINE reference manual, and you should also look at the section on synonyms in the INFORMIX-SQL and INFORMIX-ONLINE reference manuals, as well as the brief discussion in Chapter 16. For the purposes of the discussion here, the important thing to note is how much easier the statements are to write if table aliases are used compared with having to write, for instance:

```
SELECT cars@osiris:abc.Stock.Registration, ...
```

12.4 Summary

This chapter has covered four 'exotic' features of the SELECT statement, namely outer joins, unions, table aliasing and self-joins. This really does conclude the discussion of the features of the SELECT statement.

Exercises

1. Find the two unspecified forms of the outer join in the example. Construct the results tables and interpret the results.

    (Hint: look in the appendix on outer joins in the reference manual.)

2. Establish which models (if any) did not change in price between successive years according to the **Prices** table. List the model, the years and the prices.

13
Advanced reports

The previous two chapters on reports have gradually extended your ability to write complex reports, but there are still several important features of ACE to be covered. One of these is to be able to do different things at different times. For example, not all the lines of all the addresses contain data, so it would be useful to be able to suppress the printing of these lines. It would also be useful to be able to modify the behaviour of a report — to control the data selected — at run-time, rather than having to change the SELECT statement and recompile the report. Both these aspects of ACE are described in this chapter, using a report to print address labels as the example. This chapter also describes the READ facility introduced with version 4.00.

13.1 Address labels

The addresses are to be printed on self-adhesive labels which, for the purposes of the exercise, are supplied three across the page and six down (see Figure 13.1). It has been established by experiment that there are eight printable lines on each label and that there are two unprintable lines between each pair of labels. Three lines are required at the top of the page to reach the first printing position on the first label, and three lines must be left at the bottom after the last label. The first label starts at column 4 (when the left margin is set to zero), the second at column 35 and the third at column 66. Each label will take up to 28 characters across.

As usual, the first step in producing the report is to get the SELECT statement correct. The WHERE clause of the SELECT statement is a little more complicated than it absolutely has to be, as shown in the following:

```
SELECT Salut, Firstname, Surname, Address1, Address2, Address3, Postcode
    FROM      Customers
    WHERE     Address1 IS NOT NULL
      AND     (Address2 IS NOT NULL OR Address3 IS NOT NULL)
      AND     (Salut IS NOT NULL OR Firstname IS NOT NULL)
    ORDER BY Surname, Firstname
END
```

There is a minor problem with the database: some parts of the address may be null. The simplest way around this problem is to stipulate that for an address to be

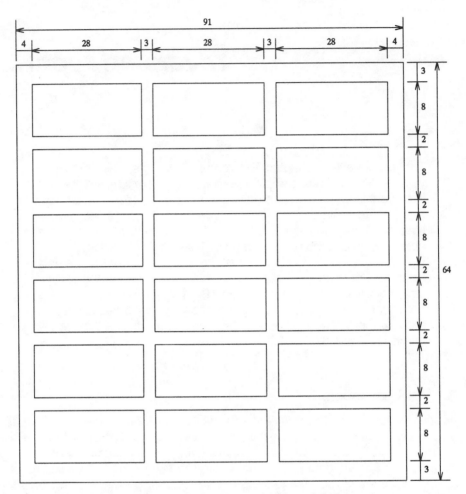

Figure 13.1 One page of address labels

complete, **Address1** must not be null, and at least one of **Address2** and **Address3** must not be null, and there must be either a salutation or a first name. The latter condition prevents letters being sent to 'Jones'; it will go to either 'Mr Jones' or 'J Jones' or 'Mr J Jones'. The SELECT statement given implements this logic.

The remaining problem is to get three addresses across the page. The only way to do this is to save at least the first two of every three rows of data and then to format the three lines at once. This requires a number of variables in which to store the data. It turns out to be straightforward to make the report configurable so that it only prints out customers who were contacted between two dates specified by the user, and also to apply a condition on the name of the customer. This will require a modified SELECT statement.

13.2 The DEFINE section

The DEFINE section is used to define variables and parameters that can be used within the report. It consists of the keyword DEFINE followed by zero or more PARAM statements, zero or more VARIABLE statements, zero or one ASCII statement and the keyword END. Version 4.00. The ASCII statement is new and is used in conjunction with the READ section of a report, described in Section 13.4.

Each PARAM statement consists of the keyword PARAM followed by an integer enclosed in square brackets, the name of a variable and a type. For example:

```
PARAM[1] early DATE
```

This defines that the first argument supplied to the report is a date, and that the value is to be stored in a variable called 'early'. The name consists of an alphabetic character followed by alpha-numeric characters, and must be distinct from all keywords, all other variables and all column names or display labels that will be used in the FORMAT section. The data type is one of the valid database types except for SERIAL; for SERIAL, use type INTEGER. The variable will be initialized from the argument on the command line indexed by the integer enclosed in square brackets. If the argument is not supplied, ACE will report an error and exit. This means that the report must be run either from the UNIX command line or from a user menu.

Similarly, each VARIABLE statement consists of the keyword VARIABLE followed by the name of a variable and a type. For example:

```
VARIABLE matchstr CHAR(30)
```

The variable name must obey the same rules as a parameter name, and the type must obey the same rules too. The variable will not be initialized to any particular value.

Version 4.00. By contrast, there can only be one ASCII statement in a report, and this consists of the keyword ASCII, followed by a comma-separated list of variable names and variable types. Only the ASCII statement allows this format, and it is mandatory for the ASCII statement. More details are supplied in Section 13.4.

For example, the following DEFINE section could be used in the address list report; it expects two dates to be passed as arguments to the report, and will prompt for a string which the surname of the customer must match in the INPUT section (see the next section). (This is a very messy interface to the report; in a production report, as opposed to this teaching report, the values should either all be passed as parameters or all be prompted for.)

```
DEFINE
    PARAM[1]    early    DATE
    PARAM[2]    late     DATE
    VARIABLE    matchstr    CHAR(30)
END
```

If the report was called addrlist, the report would have to be invoked from the UNIX command line as:

```
$ sacego -q addrlist 01/01/87 31/12/88
```

13.3 The INPUT section

The INPUT section is used to make ACE prompt the user for information which can subsequently be used in the report. It consists of the keyword INPUT followed by one or more PROMPT statements followed by the keyword END. Each PROMPT statement has the syntax:

PROMPT FOR *variable* USING *"prompt string"*

The variable must have been defined in the DEFINE section. ACE will print the prompt string and then read a line of input from the user.

Any variables which have been initialized with a PROMPT statement (and any parameters) can be used in the SELECT statement provided that they are prefixed by a dollar sign '$'. The PROMPT statement is executed before the SELECT statement in the report, so the user can enter one or more values when the report is executed and these can be used in the SELECT section. For example, given the DEFINE section shown earlier, the following INPUT and SELECT sections would be sensible:

```
INPUT
     PROMPT FOR matchstr USING "Enter pattern for surnames: "
END

SELECT Salut, Firstname, Surname,
       Address1, Address2, Address3, Postcode
   FROM      Customers
   WHERE     Address1 IS NOT NULL
     AND     (Address2 IS NOT NULL OR Address3 IS NOT NULL)
     AND     (Salut IS NOT NULL OR Firstname IS NOT NULL)
     AND     Contactdate BETWEEN $early AND $late
     AND     Surname MATCHES $matchstr
   ORDER BY Surname, Firstname
END
```

13.4 The READ section

Version 4.00. As an alternative to using a SELECT section in the report, it is now possible to use a READ section which will interpret files in UNLOAD format. This is also described in Chapter 15, but it consists of one line of data for each record. Each line consists of one or more variable-length fields, each of which is terminated by a specifiable character, the default one being '|'. As an example, the line below is a record from the **Stock** table in UNLOAD format:

```
A1 BJX|34|Red|X|05/06/1990|12000.0|37534|A nice car||
```

The first column is the registration, 'A1 BJX', the second the model number, the third the colour and so on. The double '| |' at the end indicates that the **Notes2** field is null. ACE can read files in this format (which could be produced by any program – the data does not have to be produced from an Informix database) and will format them in the same way as it does any other data.

If there is a READ section in the report, there must be a DEFINE section too, and the DEFINE section must contain an ASCII statement to define the data that is in the file. The first item in the ASCII statement must correspond to the first column in the data file, the second item to the second column and so on. Any column can be defined as a CHAR type, but columns of other types must be handled carefully to ensure that they are correct.

The READ section itself consists of the READ keyword, followed by the name of the file to be read, optionally followed by a delimiter declaration, which is optionally followed by an ORDER BY clause. The data can either be sorted by ACE or be declared to be in sorted order in the data file.

To illustrate this facility, the password file on UNIX can be read and neatly formatted using the report below:

```
{
    @(#)password.ace      5.4 91/02/26
    @(#)Report illustrating READ section
}

DATABASE ASCII END

DEFINE
    ASCII
        username CHAR(8),   password CHAR(13),
        uid      SMALLINT, gid       SMALLINT,
        comment  CHAR(20), homedir   CHAR(20),
        shell    CHAR(20)
END

OUTPUT
    LEFT MARGIN   0
    TOP MARGIN    0
    BOTTOM MARGIN 0
END

READ "/tmp/ace.password" DELIMITER ":" ORDER BY uid, gid, username END

FORMAT

    PAGE HEADER
        PRINT "/etc/passwd dissected"
        SKIP 1 LINE
        PRINT
            COLUMN  1, "User",
            COLUMN 10, "UID",
            COLUMN 15, "GID",
            COLUMN 20, "Who",
            COLUMN 42, "Home",
            COLUMN 64, "Shell"

    ON EVERY ROW
        PRINT
            COLUMN  1, username,
            COLUMN 10, uid USING "##&",
            COLUMN 15, gid USING "##&",
            COLUMN 20, comment,
            COLUMN 42, homedir,
            COLUMN 64, shell CLIPPED

END
```

The DATABASE section uses the special database ASCII to indicate that it is not reading from a real database. The data in the password file is not necessarily sorted in the required manner (by user ID number, group ID number and then user login name), so the report specifies the order. If the data in the input file was actually in the correct sorted order, the READ clause would be rewritten as:

```
READ "/tmp/ace.password" DELIMITER ":"
    ORDER EXTERNAL BY uid, gid, username
END
```

The FORMAT section of the report has no special features associated with it; the data selection is different, but once selected, it is treated in the same way as any other selected data. Note that the encrypted password is not included in the output.

This report neatly illustrates one of the minor problems with UNLOAD format, namely that every field, including the last, must have a delimiter. The password file only has ':' separator characters, so the last field is not terminated. To get around this minor problem, the report is never run directly; it should always be run by the simple shell script shown below, which uses the program **sed** to add a colon to the end of each line:

```
:        "@(#)password.sh 5.3 90/09/16"
#
#        Script to run password formatting report
DBPATH=/consult/john/cars/isql/arc:$DBPATH
export DBPATH
tmp=/tmp/ace.password
trap "rm -f $tmp ; exit 1" 1 2 3 13 15
sed 's/$/:/' /etc/passwd >$tmp
sacego password
rm -f $tmp
exit 0
```

13.5 Expressions and manipulating variables

It is possible to write expressions in many places where simple values have been used so far. There were some examples of this in Chapter 9. An expression may be any valid combination of column values, variables, parameters and constants, and may use any of the operators shown in Table 13.1. When the MATCHES operator is inverted in ACE, the whole expression is negated:

```
NOT (column_name MATCHES "string_expr")
```

Expressions with an integer value may be used in NEED, SKIP and COLUMN statements, and a character variable can be used with a USING statement.

13.5.1 Manipulating variables

There are four statements which can be used to manipulate variables in any of the control blocks, namely LET, FOR, WHILE and IF/THEN/ELSE.

Operator	Interpretation
-	Unary minus
**	Exponentiation
*	Multiplication
/	Division
+	Addition
-	Subtraction
MATCHES	Fuzzy match for strings
IS [NOT] NULL	Presence of value
=	Logical equal
!=	Logical not equal
<>	Logical not equal
>	Logical greater than
<	Logical less than
>=	Greater than or equal
<=	Less than or equal
NOT	Logical NOT
AND	Logical AND
OR	Logical OR

Table 13.1 ACE operators

LET – assignment

LET is used to assign a value to a variable (or parameter); its syntax is:

```
LET var = expr
```

FOR – counted loop

The FOR loop is used to repeat an operation a fixed number of times; its syntax is:

```
FOR var = expr1 TO expr2 [STEP expr3] DO
      statement
```

This construct will assign *var* the values from *expr1* to *expr2* in turn and executes the *statement* for each value. If a step size was not specified, it will be 1.

It is important to note that *expr2* and *expr3* are executed each time around the loop. Hence the number of times the loop is executed may be changed by altering a value that changes the result of one of the expressions.

The statement may be one single statement or a set of statements enclosed between the keywords BEGIN and END. This also applies to the WHILE loop and the IF/THEN/ELSE construct.

WHILE – conditional loop

The WHILE loop is used to loop for an indefinite number of times. The syntax is:

```
WHILE expr DO
      statement
```

IF/THEN/ELSE – general condition
The IF/THEN/ELSE statement provides conditional branching. The syntax is:

```
IF expr THEN
        statement1
ELSE
        statement2
```

The ELSE clause is optional. If the expression evaluates to true, *statement1* will be executed. If it evaluates to false and there is an ELSE clause, *statement2* will be executed.

Using the statements
Each of the statements after the control statements may be a compound statement which, like Pascal, uses the keywords BEGIN to mark the beginning of the compound statement and END to mark the end of it.

These control statements may be used anywhere within a control block and provide a very general means for controlling the output of a report. One of the important uses of the FIRST PAGE HEADER is to initialize variables. It is also possible to ensure that the report has a cover page by setting a flag variable to 0 (say) in the FIRST PAGE HEADER, and by inserting a test on that variable in the outermost BEFORE GROUP OF control block (or ON EVERY ROW control block if there are no BEFORE GROUP OF blocks) and doing a SKIP TO TOP OF PAGE if the variable is not set. (Do not forget to set the variable to 1 (say) inside the conditional statement.)

Another possible use for conditional statements is to arrange that the odd pages of a report have a different title from the even pages. In all three PAGE control blocks, the same number of lines must be printed regardless of which conditions are false or true. This means that all IF statements in a page control block that print anything *must* have an ELSE part which prints the same number of lines.

13.6 The address label report continued

As was suggested previously, the address label report needs to store two addresses before printing one row of three address labels. It turns out to be more convenient to actually store all three addresses in variables because the same processing can then be applied to each address in a uniform way, and the actual printing operation is uniform. For convenience, all the values for the first column are stored in variables whose names begin 'a', those for the second address start 'b' and those for the third address start 'c'. There are also a number of auxiliary variables; the most important of these is n_address which keeps a count of the number of addresses.

The OUTPUT section of the report has to set the page length and the top, bottom and left margins. Although the left margin could be set to 4, the experiments assumed that the left margin was zero, so all the figures are quoted assuming this and the report sets it to zero too. The page length is built up from:

$$L_{page} = L_{header} + (N \times L_{label}) + ((N - 1) \times L_{gap}) + L_{trailer}$$

where N is the number of labels down the page, L_{header} is the number of lines at the top of the page, L_{label} is the number of lines on one label, L_{gap} is the gap between two labels and $L_{trailer}$ is the amount of space after the last label. For this report, the result is:

$$L_{page} = 3 + (6 \times 8) + ((6 - 1) \times 2) + 3 = 64$$

The PAGE HEADER and PAGE TRAILER blocks are not needed, but the FIRST PAGE HEADER block has to initialize some of the variables, even though it does no printing. The ON EVERY ROW control block has five parts:

1. Sort out the name line and address.
2. Store the first of three rows.
3. Store the second of three rows.
4. Store the third of three rows.
5. Print stored and current rows and clean up.

The first section takes the three parts of the name and converts it into a salutation, first initial and surname, and allows for nulls. The second, third and fourth parts are substantially identical and conditionally copy data to the relevant variables. The printing is also essentially straightforward. Note the use of variables to store the column numbers where the printing starts. These were initialized in the FIRST PAGE HEADER section to the values determined by experiment, but using the variables, any further adjustments can be made uniformly by just adjusting the one assignment, rather than having to locate all the instances of a constant number. The clean-up code needs to be executed conditionally too.

The final complication is that there is no guarantee that the report will have to print an exact multiple of three addresses. The ON LAST ROW block flushes out any stored addresses. The variables for the third column are not printed since, by definition, they must be null.

Putting all these parts together leads to the (substantial) report shown in Figure 13.2. *Note*: to keep the printout to a reasonable length, a number of assignments have been put two-on-a-line, and so have some of the declarations. This reduces the length of the listing, but it does mean that the listing is not as tidy as it could be.

```
{
    @(#)addrlist.pt1     5.2 91/03/08
    Address label generating report
}

DATABASE Cars END

DEFINE
    { Restrict data selected by report }
    PARAM[1]    early   DATE
    PARAM[2]    late    DATE
    VARIABLE    matchstr    CHAR(30)
```

Figure 13.2 The address label report

```
        VARIABLE  col1    INTEGER    { Column for 1st label }
        VARIABLE  col2    INTEGER    { Column for 2nd label }
        VARIABLE  col3    INTEGER    { Column for 3rd label }
        VARIABLE  aname   CHAR(28)   { Storage for 1st label }
        VARIABLE  aline1 CHAR(28) VARIABLE aline2 CHAR(28)
        VARIABLE  aline3 CHAR(28) VARIABLE aline4 CHAR(28)
        VARIABLE  bname   CHAR(28)   { Storage for 2nd label }
        VARIABLE  bline1 CHAR(28) VARIABLE bline2 CHAR(28)
        VARIABLE  bline3 CHAR(28) VARIABLE bline4 CHAR(28)
        VARIABLE  cname   CHAR(28)   { Storage for 3rd label }
        VARIABLE  cline1 CHAR(28) VARIABLE cline2 CHAR(28)
        VARIABLE  cline3 CHAR(28) VARIABLE cline4 CHAR(28)
        VARIABLE  n_addr INTEGER     { No. of stored addresses }
        VARIABLE  xname   CHAR(28)   { Used to build label }
        VARIABLE  xline1 CHAR(28) VARIABLE xline2 CHAR(28)
        VARIABLE  xline3 CHAR(28) VARIABLE xline4 CHAR(28)
    END

    INPUT
        PROMPT FOR matchstr USING "Enter pattern for surnames: "
    END

    OUTPUT
        REPORT TO PRINTER
        PAGE LENGTH    64
        TOP MARGIN     3
        BOTTOM MARGIN  1
        LEFT MARGIN    0
    END

    SELECT Salut, Firstname, Surname,
           Address1, Address2, Address3, Postcode
        FROM    Customers
        WHERE   Address1 IS NOT NULL
          AND   (Address2 IS NOT NULL OR Address3 IS NOT NULL)
          AND   (Salut IS NOT NULL OR Firstname IS NOT NULL)
          AND   Contactdate BETWEEN $early AND $late
          AND   Surname MATCHES $matchstr
        ORDER BY Surname, Firstname
    END

    FORMAT

        FIRST PAGE HEADER
            LET col1   = 13
            LET col2   = 44
            LET col3   = 75
            LET n_addr = 0
            LET aname  = ""  LET bname  = ""  LET cname  = ""
            LET aline1 = ""  LET aline2 = ""  LET aline3 = ""  LET aline4 = ""
            LET bline1 = ""  LET bline2 = ""  LET bline3 = ""  LET bline4 = ""
            LET cline1 = ""  LET cline2 = ""  LET cline3 = ""  LET cline4 = ""

        ON EVERY ROW
            { Sort out label into x-variables }
            IF salut IS NOT NULL THEN { Sort out name }
                LET xname = salut CLIPPED, " ", firstname[1]
            ELSE
                LET xname = firstname[1]
            LET xname = xname CLIPPED, " ", surname CLIPPED
            LET xline1 = address1
```

Figure 13.2 *(cont.)*

```
    IF address2 IS NULL THEN BEGIN
        LET xline2 = address3
        LET xline3 = postcode
    END ELSE BEGIN
        LET xline2 = address2
        IF address3 IS NULL THEN BEGIN
            LET xline3 = postcode
        END ELSE BEGIN
            LET xline3 = address3
            LET xline4 = postcode
        END
    END
    IF n_addr = 0 THEN BEGIN { Store 1st address }
        LET aname  = xname
        LET aline1 = xline1
        LET aline2 = xline2
        LET aline3 = xline3
        LET aline4 = xline4
    END
    IF n_addr = 1 THEN BEGIN { Store 2nd address }
        LET bname  = xname
        LET bline1 = xline1
        LET bline2 = xline2
        LET bline3 = xline3
        LET bline4 = xline4
    END
    IF n_addr = 2 THEN BEGIN { Store 3rd address }
        LET cname  = xname
        LET cline1 = xline1
        LET cline2 = xline2
        LET cline3 = xline3
        LET cline4 = xline4
    END
    LET n_addr = n_addr + 1
    IF n_addr = 3 THEN BEGIN { Print data if required }
        SKIP 2 LINES
        PRINT COLUMN col1, aname,  COLUMN col2, bname,  COLUMN col3, cname
        PRINT COLUMN col1, aline1, COLUMN col2, bline1, COLUMN col3, cline1
        PRINT COLUMN col1, aline2, COLUMN col2, bline2, COLUMN col3, cline2
        PRINT COLUMN col1, aline3, COLUMN col2, bline3, COLUMN col3, cline3
        PRINT COLUMN col1, aline4, COLUMN col2, bline4, COLUMN col3, cline4
        SKIP 3 LINES
        LET n_addr = 0
        LET aname  = "" LET bname  = "" LET cname  = ""
        LET aline1 = "" LET aline2 = "" LET aline3 = "" LET aline4 = ""
        LET bline1 = "" LET bline2 = "" LET bline3 = "" LET bline4 = ""
        LET cline1 = "" LET cline2 = "" LET cline3 = "" LET cline4 = ""
    END

ON LAST ROW
    { Flush outstanding addresses }
    IF n_addr > 0 THEN BEGIN
        SKIP 2 LINES
        PRINT COLUMN col1, aname,  COLUMN col2, bname
        PRINT COLUMN col1, aline1, COLUMN col2, bline1
        PRINT COLUMN col1, aline2, COLUMN col2, bline2
        PRINT COLUMN col1, aline3, COLUMN col2, bline3
        PRINT COLUMN col1, aline4, COLUMN col2, bline4
        SKIP 3 LINES
    END
END
```

Figure 13.2 (*cont.*)

13.7 Summary

ACE is a very powerful reporting language which can be used to produce almost any report that is required from an INFORMIX-SQL database. ACE allows you to pass parameters to a report, and it also provides the PROMPT FOR mechanism which means that the user supplies values for variables. Either parameters or variables (or both) can be used in the SELECT section of the report to alter the output produced by the report. Additionally, variables can be manipulated extensively within a report, and the expressions used in formatting a PRINT line can also be used in assignments. With version 4.00, ACE has been extended so that it can process files in UNLOAD format, and these files need not have been created from an Informix database.

Exercises

1. Generate a report for the **Customers** table. Tailor the report so that it:

    i.   Handles names sensibly.
    ii. Copes with the salutation 'Esq'.
    iii. Prints the postcode on the same line as the last part of the address.
    iv. Has a cover page, page header and page trailer.
    v.   Includes the date of the listing and the page number on each page.

    Modify the report to print sensibly on the screen.

2. Modify the address label report so that the addresses which are printed can be controlled when the report is run. It should be able to produce a set of address labels for the customers who bought, say, Fords. Devise a method to enable the user to stipulate the maker and/or model. Also, allow the user to specify a range of surnames, such as all those beginning with the letters K to Z. This would be very useful for restarting the report part way through the output if the printer jammed while printing a set of labels.

Part V
Database administration

14

Tables, indexes and permissions

The rest of this book is of most concern to database administrators. Database administration includes many separate tasks, such as creating the database, modifying it to take into account changes in the data it should store, controlling who can access the database, ensuring the data stored is valid, making sure that the database is properly backed up and so on.

This chapter will cover those aspects of handling a database which are related to creating the database tables and indexes, and will deal with access control – who can do what with the database. It also gives some extra detailed information about the various data types that can be used in tables. Chapter 15 discusses the methods of loading and unloading data from the database, how to use transaction logs as a database integrity tool, along with some suggestions about how to organize database back-ups. The final chapter, Chapter 16, explains all the environment variables which are used by INFORMIX-SQL, how to use the various INFORMIX-SQL tools from the command line, how to install the product, how to use the extra tools provided with INFORMIX-SQL for helping manage databases and how to use the information from the system catalogue.

14.1 Data types

This section covers all the data types recognized by INFORMIX-SQL, including those introduced with version 4.00, whereas Section 3.5.1 only gave an overview of the types. It will not cover blobs in much detail because they are most relevant to programs written in INFORMIX-4GL or ESQL/C.

14.1.1 CHAR

The CHAR data type is used to store text such as names, alpha-numeric codes and similar things. The maximum number of characters to be stored in a CHAR column is fixed when the table is created and must be specified in parentheses –

CHAR(20). The maximum permitted number of characters in one string is 32767, but the maximum length of a row in the database is also 32767 bytes, so if a string of this length was specified, it would be the only column in the table. Neither restriction causes any problem in practice. The CHAR(1) data type can be used to store flag values as it uses less disk space than even a small integer. A CHAR(n) column uses n bytes of disk space. (All records are stored in fixed-length records in C-ISAM data files – there are no variable-length records in INFORMIX-SE or INFORMIX-TURBO, but there are VARCHAR fields in INFORMIX-ONLINE.) Character fields are expected to hold printable characters and cannot be used to hold arbitrary binary data.

Version 4.00. The synonym CHARACTER was introduced for the type CHAR in order to conform with the ANSI standard.

14.1.2 INTEGER and SMALLINT

The INTEGER and SMALLINT data types are used for storing whole numbers. An INTEGER uses 4 bytes of disk space and can store values in the range -2147483647 .. 2147483647. Similarly, a SMALLINT uses 2 bytes of disk space and can store values in the range -32767 .. 32767.

Version 4.00. The synonym INT was introduced for the type INTEGER, also in order to conform with the ANSI standard.

14.1.3 SERIAL

The SERIAL type is a special case of INTEGER. When the special value of zero is inserted into a SERIAL column, the value actually stored is one greater than the maximum number previously inserted into the table. It is possible to specify the first serial number which will be assigned to a SERIAL column by enclosing the number for the first row in parentheses – SERIAL(1000). A SERIAL column gives a simple way of generating a unique number for a row of data. It is, of course, possible to insert a value other than zero; if this happens, the value is stored in the SERIAL column unchanged, and if the number is higher than the previous maximum value, the maximum value is changed accordingly. Although the schema editor automatically creates a unique index on a SERIAL column, if you create the table using SQL, you must create the index yourself. There can only be one SERIAL field in any table.

14.1.4 FLOAT and SMALLFLOAT

FLOAT and SMALLFLOAT are used for storing floating-point numbers, but the precision varies between machines. Normally, these are implemented by the hardware on the machine, in which case FLOAT is the machine's double-precision floating-point type (in C, double) and SMALLFLOAT is the machine's single-precision floating-point type (in C, float). On some small machines, these types are implemented as DECIMAL types. These types should not be used for storing money values, or where any guaranteed precision is required. A FLOAT normally uses 8 bytes of disk space, while a SMALLFLOAT normally uses 4 bytes.

Because the internal format of FLOAT and SMALLFLOAT data types is machine dependent, it is not possible to transfer a database created on one type of machine to another without going through the LOAD and UNLOAD process. However, Informix has carefully defined the DECIMAL and MONEY types in such a way that even if a binary copy of the data from an INFORMIX-SE database is transferred from a machine with, say, an Intel 80386 chip to another machine with a Motorola 68030 chip, the data can be interpreted correctly without any further change. Therefore, if a database has to be portable, it is a good idea to avoid the FLOAT and SMALLFLOAT data types.

Version 4.00. REAL is a synonym for SMALLFLOAT and DOUBLE PRECISION is a synonym for FLOAT, again in order to conform with the ANSI standard.

14.1.5 DECIMAL and MONEY

The DECIMAL and MONEY types are used for storing floating-point values to a guaranteed accuracy. Internally, they use the same data type, but ISQL displays a MONEY column with a currency symbol whereas a DECIMAL column is displayed as a pure number.

The DECIMAL and MONEY types can have a precision and scale specified using the notation DECIMAL(p,s), where p represents the precision and s the scale. The scale is optional. The precision is the number of decimal digits preserved, while the scale is the number of digits after the decimal point. The maximum number of digits is 32, with the default being 16. If no scale is specified, the number is floating point rather than fixed point. The default scale for MONEY is 2 – that is, there are two digits after the decimal point. These types use from 2 to 17 bytes of disk space, depending on the precision and scale. The formula is:

$$n = \left\lfloor \frac{p - s + 1}{2} \right\rfloor + \left\lfloor \frac{s + 1}{2} \right\rfloor + 1$$

The final result n is restricted to a maximum of 17, which means that it is not possible to use the full 32 digits of precision *and* have an odd number of digits after the decimal point. This is a consequence of the fact that DECIMAL numbers are implemented in base 100 floating-point arithmetic, with up to 16 centesimal (base 100) digits and 1 byte for the exponent.

Version 4.00. Both DEC and NUMERIC are synonyms for DECIMAL, once more in order to conform with the ANSI standard.

14.1.6 DATE

Either the DATE type or the DATETIME type should be used whenever dates are stored. This section discusses the DATE type which is available on all versions of INFORMIX-SQL, whereas the DATETIME type is new with version 4.00.

A DATE is stored internally as an INTEGER (actually the number of days since 31 December 1899, so that the 1 January 1900 is day 1), and therefore occupies 4 bytes of disk space. ISQL provides a powerful collection of facilities for formatting and converting dates when needed. These include the DATE, MDY, YEAR, MONTH, DAY and WEEKDAY functions which can be used in both SQL and ACE.

14.1.7 DATETIME and INTERVAL

Version 4.00. These data types were added for conformity with the ANSI standard and are available in both INFORMIX-SE and INFORMIX-ONLINE. The DATETIME type, in particular, is extremely valuable; the INTERVAL type complements it.

The DATETIME type can be used to store a value which represents both a date and a time, or just a date, or just a time. The date can be expressed as YEAR TO DAY, YEAR TO MONTH, YEAR TO YEAR, MONTH TO DAY, MONTH TO MONTH or DAY TO DAY. Similarly, the time component can be any range from HOUR down to FRACTION(5). The FRACTION qualifier has a default precision of 3, corresponding to milliseconds; the maximum precision of 5 corresponds to tens of microseconds. If no qualifier is added, the qualifier is assumed to be YEAR TO FRACTION(3). A one-second accuracy DATETIME column would have the type:

    Column_name DATETIME YEAR TO SECOND

In general terms, an INTERVAL is the difference between two DATETIME values. You can also store INTERVAL values in the database, but there is a restriction on the range of values that you can store. An INTERVAL can have components from either the set YEAR, MONTH or from the set DAY, HOUR, MINUTE, SECOND, FRACTION. Under no circumstances can an INTERVAL mix the two sets because, of course, without knowing the two end dates, it is not possible to know how many days there are between two dates, simply because the calendar has such an irregular structure. You can specify the precision of the leading component of an INTERVAL, as well as the precision of the final component if it is a FRACTION. For example, it would be possible to have an INTERVAL which could store intervals of up to about 300 years, accurate to a second:

    Column_name INTERVAL DAY(6) TO SECOND

Using DATETIME and INTERVAL

On forms, the data format for both DATETIME and INTERVAL data is rigidly defined and cannot be varied. The components YEAR, MONTH and DAY are separated from each other by hyphens '–'; the DAY and HOUR components are separated by a space; the HOUR, MINUTE and SECOND components are separated by colons ':'; and the SECOND and FRACTION components are separated by a period '.'. Thus, if a

DATETIME YEAR TO FRACTION(5) value was being entered, you would have to type:

```
1990-10-31 15:03:39.51542
```

Note that you cannot enter a name for the month – you must always enter a number. Similarly, there is no special treatment for the twentieth century; if you want a year 1990, you must enter the year 1990 because the year 90 was AD 90.

Just as the keyword TODAY signifies the current DATE, the keyword CURRENT indicates the current DATETIME. It is therefore possible to specify a default value for a DATETIME field in a form such as:

```
f003 = some_table.some_column,
       DEFAULT = CURRENT YEAR TO SECOND;
```

Note that if you specify CURRENT YEAR TO FRACTION(5), the accuracy of your answer depends on the machine you are running on; indeed, even the time to the second depends on the system clock. One unfortunate oversight on the part of Informix Software is that the DATETIME types do not take into account the time-zone in any clearly defined way, although it seems to get the default time correct in the UK. This is due to be fixed in version 4.10.

In the same way that there is a constructor function DATE for DATE types, so there are constructor functions for both INTERVAL and DATETIME types, although the manuals only mention them in one of the appendices, except for one place where DATETIME is used in an example. The DATETIME constructor is used as:

```
DATETIME(1990-9-29 19:31:41) YEAR TO SECOND
```

Note that there are no double quotes in this; they cause a syntax error. In the same general style, the INTERVAL constructor is used as:

```
INTERVAL(19-9) YEAR TO MONTH
INTERVAL(399 16:54) DAY(3) TO MINUTE
```

There is a function called EXTEND which is used to alter the precision of DATETIME values.

```
EXTEND (DATETIME(16 19) DAY TO HOUR, YEAR TO SECOND)
```

The value returned by this will be a DATETIME value with the year and month extracted from the corresponding values of CURRENT, and the minutes and seconds set to zero.

```
EXTEND (DATETIME(1991) YEAR TO YEAR, YEAR TO SECOND)
```

The value returned here will be '1991-01-01 00:00:00'; if the last qualifier specifies a field which is less significant than that in the value being converted, then the missing day or month values are set to 1, and missing time values are set to zero.

It is possible to combine DATETIME and INTERVAL types in sensible ways. This means that: the difference between two DATETIME values is an INTERVAL; a DATETIME can have an INTERVAL added or subtracted giving a DATETIME; two INTERVAL values can be added or subtracted giving another INTERVAL; and an INTERVAL can be multiplied or divided by a scalar (simple number) to give another INTERVAL. The EXTEND function can also be used to handle conversions from

DATE types and strings. Thus, the examples below all work:

```
EXTEND ("1989-09-09", YEAR TO DAY),
EXTEND (EXTEND ("1989-09-09", YEAR TO DAY), YEAR TO SECOND),
EXTEND (TODAY, YEAR TO SECOND),
```

However, it is critical that a character string should have all the specified components. The second of the examples above cannot be written as:

```
EXTEND("1989-09-09", YEAR TO SECOND)    { Invalid }
```

Similar constraints apply when trying to insert a literal string into a database column in an INSERT statement.

There is one more useful facility for DATETIME and INTERVAL manipulation, namely the UNITS keyword. This can be used as a shorthand notation for an INTERVAL, and consists of a number, the keyword and a field name (YEAR, etc). The example below returns '1990-11-16':

```
DATETIME(1990-09-30) YEAR TO DAY + 47 UNITS DAY
```

14.1.8 VARCHAR

OnLine. The VARCHAR type is only available with INFORMIX-ONLINE. As its name implies, it uses a variable number of characters to store the data in the field. This is most useful when the data sometimes needs a large number of characters, but the vast majority of cases only need a few characters. A column is declared to be a VARCHAR column using the notation:

```
Column_name VARCHAR(max [, min])
```

The maximum size of the column must be expressed, with the upper bound on the size being 255. The lower limit need not be specified and defaults to zero. However, if the minimum size can be specified as some larger value, all rows of data will have at least the minimum amount of space allocated for each VARCHAR column. This can lead to a (slight) performance improvement over not specifying a lower limit. A VARCHAR column uses 1 byte to store the length of the actual column and 1 byte for every character actually stored.

14.1.9 BYTE and TEXT

OnLine. The other new type introduced with INFORMIX-ONLINE is the *blob* (*binary large ob*ject). These come in two flavours: BYTE and TEXT. A TEXT blob contains printable characters plus tabs, newlines and form-feeds. A BYTE blob can contain any type of data. These types are usually used to support multi-media applications because BYTE blobs in particular can be used to store any data that can be stored in a computer. One example application used BYTE blobs to store digitized pictures, while another used them to store music which was subsequently played back through a MIDI music system. However, there is a distinct limit to what can be done with blobs in INFORMIX-SQL – they really come into their own in applications written in INFORMIX-4GL and ESQL/C – so this section just summarizes what is possible. For more information about blobs, you will need to refer to the INFORMIX-ONLINE programmer's manual.

PERFORM can handle blobs. They are retrieved and stored in more or less the same way as any other data type. However, the only editing action that can be used on a blob in a form is to run a program to edit the blob. The program can be specified by the PROGRAM attribute in the form:

```
f006 = tablename.blob_column, PROGRAM = "progname";
```

You could also specify the WORDWRAP attribute if required. If you do not specify a program, the DBEDIT program will be used instead. During input and update, the program is run by typing an exclamation mark '!' in the display field for the blob column. To inspect a blob, use the **View** option; you activate the viewing program in the same way as during input. The specified program is given the name of a file containing a copy of the blob as an argument. A TEXT blob can be manipulated by any suitable program (eg **vi**), but a BYTE blob has to be handled by a program which understands the data structure. The first characters in a TEXT blob will be displayed in the corresponding display field on the form, although any non-printable characters will be displayed as a question mark '?'. The only information that will appear in a BYTE blob field will be '<BYTE value>'. (The default field size for a blob is 12 characters.)

ACE can handle TEXT blobs, but not BYTE blobs. A TEXT blob can be printed using the normal ACE PRINT statement. It is normally sensible to use WORDWRAP and RIGHT MARGIN when printing a TEXT blob:

```
PRINT COLUMN 20, blob_column WORDWRAP RIGHT MARGIN 75
```

A BYTE blob cannot be printed within an ACE report. The utility programs such as **dbload**, **dbimport** and **dbexport** understand blobs, and are discussed in Chapter 15.

14.2 Tables

Chapter 3 discussed the basic features of the CREATE TABLE statement. The previous section discussed in great detail the types of data that can be stored in a table. This section describes some other things that can be done when creating tables. For example, it is possible to create temporary tables explicitly (as well as with the INTO TEMP clause of the SELECT statement), and it is also possible to create a table in a directory other than the main database directory. The ALTER TABLE statement can be used to change the structure of a table, automatically transferring the contents between the old version and the new.

OnLine. There are still more ways of controlling tables with INFORMIX-ONLINE, but they are not covered here; you should look in the INFORMIX-ONLINE programmer's manual.

14.2.1 Creating temporary tables

Explicitly creating a temporary table is occasionally useful. The main advantage over an implicitly created temporary table is that the types of the columns can be controlled. Thus, it is possible to have a temporary table with a SERIAL column so that when the data is inserted, each row can be given as unique number – something which is impossible to do with a temporary table created by an INTO TEMP clause. It also gives you control over the scale and precision of DECIMAL and MONEY types, and over the qualifiers for DATETIME and INTERVAL types.

A temporary table is created by specifying CREATE TEMP TABLE instead of simply CREATE TABLE. Like any other table, the columns can store nulls or not as required; like any other temporary table, it is private to the database engine which creates it and disappears when that process terminates. Regardless of how it is created, a temporary table is only accessible to the program which created it; other users could create a table with the same name but would use a different physical table. The name is not recorded in the system catalogue. The data file is created in the temporary directory nominated by the environment variable DBTEMP, which defaults to /tmp.

Version 4.00. When a temporary table is created, all the statements that affect the table are logged in the transaction log, if there is one. (See Chapter 15 for more details of transaction logs.) This is somewhat wasteful since they are purely temporary phenomena, so it is now possible to suppress logging on a temporary table by specifying:

```
CREATE TEMP TABLE table_name
(
    column_name   column_type,
    ...
) WITH NO LOG
```

This option can also be appended to the end of an INTO TEMP clause of a SELECT statement. Using this cuts down the rate at which the log file grows, which speeds operations up (because there is less disk activity), and reduces the chance of running out of disk space.

14.2.2 Creating tables in remote directories

Standard Engine. Creating a table in a specified directory is another extension of CREATE TABLE which is occasionally useful. On UNIX, this would be most relevant if you knew that a particular table was going to grow very large and you wanted it to be placed on a different file system from the rest of the database. It is important that the table is as well protected as the rest of the database, so the place where it is put should be considered carefully. The best way of handling this would be to create a new directory on the other file system with the same permissions as the main database directory (see later in this chapter for more information on directory permissions), as shown in the example which follows:

```
$ pwd
/consult/john/cars
$ ls -ld cars.dbs
drwxrwx---   2 john    informix    448 Apr 17 15:26 cars.dbs
$ cd /sphinx/john
$ mkdir cars.ext
$ chmod 770 cars.ext
$ chgrp informix cars.ext
$ chown john cars.ext
$ ls -ld cars.ext
drwxrwx---   2 john    informix     32 Apr 17 15:54 cars.ext
$
```

To create a table in that directory, use the syntax:

```
CREATE TABLE Models
(
        Model       SERIAL(1) NOT NULL,
        Maker       INTEGER   NOT NULL,
        Modelname   CHAR(20)  NOT NULL,
        Details     CHAR(20),
        Price       MONEY(6,0),
        Maxspeed    INTEGER,
        Accel       DECIMAL(3,1),
        Tanksize    DECIMAL(3,1),
        Urban       INTEGER,
        Mpgat56     INTEGER
)
IN "/sphinx/john/cars.ext/models";

CREATE UNIQUE INDEX pk_models ON Models(Model);
CREATE INDEX f1_models ON Models(Maker);
CREATE INDEX i1_models ON Models(Modelname);
```

The IN clause of the CREATE TABLE statement specifies the name of the C-ISAM file in which the table is to be stored. Note that the name is specified without any extension, and the directory must be accessible to group informix and the owner of the database: the elaborate steps taken to create a directory with the standard permissions ensures that the new table is as well protected as the original. There is nothing to stop you creating the new table in /tmp, but anyone could delete it from there; if the system was rebooted, the new table would (probably) be removed automatically anyway.

Sometimes a table grows too big for the file system which holds the database. This is one occasion when it would be sensible to create the table in a named file on another file system. However, before creating a table on another file system, check whether all the data is really needed on-line. Can any of it be stored on back-up media only? Can any of it simply be deleted? Can any of it be summarized and stored only in summarized form? If it is still necessary to move the table, there are several methods of doing it, although only one of them is strictly orthodox and uses just Informix tools, so this is the only one described. The sequence of operations is important: the new table should be created and loaded from the old table; the old table should be renamed, then the new table; and the old table should be dropped before creating the indexes because this automatically deletes the indexes and allows them to be recreated with the same names as the (now deleted) original indexes.

Another advantage of not creating the indexes on the new table until after the data is loaded is that it is quicker to create the indexes rather than to repeatedly update the indexes, as would be necessary if the indexes were created before the data was loaded. The ORDER BY clause in the SELECT statement means that the data will be inserted in the same order as the primary key for the table, which means that accessing the data in primary key order should be faster. When one table grows too big for any single file system, there is nothing that can be done except get more disk space, or re-evaluate the decision that there is no way of reducing the size of the table.

```
DATABASE Cars EXCLUSIVE;

CREATE TABLE N_models
(
       Model        SERIAL(1) NOT NULL,
       Maker        INTEGER   NOT NULL,
       Modelname    CHAR(20)  NOT NULL,
       Details      CHAR(20),
       Price        MONEY(6,0),
       Maxspeed     INTEGER,
       Accel        DECIMAL(3,1),
       Tanksize     DECIMAL(3,1),
       Urban        INTEGER,
       Mpgat56      INTEGER
)
IN "/sphinx/john/cars.ext/models";

INSERT INTO N_models SELECT * FROM Models;

RENAME TABLE Models TO O_models;
RENAME TABLE N_models TO Models;
DROP TABLE O_models;

CREATE UNIQUE INDEX pk_models ON Models(Model);
CREATE INDEX f1_models ON Models(Maker);
CREATE INDEX i1_models ON Models(Modelname);
```

14.2.3 Changing tables

There are three ways of changing tables in a database without having to drop and recreate them. The simplest two are renaming a table or a column.

```
RENAME TABLE Companies TO Makers;
RENAME COLUMN Makers.Company TO Maker;
```

These operations are quick to implement; changing a column name simply involves changing an entry in the **Syscolumns** table; changing a table name changes an entry in the **Systables** table and also the name of the C-ISAM file for that table.

The other way of changing a table is to use ALTER TABLE to add or drop a column, or to change the type of a column. This process rebuilds the table completely and preserves the data in the original table as far as possible. If a CHAR column has its length reduced, the original data is truncated; if an INTEGER column is changed to a SMALLINT column, all the existing values must be small enough to fit into a SMALLINT, and if a DECIMAL or MONEY column is changed to FLOAT or SMALLFLOAT (or vice versa), as many significant digits as possible are preserved. For example, it might be necessary to reorganize the **Stock** table so that:

1. It has a serial column **Stock_id** as the first column.
2. It can have a null registration number (for a new car).
3. It does not record the price the car was bought for (it was embarrassing when customers saw what sort of profit we were making).
4. It makes sure that a mileage figure must be entered.

To reorganize the **Stock** table like this, run this ALTER TABLE statement:

```
ALTER TABLE Stock
    ADD     (Stock_id INTEGER BEFORE Registration),
    MODIFY (Stock_id INTEGER NOT NULL),
    MODIFY (Stock_id SERIAL),
    DROP    (Boughtfor),
    MODIFY (Registration CHAR(7),
            Mileage INTEGER NOT NULL);
```

Note that this will only work if the **Stock** table is empty; you cannot add a SERIAL column if the table is not empty. The BEFORE is optional – if it is omitted, the new column will go at the end of the list of the columns. (*Note*: although the manual states that a SERIAL column cannot be added to a non-empty table, it neglects to say that you cannot directly add a SERIAL column at all. If you try to add a SERIAL column in line one, error number -287 stops the statement working. The corrective action in the manual indicates that the steps to be taken are as shown above.) Changing a column to allow nulls always works, but changing a column so that it does not allow nulls only works if there are no rows in the table where that column has a null value. In general, adding a column to a non-empty table causes nulls to be inserted in that column for all existing rows. One obvious implication is that the column cannot be a not-null column. All the changes are made at once, and the whole operation succeeds or fails. The entire table is rebuilt when the ALTER TABLE statement is run, and the table number changes in the system catalogue.

An alternative way of preventing customers from seeing the cost of the car would be to create a VIEW on the **Stock** table which did not include this column. When the sale was made, the data from this view would be used. When the client had left, the cars would be deleted from the **Stock** table after the purchase price had been transferred to the **Sales** table.

In the ALTER TABLE statement, each of the clauses ADD, DROP and MODIFY is optional, but at least one must be present. The order in which the clauses occur is optional, but they are executed in order of appearance. If a new column should not accept null values, the new column should be updated immediately after the ALTER TABLE statement, so that there is a non-null value in that column in every row of the table, and then a second ALTER TABLE statement can be executed to change the type of the column to NOT NULL. Columns are deleted from the table when the DROP keyword is used. When a column is dropped, the data contained within the column is lost, and is not recoverable.

Be careful when making changes to the database using any of these statements. Many forms and reports will cease to work and will need to be recompiled, and if a column was added or dropped, the forms and reports will also need to be modified.

14.3 Query optimization

In general terms, the manner in which the database system produces the answer to a query is totally irrelevant to the user, but an appreciation of how the database system handles queries helps to indicate the set of indexes which will be useful. Whenever you execute a SELECT statement, the database engine (either **sqlexec** or **sqlturbo**) has to decode it and decide what strategy to use to produce the answer requested. When it is analysing a statement, it looks at the FROM clause and the WHERE clause. It splits the conditions in the WHERE clause into two types: *filter* conditions apply to column(s) of one table and potentially restrict the number of rows selected from that table, and *join* conditions relate columns from two different tables.

```
SELECT Coname, Modelname, Details
    FROM  Companies, Models
    WHERE Companies.Company = Models.maker  { Join }
      AND Models.Price >10000;              { Filter }
```

The information in this section came from ISI (1987) and applies to INFORMIX-SE and INFORMIX-TURBO. The optimizer for INFORMIX-ONLINE has been extensively modified to make use of extra statistics and to do a better cost estimate of which is the best way of doing the enquiry. This means that some of the details of the strategy outlined below no longer apply in quite the order described. The basic points are still valid, but the application of them may have changed. Another new statement with version 4.00 is the invaluable SET EXPLAIN ON statement, which is discussed in a later section.

When INFORMIX-SE looks at a query, it applies five criteria to decide which order it should use to process the tables. First, it examines the FROM clause for OUTER JOINS – see Chapter 12. If there is an outer join, it gives priority to the dominant table(s) as this allows it to ensure that rows from these tables are not discarded prematurely. If there are several tables at the same level of priority after examining the FROM clause, the other criteria are used to determine the ordering. In the query below, tables A and B are at the same level of priority, and so are C and D, but the two pairs cannot be further ordered by this rule:

```
SELECT column-list
    FROM A, B, OUTER (C, D)
    WHERE conditions
```

The second criterion looks at the indexes on the joining columns. If only one table has an index on the joining column, it is most efficient for INFORMIX-SE to search sequentially through the unindexed table, using the index to locate the joining rows from the indexed table. If both columns are indexed, but one has a unique index and the other does not, INFORMIX-SE will search through the non-uniquely indexed table and use the uniquely indexed table to speed up the search for joining rows. If both tables have an index on the joined columns and both are non-unique (or both unique, although this is less likely), but the index on one table contains fewer columns than the index on the other, INFORMIX-SE gives priority to the table with the 'smaller' index. With version 2.10 and later, if there is no way of choosing between the two tables because none of the columns involved is indexed, the optimizer creates a temporary table which is a copy of the larger of the two tables, and then creates an advantageous index on this temporary table and uses this when answering the query. The temporary table is dropped when the query is complete. This process is called *auto-indexing*. Note that this only occurs if there are no relevant indexes on either of the two tables. If the enquiry is a one-off job, this is ideal, but if a particular query is executed frequently and needs auto-indexing, it is distinctly quicker in the long run to create a suitable permanent index on at least one of the tables.

   In a join between the **Models** and **Companies** tables, both **Models.Maker** and **Companies.Maker** are indexed, but the index on **Companies** is unique (because it is the primary key), so according to this rule, **Models** is given priority over **Companies**. On the other hand, if the **Sales** and **Stock** tables were being joined by **Stock.Model** and **Sales.Model** – it would be a rather weird query – then both columns are non-uniquely indexed so this rule could not determine the ordering. In the **Cars** database, this rule does normally determine the ordering of the tables. There should not be any auto-indexing as all the primary and foreign keys are already indexed.

   If INFORMIX-SE cannot decide the ordering on the first two criteria, it looks at the filter conditions. If only one table has a filter condition applied, that table is given priority. If both tables have filter conditions but only one of the filter columns is indexed, the table with the index is given priority. If both tables have indexes on the filter columns, but only one of the indexes is unique, the table with the unique index is given priority. If both tables have indexes and both tables are either unique or non-unique but the indexes do not cover the same number of columns, the table with the 'larger' index is given priority.

   Occasionally, INFORMIX-SE will still be unable to choose between the two tables, in which case it gives priority to the table with the fewest rows. If both tables have the same number of rows (either because it is a self-join, the UPDATE STATISTICS command has never been run, or because it just so happens that the two tables *do* have the same number of rows), INFORMIX-SE will give priority to the table listed first in the FROM clause. The fifth criterion – order in the FROM clause – should seldom be used; one of the previous conditions will normally decide the ordering. Once INFORMIX-SE has worked out the order for processing the tables, it can execute the query.

14.4 Indexes

The judicious use of an index can increase the speed with which information can be retrieved from a database. To a lesser extent, however, an index can slow down the process of adding data to and updating data in a database.

In general, indexing is a trade-off between time gained during some operations and time lost during others. Every modification to an indexed column involves updating the corresponding '.idx' file. Thus, in a very large database, an index that helps performance during complex queries and sorting operations may hinder performance during operations that add, change or delete data. The greater the number of rows that are modified at a time, the greater the impact.

Indexes may be added and removed at will in INFORMIX-SQL, until the most efficient indexing structure is achieved. This may involve the creation of indexes for certain times of the day which may subsequently be dropped at a later stage, and then re-created the next day. This can be handled by **cron**, which could also be used to run UPDATE STATISTICS periodically. The performance trade-offs must be carefully evaluated on the basis of first-hand knowledge of the database and application.

Composite indexes may be created on two or more columns in a table either to provide uniqueness or so that the columns may be used as COMPOSITES in the INSTRUCTIONS section of a PERFORM screen. Up to eight columns may be included in a composite index, but the total length of all columns indexed in a single CREATE INDEX statement may not exceed 120 bytes.

14.4.1 Clustered indexes

Version 2.10 and later. When a clustered index is created, the table is rebuilt so that the records in the new table are in the same physical order as they occur in the clustered index. This can improve the speed of access to the data in that table via that index. However, it is important to note that the user cannot dictate whether any index will be used in any given query – the database agent optimizes the query and will use the index if it thinks there will be any advantage to doing so. There can be at most one clustered index on a table. (At least one port of version 2.10.03 only allowed one clustered index per database; to have several clustered indexes on this machine, it was necessary to create each clustered index and immediately alter it back to non-clustered. This was a bug.) To create a clustered index on the **Models** table, use:

```
DROP INDEX pk_models;
CREATE UNIQUE CLUSTER INDEX pk_models ON Models(Model);
```

To change an existing index to unclustered, use:

```
ALTER INDEX pk_models TO NOT CLUSTER;
```

To change it back to clustered, use:

```
ALTER INDEX pk_models TO CLUSTER;
```

Altering an index to unclustered is a quick operation; changing it to clustered means rebuilding the table.

It is important to note that a clustered index is created once and that immediately afterwards the physical order of the records corresponds to the logical order of the records, but as more records are inserted and deleted, the order becomes increasingly scrambled. To restore the ordering, simply run the ALTER INDEX commands.

Incidentally, the proof that the table is rebuilt is in the system tables; the table ID changes when a clustered index is created. Also, creating a clustered index on a large table makes the transaction log grow very fast.

14.5 SET EXPLAIN

Version 4.00. One of the powerful features of the new optimizer is that it can be persuaded to give an explanation of how it processes a particular enquiry. Studying this explanation can then help modify the indexes on the tables involved (if this is appropriate). The explanations are turned on and off using the statements:

```
SET EXPLAIN ON;
SET EXPLAIN OFF;
```

When explain mode is on, the explanation of each query processed is written to a file `sqexplain.out`. As an example of the output, consider the enquiry shown below:

```
QUERY:
------
SELECT DISTINCT Salut, Firstname, Surname, Company,
       Modelname, Details
   FROM  Customers, Models, Companies, Stock
   WHERE Customers.Lastmodel = Stock.Model
   AND Customers.Lastmodel = Models.Model
   AND Models.Maker = Companies.Maker;

Estimated Cost: 105
Estimated # of Rows Returned: 1

1) john.customers: SEQUENTIAL SCAN

2) john.models: INDEX PATH

   (1) Index Keys: model
       Lower Index Filter: john.models.model = john.customers.lastmodel

3) john.companies: INDEX PATH

   (1) Index Keys: maker
       Lower Index Filter: john.companies.maker = john.models.maker

4) john.stock: INDEX PATH

   (1) Index Keys: model   (Key-Only)
       Lower Index Filter: john.stock.model = john.customers.lastmodel
```

This query is one of the more complex ones in this book because it contains four tables joined; however, it has no filter conditions on any of the tables, which simplifies it for the optimizer. When this query was run, the data had only just been loaded into the database, and the UPDATE STATISTICS statement had not been run.

The interpretation of the `sqexplain.out` file is fairly simple: the primary table being scanned is the **Customers** table which will be searched sequentially. For each row in that table, the **Models** table will be cross-referenced via the **lastmodel** and **Model** columns, and the index on **Models.Model** will be used. Similarly, the value of the **Companies.Maker** column will be joined with the value retrieved from **Models**. The final join has the comment '(Key-Only)' attached. The database does not need to read the data file for the **Stock** table because all the information it needs is in the index file.

For comparison, the same query was run again after the statistics had been updated. There were 126 **Customers** records, 55 **Companies** records, 157 **Models** records and 6 **Stock** records. This produced the following somewhat different report:

```
QUERY:
------
SELECT DISTINCT Salut, Firstname, Surname, Company,
       Modelname, Details
    FROM  Customers, Models, Companies, Stock
    WHERE Customers.Lastmodel = Stock.Model
    AND Customers.Lastmodel = Models.Model
    AND Models.Maker = Companies.Maker;

Estimated Cost: 59
Estimated # of Rows Returned: 5

1) john.stock: INDEX PATH

    (1) Index Keys: model    (Key-Only)

2) john.customers: INDEX PATH

    (1) Index Keys: lastmodel
        Lower Index Filter: john.customers.lastmodel = john.stock.model

3) john.models: INDEX PATH

    (1) Index Keys: model
        Lower Index Filter: john.models.model = john.customers.lastmodel

4) john.companies: INDEX PATH

    (1) Index Keys: maker
        Lower Index Filter: john.companies.maker = john.models.maker
```

The optimizer has seized on the fact that there are only six rows in the **Stock** table and that it only uses the index file to work with this table first; it then uses the index on **Customers.Lastmodel** to locate customers which match each model, and then does the joins to **Models** and **Companies** as before. Note the reduced estimated cost and the altered estimated number of rows returned. As a matter of idle fact, two rows were returned. This difference emphasizes the importance of maintaining moderately up-to-date statistics on the database. It should also be mentioned that the UPDATE STATISTICS operation is more expensive in version 4.00 than it was in previous versions because a more comprehensive set of statistics is maintained. However, there is more than enough potential gain in performance from having good statistics to offset the cost of updating the statistics, providing the update is done sensibly. On a fast changing database, it may be appropriate to do it every hour; on most databases, once a day is likely to suffice; some exceptionally static databases may not need the statistics updated more than once a week.

To illustrate the use of SET EXPLAIN as a diagnostic tool, suppose that the index on **Models.Model** was dropped for some reason. This produced the following version of `sqexplain.out`:

```
QUERY:
------
SELECT DISTINCT Salut, Firstname, Surname, Company,
       Modelname, Details
   FROM  Customers, Models, Companies, Stock
   WHERE Customers.Lastmodel = Stock.Model
     AND Customers.Lastmodel = Models.Model
     AND Models.Maker = Companies.Maker;

Estimated Cost: 134
Estimated # of Rows Returned: 8

1) john.stock: INDEX PATH

    (1) Index Keys: model    (Key-Only)

2) john.customers: INDEX PATH

    (1) Index Keys: lastmodel
        Lower Index Filter: john.customers.lastmodel = john.stock.model

3) john.models: AUTOINDEX PATH

    (1) Index Keys: model
        Lower Index Filter: john.models.model = john.customers.lastmodel

4) john.companies: INDEX PATH

    (1) Index Keys: maker
        Lower Index Filter: john.companies.maker = john.models.maker
```

The cost has increased, but only slightly compared with the first example, and the sequence of operations has not changed, but the optimizer has identified that it will be most effective if it automatically creates the missing index on the **Models** table. If the database is further damaged by deleting the foreign key index on **Customers.Lastmodel**, the changes are much more marked:

```
QUERY:
------
SELECT DISTINCT Salut, Firstname, Surname, Company,
       Modelname, Details
   FROM  Customers, Models, Companies, Stock
   WHERE Customers.Lastmodel = Stock.Model
     AND Customers.Lastmodel = Models.Model
     AND Models.Maker = Companies.Maker;

Estimated Cost: 5131
Estimated # of Rows Returned: 1188

1) john.companies: SEQUENTIAL SCAN

2) john.models: INDEX PATH

    (1) Index Keys: maker
```

```
              Lower Index Filter: john.models.maker = john.companies.maker

3) john.customers: AUTOINDEX PATH

    (1) Index Keys: lastmodel
        Lower Index Filter: john.customers.lastmodel = john.models.model

4) john.stock: INDEX PATH

    (1) Index Keys: model   (Key-Only)
        Lower Index Filter: john.stock.model = john.customers.lastmodel
```

The optimizer now scans the **Companies** table sequentially, uses the foreign key index on **Models.Maker** to join with the **Models** table, creates an automatic index on **Customers.Lastmodel** and finally uses the index on **Stock** to check the final join condition. The cost is enormous by comparison with what went before, being about 50 times larger.

In each of these last two cases, the auto-indexed columns are prime candidates for having a permanent index placed on them. The example below, which has just the primary key index on **Models** in place (but the index on **Customers.Lastmodel** still dropped), shows some improvement in performance, but the auto-index on **Customers.Lastmodel** is necessary to cut down the cost and speed up the enquiry:

```
QUERY:
------
SELECT DISTINCT Salut, Firstname, Surname, Company,
       Modelname, Details
    FROM  Customers, Models, Companies, Stock
    WHERE Customers.Lastmodel = Stock.Model
      AND Customers.Lastmodel = Models.Model
      AND Models.Maker = Companies.Maker;

Estimated Cost: 715
Estimated # of Rows Returned: 77

1) john.stock: INDEX PATH

    (1) Index Keys: model   (Key-Only)

2) john.customers: AUTOINDEX PATH

    (1) Index Keys: lastmodel
        Lower Index Filter: john.customers.lastmodel = john.stock.model

3) john.models: INDEX PATH

    (1) Index Keys: model
        Lower Index Filter: john.models.model = john.customers.lastmodel

4) john.companies: INDEX PATH

    (1) Index Keys: maker
        Lower Index Filter: john.companies.maker = john.models.maker
```

This sort of diagnostic information is utterly invaluable to all database developers because it is often not obvious what effect adding or deleting an index will have.

14.6 Constraints

Version 4.00.   To conform with the ANSI standard, INFORMIX-SQL has introduced
constraints which can be specified when the table is created, or when a table is
altered. All constraints are unique and may optionally be given a name. A
constraint may be specified on a single column or for a set of columns. For example,
the schema for the **Stock** table could be modified to:

```
{
    a(#)stock4.sql       5.4 91/02/26
    Database Cars: Table Stock using constraint
}

CREATE TABLE Stock
(
    Registration  CHAR(7)     NOT NULL UNIQUE CONSTRAINT Pk_stock,
    Model         INTEGER.    NOT NULL,
    Colour        CHAR(8),
    Condition     CHAR(1),
    Datebought    DATE        NOT NULL,
    Boughtfor     MONEY(8,2)  NOT NULL,
    Mileage       INTEGER,
    Notes1        CHAR(60),
    Notes2        CHAR(60)
);
{
    PRIMARY KEY Stock(Registration)
    FOREIGN KEY Stock(Model)
        REFERENCES Models(Model)
}
CREATE INDEX F1_stock ON Stock(Model);
```

There are two changes here compared with what was used to create the table in the
database. First, the tag UNIQUE CONSTRAINT indicates that all the values in the
Registration column must be distinct from each other. The name of the constraint is
Pk_stock which is a reminder of its function; it is the primary key of the **Stock** table.
The second change is that there is no explicit index created on the **Registration**
column. This is partly because it is redundant − the unique constraint does the same
job as the index would do − and partly because it is not allowed. Internally, a
constraint is implemented as a unique index on the set of columns. The index is
given a name which starts with a blank so that users can never successfully refer to
the index in any SQL statement. If no constraint name is specified, then a name is
created from the letter 'u', the table number and the index number separated by an
underscore '_'.

Similarly, it is possible to create a constraint on several columns at once. This
is illustrated with the **Models2** table which was used, if you remember, in Chapter 11
to illustrate COMPOSITES in forms. This could be specified as shown overleaf. Note
again that the only index specified explicitly is the one on **Modelname**. If necessary,
a table could have several constraints on it, presumably one for each candidate key.

```
{
    @(#)models4.sql      5.2 90/09/16
    Database Cars: Table Models2 using constraint
}

CREATE TABLE Models2
(
    Model            INTEGER        NOT NULL,
    Maker            INTEGER        NOT NULL,
    Modelname        CHAR(20)       NOT NULL,
    Details          CHAR(40),
    Price            MONEY(6,0),
    Maxspeed         SMALLINT,
    Accel            DECIMAL(3,1),
    Tanksize         DECIMAL(3,1),
    Urban            DECIMAL(3,1),
    Mpgat56          DECIMAL(3,1),
    Enginesize       SMALLINT,
    UNIQUE (Model, Maker) CONSTRAINT Pk_models2
);
{
    PRIMARY KEY Models2(Maker, Model)
    FOREIGN KEY Models2(Maker)
        REFERENCES Companies(Company)
}
CREATE INDEX I1_models2 ON Models2(Modelname);
```

It is possible to add and drop constraints using the ALTER TABLE statement. If you need to drop a constraint and you did not specify a name for the constraint when you created it, you should look in the **Sysconstraints** table to find the name given to the constraint by the system. You cannot add a unique constraint to a new column unless the table is empty. If you drop a column that is part of a multi-column constraint, the constraint is dropped automatically. For example, the following statements could have been used to modify the **Stock** and **Models2** tables:

```
DROP INDEX Pk_stock;
ALTER TABLE Stock
    ADD CONSTRAINT UNIQUE (Registration) CONSTRAINT Pk_stock;

DROP INDEX Pk_models2;
ALTER TABLE Models2
    ADD CONSTRAINT UNIQUE (Maker, Model) CONSTRAINT Pk_models2;
```

14.7 Controlling access to a database

System security is a vital part of any database system which is often overlooked. Some users of the system should not be able to read, add, update or delete certain tables or even columns. INFORMIX-SQL has the ability to restrict access to specific users, which supplements the usual operating system permissions. This section is about how to control what people can do to the data in the database and is split into three sections: what people can do without using Informix tools and how Informix accesses the database; how to control who can access the database using the Informix tools; and how to control which particular tables people can change. The subject is discussed in terms of UNIX; DOS does not have users in the same way.

14.7.1 Access without using Informix tools

Whether a user can gain access to a database without using any database tools is governed by the normal UNIX permissions system. This section assumes a good knowledge of standard UNIX file and directory permissions: it does not explain them (see Bourne (1987)) but it does point out the consequences of the permissions used to protect databases. Similarly, there is no explanation of SUID and SGID programs.

On UNIX, there are two categories of user: superuser and everyone else. On a system with Informix, there is a third category of user, namely user informix and members of group informix, and the roles of these users are the subject of this section.

Since a superuser can access any file on the system at any time, it is important to realize that (a) if a superuser really tries, he can read, delete or do anything with the files in the database and there is nothing anyone can do to stop this, and (b) if everyone on the system knows how to become a superuser, anyone can get at the database. For these reasons, and many others, the superuser privileges should be strictly limited to two or three trustworthy users only.

Other users can be kept from directly accessing a database by standard UNIX file permissions. The default access permissions allow the owner of the database (the person who created it) and members of group informix to find out which files are in the database, to create or delete files in the directory, and to read or modify the files. The C-ISAM files are all set up so that the owner and members of group informix can read or modify those files. Other people have no access rights of any sort on the database, nor on the files in the database, and those permissions should *not* (repeat *NOT!*) be changed. It is not necessary, and it is silly to do so.

It is not necessary to change the default permissions on a database because the database engine has special permissions. This program is owned by root, belongs to group informix, and is both SUID and SGID. With INFORMIX-SQL version 2.10 on UNIX System V, it is the only SUID program in the Informix distribution. (With INFORMIX-SQL versions 1.10 and 2.00, the **sperform** program did not use **sqlexec** – for a variety of technical reasons – and it also had the same SUID root, SGID informix permissions. There are two other programs which are only supplied when the version of UNIX is derived from BSD UNIX. These programs are mkdbsdir and changrp which are used when creating the database and when creating tables respectively. Both these programs are always SUID to root. All the other programs distributed with Informix are owned by user informix, and all the programs and files, without exception, belong to group informix.) The database engine program only uses the superuser privileges to reset some system limits (specifically, it increases the maximum size of file it is allowed to create) before it resets its UID to that of the user who started it. Thereafter, the database engine runs SGID informix, which means that when it runs, it uses the permissions for group informix to read and modify the database files. It does not matter which group the user belongs to because the database engine always uses the group informix permissions to access the database. (If you know enough about UNIX permissions to spot the simplification in this argument, you will know that it does not normally make any difference to what the user perceives.) This is why the database and its

Permissions	Owner	Group	Directory
drwxrwxr-x	root	sys	/
drwxrwxr-x	root	sys	/usr
drwxr-x---	john	consult	/usr/john
drwxr-x---	john	consult	/usr/john/cars
drwxrwx---	john	informix	/usr/john/cars/cars.dbs

Table 14.1 Restricted access to a database

contents belong to group informix, and why group informix can create, read, write and delete those files.

On a system which only uses INFORMIX-SE, no user should be allowed to login as user informix, and no user should be allowed to belong to group informix. To prevent users logging in as user informix, set the password field in /etc/passwd to 'No login': this is guaranteed to be an invalid password because it is not 13 characters long. To prevent people running with group informix permissions, make sure that no one is given the login group number which is the informix group number, and also make sure that no one can change their group to group informix by making sure that the entry in /etc/group has no password and no users listed. If there is no password, only users listed can change to that group; if there are no users listed either, no one (except the superuser) can change to that group.

With INFORMIX-ONLINE and INFORMIX-TURBO, the user informix has an important role as controller of the resources available to the database administrators who control the individual databases. This user needs to be able to login to supervise some of the operations, so it should be treated in the same way as root; very few people should know the password, which should be changed frequently and recorded somewhere secure. The previous comments about group informix still apply.

If you run a secure system where others are not allowed access to user directories by default (eg the default value for the file creation mask **umask** is 007, 027 or 077), ISQL will not work on a database unless the user is also the database owner, or the directory permissions are relaxed slightly.

For example, given the directories and permissions shown in Table 14.1, user john can access the **Cars** database, but no one else can. This is because: (1) john has full access rights (the owner permissions are 'rwx' from /usr/john downwards; (2) members of group consult can find that there is a database in /usr/john/cars but since they are not in group informix and group informix does not have any access rights on /usr/john, they cannot get at the database; and (3) everyone else is barred from accessing /usr/john as well as the files in the sub-directories. So, if user pat in group sphinx tries to access this **Cars** database, she will fail because of the permissions. To let anyone access the database, the permissions need to be changed as shown in Table 14.2.

All that has happened is that others now have permission to access files in /usr/john and /usr/john/cars, but only if they know the name of the file and the permissions on the file let them. Now when pat runs the **sqlexec** program, it

Permissions	Owner	Group	Directory
drwxrwxr-x	root	sys	/
drwxrwxr-x	root	sys	/usr
drwxr-x--x	john	consult	/usr/john
drwxr-x--x	john	consult	/usr/john/cars
drwxrwx---	john	informix	/usr/john/cars/cars.dbs

Table 14.2 General access to a database

can access the database directory because (asuming /usr/john/cars is one of the directories included in the environment variable DBPATH) it will look for /usr/john/cars/cars.dbs explicitly. Anybody can find that the database exists if they know where to look for it, and **sqlexec** is in group informix so it can use the files inside the database. However, neither pat nor anyone else not in group consult can find out what other databases or files exist in either of the directories /usr/john or /usr/john/cars because they cannot list the files in those directories, nor can they create or delete files in the directories. And note that the permissions on the database directory itself have not been changed! The rule is: others must have at least execute (search) permission on each directory down to but not including the database directory; read permission may be helpful but is not necessary, and write permission should (almost) never be granted to others anyway.

These rules and observations about users and access privileges can be summarized as follows:

1. A superuser cannot be stopped.
2. Standard Engine. No one should be able to login as user informix.
3. OnLine and Turbo. The informix login should be as carefully controlled as the root login.
4. No one except informix should be logged in to group informix.
5. No one should be able to change to group informix.
6. The default permissions on a database directory should not be changed.
7. For anyone to be able to access the database at all, others must have execute permission on all directories down to but not including the database directory.

OnLine and Turbo. The databases for INFORMIX-ONLINE and INFORMIX-TURBO are normally stored on what are called raw disk partitions which are not used by anything else on the machine. There may be one or more partitions which hold the databases. The format of the data within the partitions is not publicly documented, and does not need to be. The partitions need to be carefully protected, as do all disk partitions, but this is very simple to arrange. The partitions are available as a device somewhere under the /dev directory, and the device is owned by user informix, belongs to group informix and has 660 permissions. The /dev directory must itself be secure (for general safety, quite apart from the security of databases) and is typically owned by root and has 755 permissions.

14.7.2 Using GRANT and REVOKE – database permissions

The previous section discussed the external security of an Informix database – who can do what with it without using the Informix database tools – and how the Informix database tools gain access to the database. Once the tools have gained external access to the database, internal security mechanisms govern who can do what with the database. Being the UNIX superuser has no direct advantage – a superuser can be forbidden to use the database, but since a superuser can become any other user without knowing the user's password, he can still get at the database by becoming the database owner. You have to be able to trust *all* your superusers. The capability to do anything with the database lies with the database administrator (DBA), or DBAs if there are several.

The default DBA is the person who creates the database, and everyone else has no permission to use the database at all – even if they have the UNIX permissions to access it, the Informix security mechanism will deny them the right to use the database. This can be changed by using GRANT and REVOKE to allow different people different levels of access to the database. There are three levels of access: DBA, RESOURCE and CONNECT. A DBA is omnipotent and can do anything to the database, including drop it – delete it completely. At the other end of the scale, users who are granted CONNECT permission may not change the structure of the database at all (except by creating temporary tables), although they can probably change the data stored in existing tables (subject to having been granted permission to change the tables). In the middle, users with RESOURCE privileges can alter the structure of the database by creating new tables or by dropping tables they own, but they cannot drop the database, nor can they drop tables which they do not own. These permissions can be granted by a DBA to anyone, but only a DBA can grant database privileges. The keywords WITH GRANT OPTION mean that `adrian` can grant RESOURCE or CONNECT privileges to other people without reference to the DBA, a licence which should not be granted to everybody:

```
GRANT CONNECT TO root, guest;
GRANT DBA TO pat;
GRANT RESOURCE TO adrian WITH GRANT OPTION;
```

There is a special user name (a reserved word), PUBLIC, which means approximately 'anyone not explicitly listed in the list of users able to user the database'.

```
GRANT CONNECT TO PUBLIC;
```

Now anyone can make use of the database, but only `pat` and `john` are DBAs, and `adrian` is the only RESOURCE-level user. To deny someone a previously granted privilege, use the REVOKE command:

```
REVOKE DBA FROM pat;
REVOKE RESOURCE FROM adrian;
REVOKE CONNECT FROM PUBLIC;
```

After this set of statements, both `root` and `guest` still have CONNECT permission (because they were explicitly granted CONNECT permission, and that has not been revoked), and so do both `pat` and `adrian`. When a high-level privilege such as DBA or RESOURCE is revoked, the named users retain CONNECT privilege. To deny the user CONNECT privileges as well, revoke CONNECT permission from the user as well. Also, john can run the command:

```
REVOKE DBA FROM john;
```

but it has no effect whatsoever – a DBA can only revoke permissions from another DBA, so there will always be one DBA for the database. (Of course, if john grants DBA privileges to sarah, sarah revokes DBA privileges from john and sarah is then removed from the system (the entry is deleted from /etc/passwd), no one will be able to login as a DBA until a user called sarah is recreated in the password file.) Finally, if PUBLIC has been granted CONNECT permission, specific people cannot be excluded from using the database.

```
GRANT CONNECT TO PUBLIC;
REVOKE CONNECT FROM root;
```

This does not prevent root from using the database because although root has no explicit privilege, root is now identified as part of PUBLIC. As a consequence, it is far better not to grant any database-level permission to PUBLIC and to explicitly grant CONNECT permission to those users who need to use the database. If anybody should be excluded from using the database, do not grant any database-level privilege to PUBLIC. See Section 16.6 on how information is stored in the database.

14.7.3 Using GRANT and REVOKE – table permissions

So far, GRANT and REVOKE are 'all-or-nothing' operations; users can either do anything with the database or they cannot do anything – there is no selectivity saying that adrian can use the **Customers**, **Models**, **Company** and **Stock** tables but not the **Sales** table, nor that pat can add to the **Customers** and **Sales** tables but cannot edit the **Sales** table once a row is entered, and that she cannot make any changes to the **Company** table.

However, GRANT and REVOKE can also be used to handle exactly these table-level conditions. By default, PUBLIC can do anything to a table except alter it (that is, alter its structure), although if PUBLIC only has CONNECT permission, people identified as PUBLIC cannot index the table either. PUBLIC can select from the table, and insert, delete and update rows in the table. To reduce these privileges so that PUBLIC can only select data from, say, **Models**, and not change it in any way, execute the following statements:

```
REVOKE ALL ON Models FROM PUBLIC;
GRANT SELECT ON Models TO PUBLIC;
```

Now the general population can only select data from the **Models** table, not change that data. The statements below set the permissions for adrian and pat:

```
REVOKE ALL ON Companies FROM pat;
GRANT SELECT ON Companies TO pat;
REVOKE ALL ON Sales FROM pat;
GRANT SELECT, INSERT ON Sales TO pat;

REVOKE ALL ON Sales FROM adrian;
```

This gives very good control over who can do what and also prevents one user from accessing a specific table even if you grant PUBLIC permission to access the same table. However, sometimes some columns should be hidden from one user, or they should only be allowed to change certain columns.

```
REVOKE SELECT, UPDATE ON Customers FROM PUBLIC;
GRANT SELECT(Customer, Salut, Firstname, Surname)
        ON Customers TO PUBLIC;
GRANT UPDATE(Salut, Firstname, Surname)
        ON Customers TO PUBLIC;
```

Now any general user can only see four of the columns in the **Customers** table, and can only update three of them. The only disadvantage of this is that if a general user executes:

```
SELECT * FROM Customers;
```

he will get an error. If this matters, you should create a view instead. You could grant update rights on a column that a user cannot select, but it seems pointless.

There is an annoying asymmetry in the GRANT and REVOKE statements (which applies to ANSI standard SQL as well as INFORMIX-SQL), namely that you can grant permissions on specified columns but you cannot revoke permissions on specified columns. The following is therefore invalid, even though it would be very useful to be able to do it:

```
GRANT UPDATE ON Customers TO adrian;           ( Valid  )
REVOKE UPDATE(Surname) ON Customers FROM adrian; ( Invalid )
```

This level of control, which can constrain any users so that they can only do exactly what they need to be able to do, is very valuable, although to set the permissions completely on a large database is a tricky (not to mention tedious) process. If, however, you need to restrict people from accessing certain rows of the table (as opposed to columns), you should create a view which only shows the required rows and then apply permissions to the view as well as the base table.

Version 4.00. It is possible for a DBA to grant table-level privileges on behalf of another user. This is done using the final qualifier 'AS user', so the example below will record the grantor (person who gives the permission) as the user abc, even if it was user john who did the typing:

```
GRANT INSERT, UPDATE, SELECT ON Models TO adrian AS abc;
```

14.8 Views

Another way of restricting user access is by the use of a view. These create what appears to the user to be a standard table which can be accessed normally with the use of SQL statements, and data added, modified or deleted. A view is created with the syntax:

```
CREATE VIEW Sale_stock (Registration, Model, Colour, Condition, Mileage, Notes1, Notes2) AS
    SELECT Registration, Model, Colour, Condition, Mileage, Notes1, Notes2
        FROM Stock;
```

A view is actually the result of a query on the database, and, as such, shows the user only what he is permitted to see. There are many restrictions on what can be done with views. In particular, some views do not allow the user to insert, delete or update the data presented by the view. For example, given the view **Stock_summary** below:

```
CREATE VIEW Stock_summary (Model, Quantity) AS
    SELECT Model, COUNT(*)
        FROM    Stock
        GROUP BY Model;
```

the data presented to the user cannot be associated with any one row in the base table, so the user cannot make any changes to the data in this view simply by editing the view; the only way is by editing the data in the base table.

Another view which is useful in the **Cars** database is **Modelnames**:

```
CREATE VIEW Modelnames (Model, Company, Modelname, Details) AS
    SELECT Models.Model, Companies.Company, Models.Modelname, Models.Details
        FROM  Models, Companies
        WHERE Models.Maker = Companies.Maker;
```

This view presents the company name, model name and details, and model number as if it were a single table. What is more, this view cannot be updated. For more information on when views are updatable and when they are not, look in the INFORMIX-SQL reference manual. For theoretical information, look in Date (1986) or Date (1983).

A view which restricts the user to a sub-set of the rows in a table still allows a user to enter data into the base table which will not be part of the view. For example, the view below restricts the user to the list of cars made by Ford:

```
CREATE VIEW Ford AS
    SELECT * FROM  Models
        WHERE Models.Maker = (SELECT Company FROM Companies WHERE Company = "Ford");
```

Using a default form generated on this view would allow the user to insert records with **Models.Maker** set to some value other than the company number for Ford; until the user executed a new enquiry, he would be able to see the non-Ford car, but once he re-executed any query, the user would not see the record again. To prevent this happening, modify the view definition to include the words WITH CHECK OPTION as below:

```
CREATE VIEW Ford AS
    SELECT * FROM  Models
        WHERE Models.Maker = (SELECT Company FROM Companies WHERE Company = "Ford")
    WITH CHECK OPTION;
```

With this view, the user cannot enter any models which are not made by Ford because the CHECK OPTION instructs the database engine to ensure that any modification made to the underlying table using the view will also satisfy the constraints defined by the view.

There are a number of odd restrictions on the definition of a view, most notably that the SELECT statement may not contain an ORDER BY clause, nor may it use UNION. For the other oddities, please read Chapter 2 in the INFORMIX-SQL reference manual.

Version 2.10 and earlier.   One word of warning: in all the early versions of INFORMIX-SQL, and even in some ports of version 2.10, PERFORM does not work properly with views. When a form was generated for the view **Ford**, it selected one row of data, but neither the `Next`, **Previous** nor **Current** options worked – they produced the error message 'Someone else has deleted a row which is in your list'. ACE works correctly, SQL works correctly, but PERFORM does not.

Version 4.00.   Where a view is a column or row sub-set of a single table, PERFORM works correctly on views. However, if the view contains a join, an aggregate function or a GROUP BY clause, PERFORM produces an error at run-time when a query is executed. The message is 'Cannot use ROWID for views with aggregates, group by or on multiple tables'. This message should not be seen by users of INFORMIX-SQL; it would make sense to INFORMIX-4GL programmers, but not to INFORMIX-SQL users. Further, PERFORM should detect that it cannot operate correctly and diagnose the problem better, preferably at compile time, but definitely when the form is run and without making the user execute a query to find out that the form will not work. It is a pity, but this problem renders views in Informix largely unworkable because the most useful views are those which combine selected columns from several tables, and because the place where this is most useful is in forms. Nevertheless, if a view is a row or column sub-set, it is now possible to use forms on the view, and the joining facilities within PERFORM are generally sufficient to enable the form designer to achieve the same effect as a join view.

14.9 Synonyms

Version 2.10 and earlier.   Users can create a set of synonyms for the tables in the database which they can use, but each user must create his own synonyms. The synonyms may not be the same as the name of a table (or view) in the database. The syntax for creating a synonym is:

```
CREATE SYNONYM p FOR Prices;
CREATE SYNONYM c FOR Customers;
```

Synonyms are not very useful because they only apply to one user, the user who created the synonym. Unless all users use the same synonyms, which is a difficult condition to enforce, a form developed by `pat` using her synonyms will not work for `adrian` using his synonyms.

Version 4.00.   The semantics of synonyms underwent a radical change with version 4.00 and became generally useful. The most important change is that a synonym defined by any user is immediately usable by everyone. This cancels the complaint made about synonyms in earlier versions. In addition, if you have INFORMIX-ONLINE, you can make a synonym refer to a table in another database on another machine altogether, and further, the administrator on the remote machine could relocate the table to a third machine and the synonym on the first machine would still locate the data correctly. The details of this are described in the documentation for INFORMIX-ONLINE. However, extending the example from

Section 12.3, it would be feasible for the DBA on each machine to set up a set of synonyms such as:

```
CREATE SYNONYM i_stock      FOR cars@isis:abc.stock;
CREATE SYNONYM i_companies  FOR cars@isis:abc.companies;
CREATE SYNONYM i_customers  FOR cars@isis:abc.customers;
CREATE SYNONYM i_prices     FOR cars@isis:abc.prices;
CREATE SYNONYM i_sales      FOR cars@isis:abc.sales;
CREATE SYNONYM i_models     FOR cars@isis:abc.models;

CREATE SYNONYM o_stock      FOR cars@osiris:abc.stock;
CREATE SYNONYM o_companies  FOR cars@osiris:abc.companies;
CREATE SYNONYM o_customers  FOR cars@osiris:abc.customers;
CREATE SYNONYM o_prices     FOR cars@osiris:abc.prices;
CREATE SYNONYM o_sales      FOR cars@osiris:abc.sales;
CREATE SYNONYM o_models     FOR cars@osiris:abc.models;
```

Now anybody who wished to could adapt the SELECT statement shown in Section 12.3 to read:

```
SELECT S1.Registration, M1.Price, C1.Manufacturer, M1.Modelname, M1.Details
    FROM  I_stock S1, I_models I_companies C1
    WHERE S1.Model = M1.Model
      AND M1.Maker = C1.Maker
UNION
SELECT S2.Registration, M2.Price, C2.Manufacturer, M2.Modelname, M2.Details
    FROM  O_stock S2, O_models M2, O_companies C2
    WHERE S2.Model = M2.Model
      AND M2.Maker = C2.Maker
ORDER BY 3, 4, 5;
```

Internally to the database, the synonym names are stored in **Systables** with a special table type. The full details of the synonym are stored in the new table, **Syssyntable**. For more details about this, see Section 16.6.

14.10 CREATE SCHEMA

Version 4.00.   The CREATE DATABASE statement is not actually part of ANSI standard SQL. The CREATE SCHEMA statement is the official ANSI method of creating a set of tables and the associated indexes and permissions. With INFORMIX-SQL, there must be a current database when the CREATE SCHEMA statement is run. It can be used by people with RESOURCE or DBA level privileges. A user with RESOURCE-level privileges can only create a schema with his own user name as the authorization identifier; a DBA can create a schema on behalf of anyone, including of course himself. The only statements that are permitted in the CREATE SCHEMA statement are CREATE TABLE, CREATE VIEW, CREATE INDEX, CREATE SYNONYM and GRANT. Note that the CREATE SCHEMA statement is a single statement with no semicolons or commas separating the components. In the example, the user who owns the table **Stock** will be abc, which is assumed to be the login name of the official DBA for ABC Cars Ltd (see also Chapter 15 on MODE ANSI databases). The CREATE SCHEMA statement would normally be used to create several tables at once, rather than the single table in the example.

```
CREATE SCHEMA AUTHORIZATION abc
  CREATE TABLE Stock
  (
      Registration  CHAR(7)     NOT NULL
                    UNIQUE CONSTRAINT Pk_stock,
      Model         INTEGER    NOT NULL,
      Colour        CHAR(8),
      Condition     CHAR(1),
      Datebought    DATE        NOT NULL,
      Boughtfor     MONEY(8,2) NOT NULL,
      Mileage       INTEGER,
      Notes1        CHAR(60),
      Notes2        CHAR(60)
  )
  CREATE INDEX F1_stock ON Stock(Model)
  CREATE SYNONYM S FOR Stock
  GRANT SELECT, INSERT, DELETE ON Stock TO bill
  GRANT SELECT, INSERT, DELETE ON Stock TO john;
```

14.11 Deleting database objects

The keyword DELETE is reserved for deleting rows of data from a table, so the keyword used to delete tables, indexes, views, synonyms and databases is DROP. Any object which can be created with a CREATE statement is removed by a corresponding DROP statement. For example, a table may be dropped by a DBA or the table's owner using the notation:

```
DROP TABLE Customers;
```

When a table is dropped, all the data in it is lost, and any indexes associated with the table are also dropped. Less obviously, any views which depend on the table are also dropped, and so are any synonyms and any permissions granted on the table. This is a good example of what is meant by the referential integrity of a database: all the extra objects which are deleted refer to the table, and so when the table is deleted, the delete cascades through the tables in the system catalogue and removes any records which refer to the deleted table.

An index is dropped using its name. The only times when the name of an index is needed are when it is created, altered or dropped. The syntax is:

```
DROP INDEX pk_stock1;
```

A view may be dropped by using the DROP VIEW statement. When a view is dropped, any other views which depend on it are also dropped, another example of referential integrity.

```
DROP VIEW Ford;
```

Synonyms may also be dropped:

```
DROP SYNONYM p;
DROP SYNONYM c;
```

In all these cases, the owner of the object or a DBA may drop the object; no one else may do so. Finally, databases can also be dropped. You cannot drop a database unless you are a DBA or you own all the tables in the database. You cannot drop the current database, so if you have been working with the database you wish to drop, you must close the database first. You cannot drop a database if anybody else is using it at the time. The syntax is:

```
DROP DATABASE Cars;
```

This deletes all the tables in the database (including the system catalogue) and removes the database directory, unless there are some files left in it which do not belong to the database.

Standard Engine. The DROP DATABASE statement is seldom used to remove INFORMIX-SE databases. It is usually easier, on UNIX, to use the ordinary UNIX command:

```
rm -fr cars.dbs
```

This is equally effective if you own the database directory and can create files in the directory containing the database directory. However, you need to be very careful about using this command. UNIX will not stop you deleting the database if someone else is using it, which would lead to weird results.

14.12 Summary

This chapter discussed how to create temporary tables explicitly and how to store a table in a directory other than the main database directory. The way in which the database engine optimizes queries was outlined so that you can see how indexing may help speed up your enquiries. The SET EXPLAIN feature available in version 4.00 was described in some detail, as was the CONSTRAINT option when creating a table. All aspects of database access and permissions were described so that you can protect any database suitably. Both synonyms and views were described, followed by a brief discussion of the CREATE SCHEMA statement introduced with version 4.00. Finally, there was a summary of how to delete parts of a database using the various DROP statements.

ransactions, audit trails and back-ups

This chapter covers the techniques for unloading ASCII data from a database into a file, and for loading ASCII data into a database, including the commands **dbload**, **dbimport** and **dbexport**. It then discusses the mechanisms provided by INFORMIX-SQL to help maintain the physical and logical integrity of the database, namely transactions and audit trails. It concludes with a discussion of the issues involved in backing up databases. This chapter does not attempt to deal with handling logs for either INFORMIX-ONLINE or INFORMIX-TURBO; that would occupy a chapter in its own right, and would require a preliminary chapter explaining a lot of other details of these types of database.

15.1 Reasons for unloading databases

INFORMIX-SQL can use data produced by other products, and can produce data for use by other products, if the data is presented as a flat ASCII file (which means a file containing only ASCII characters with each line in the file representing one record). This is very useful for:

1. Transferring data from ISQL to a spreadsheet, say.
2. Transferring data from a spreadsheet to ISQL.
3. Transferring data between two different types of machine.
4. Storing data in a human-readable form.
5. Manipulating the data outside the database.

An example of the latter is converting data about real customers into imaginary data. To do this, the data is unloaded in sections – the salutation and first name in one block, the surname in another, the first line of the address in a third and so on. Each row in each block is assigned a random number and sorted into order. The resulting blocks are then recombined to form a shuffled table and every digit has a random digit added to it. Finally, the data is reloaded into the database. All this would have been impossible in INFORMIX-SQL, but was not difficult using a couple of simple C programs to generate random numbers and UNIX commands such as **cut**, **sort**, **paste** and **awk** to manipulate the data unloaded by INFORMIX-SQL.

15.2 Unloading the database

INFORMIX-SQL has four ways of producing ASCII text files which can subsequently be transferred to another system (or edited, or printed, or simply stored), namely ACE reports, the OUTPUT statement, the UNLOAD statement and the **dbexport** utility.

15.2.1 Reports

One of the ways of producing ASCII data, writing a report, has already been covered in detail. A report used for this purpose is usually relatively easy to write; it will usually only have an ON EVERY ROW control block, which will typically print only a single line for each row of data.

As an example, which will be used later in discussing the **dbload** command, the report `custfix.unl` shown below unloads the **Customers** table into a file called `custfix.unl`:

```
DATABASE Cars END

OUTPUT
    TOP MARGIN      0
    BOTTOM MARGIN   0
    LEFT MARGIN     0
    PAGE LENGTH     1
    REPORT TO "custom.fix"
END

SELECT *
    FROM     Customers
    ORDER BY Surname, Firstname, Salut
END

FORMAT

ON EVERY ROW
    PRINT
        Customer USING "###&", 1 SPACE,
        Salut, 1 SPACE,
        Firstname, 1 SPACE,
        Surname, 1 SPACE,
        Address1, 1 SPACE,
        Address2, 1 SPACE,
        Address3, 1 SPACE,
        Postcode, 1 SPACE,
        Phone, 1 SPACE,
        Maxmoney USING "######", 1 SPACE,
        Enquiry, 1 SPACE,
        Lastmodel USING "###&", 1 SPACE,
        Contactdate USING "dd/mm/yyyy"

    END
```

This report prints each field using a fixed format; the character fields are printed with all trailing spaces, and the number and date fields have a fixed format. This will allow the **dbload** command to pick up the fields correctly.

15.2.2 OUTPUT

The other two ways of producing ASCII data – namely the OUTPUT statement and the UNLOAD statement – are also ways of capturing the output from a SELECT statement, but the user has almost no control over the format of the output.

It is perhaps stretching things a little to say that the OUTPUT statement can be used to produce an ASCII dump of a table, although it can certainly be used for that purpose. The OUTPUT statement is effectively a prefix to a SELECT statement which specifies where the results are to go – and whether headings should be included. Thus, the contents of the **Stock** table could be dumped using any of the following statements:

```
OUTPUT TO "stock.dump" SELECT * FROM Stock;
OUTPUT TO PRINTER WITHOUT HEADINGS SELECT * FROM Stock;
OUTPUT TO PIPE "mailx john@sphinx.co.uk" SELECT * FROM Stock;
```

The output format closely resembles a default report layout; that is, the data will be printed in columns if it will fit across the page (generally regarded as 80 columns wide), and if it won't fit, each row of data will be printed as a series of lines and one row will be separated from the next by a blank line.

As the syntax suggests, the optional clause WITHOUT HEADINGS is used to modify the layout so that the headings are not printed. This cuts down the amount of white space in the output, but the layout is no more predictable than before.

15.2.3 UNLOAD

The other, more orthodox, way of producing an ASCII file is to use the UNLOAD statement. This, too, is a prefix to a SELECT statement, the format of which is:

```
UNLOAD TO "stock.unl" SELECT * FROM Stock;
```

The SELECT statement can of course be as complicated as required. The output from this statement is strictly disciplined: it consists of one line for each row of data, with each field terminated by a delimiter, and all the fields are of variable length (so that character fields, for example, are clipped of trailing blanks), and null fields are represented by adjacent delimiters. By default, the delimiter character is a vertical bar '|', but it can be reset to anything using the environment variable DBDELIMITER. Any instance of DBDELIMITER occurring in a character field is escaped with a backslash '\'. Be careful though if you use something eccentric as a delimiter (eg '8'); it will unload without any trouble, but any 8s in the numeric fields will not be escaped and will prevent the file from loading.

15.2.4 dbexport

Version 4.00. The **dbexport** and **dbimport** facilities work as a pair and greatly facilitate the transfer of databases between machines (or on the same machine). The **dbexport** command is used to unload all the data from a database in a form which

can be used by **dbimport** to recreate the database elsewhere. The simplest use of
dbexport is:

```
$ dbexport cars
```

This will produce a lot of information on the screen, a copy of all that information in
a file dbexport.out, and a directory called cars.exp containing a file
cars.sql and a number of unloaded data files, each of which consists of the first
seven characters of the table name (padded with underscores if the table name is
shorter than seven characters) followed by the three-digit table number and the
extension '.unl'. The cars.sql file contains all the statements necessary to
duplicate the database. While the export is happening, the database is locked in
exclusive mode so that no one else can alter it at the same time; if this were not the
case, someone might easily alter several rows of data, some in tables which were
already unloaded and others in tables still to be unloaded, which would lead to an
inconsistent database.

There are a number of options which can be used to modify the behaviour of
dbexport. The '-c' option tells the program to continue even if errors occur; this
does not override the exclusive lock test. The '-q' option suppresses the output to
standard output, but the file dbexport.out is still written. The '-o' option allows
you to specify the directory where cars.exp will be created; by default it is created
in the current directory. Instead of using the '-o' option, the data can be written to
tape directly by specifying all three of the options '-t', '-b' and '-s'. The '-t'
option is followed by the name of the tape device (which could be a floppy disk or
some other device); the '-b' option is followed by the block size in kilobytes; and the
'-s' option is the capacity of one reel, also in kilobytes. When the '-t' option is
used, it is possible to add the '-f' option, which specifies the name of a disk file
where the contents of cars.sql should be written. This allows the contents to be
edited before transferring the database to the new system. This is advantageous
because it allows you to clean up the ownerships and permissions in particular.

15.3 Loading the database

There are two different ways of reading the ASCII files produced by UNLOAD (or,
indeed, ASCII files from any other source, whether that is a spreadsheet or a
different database product), namely the LOAD statement in SQL and the **dbload**
command. Additionally, version 4.00 provides the **dbimport** command which
creates and loads a database from the data produced by **dbexport**.

15.3.1 LOAD

The LOAD statement is a variant of the INSERT statement:

```
LOAD FROM "stock.unl" INSERT INTO stock;
```

With this syntax, the first field in the file `stock.unl` is loaded into the first column of the table **Stock**, the second field into the second column and so on. There must be as many delimiters in each line of data as there are columns in the table being loaded, and the data types must match too. If there are too many fields, or too few, an error occurs. If required, the columns in the input file can be assigned to particular columns in the table:

```
LOAD FROM "stock.unl" INSERT INTO stock (model, boughtfor, registration);
```

Now the first field of a row of input will go into the **Model** column of the table, the second field into the **Boughtfor** column and the third field into the **Registration** column. This is the inverse operation to the UNLOAD statement, and again the environment variable DBDELIMITER governs the field delimiter, with the default delimiter character being a vertical bar '|'. If there are not as many fields of data as there are columns in the table, the remaining columns are assigned null values, but only if nulls are acceptable.

15.3.2 dbload

The other way of loading data is using the **dbload** command. This is a program in its own right with a large set of command-line arguments and an input syntax which is both complex and powerful. **dbload** can handle files with variable-length fields terminated by a delimiter or files with fixed-length fields. **dbload** is driven by a command file which consists of a sequence of (one or more) control units. A control unit is either a file description or a modified INSERT statement, both of which are terminated by a semicolon. A command file can also contain comments enclosed in braces '{ }'.

dbload command file – FILE

A FILE description control unit takes one of two forms depending on whether the input file has fixed-length fields or variable-length fields. If the file is of variable-length fields, the FILE statement simply specifies the file, the field delimiter and the number of fields in each row, thus:

```
FILE "custom.unl" DELIMITER "|" 13;
```

If the file is of fixed-length records, each field is described in turn and the descriptions are separated by commas. A field description consists of a name followed by a specification of which columns make up the field, optionally followed by a specification of the string which should be regarded as the null value. Thus, if the file `custom.fix` contained the customer data in fixed-length fields, the file description might look like Figure 15.1. The field names are f01 etc, and this version has simple, contiguous fields for the different columns. If a complex field was needed with parts from several disjoint fields (possibly overlapping, possibly reusing fields), the syntax would be modified, thus:

```
FILE "custfix.unl" (f_of_5  15-70 : 1-3 : 7-11 : 9 : 10-20, f_of_3  13-25 : 2 : 19-25);
```

```
FILE "custom.fix"
( f01    1 -   4,                        ( Customer )
  f02    6 -  10  NULL "      ",         ( Salut )
  f03   12 -  21,                        ( Firstname )
  f04   23 -  37,                        ( Surname )
  f05   39 -  62,                        ( Address1 )
  f06   64 -  87,                        ( Address2 )
  f07   89 - 102,                        ( Address3 )
  f08  104 - 113,                        ( Postcode )
  f09  115 - 130,                        ( Phone )
  f10  132 - 137,                        ( Maxmoney )
  f11  139,                              ( Enquiry )
  f12  141 - 144,                        ( Lastmodel )
  f13  146 - 155                         ( Contactdate )
);
```

Figure 15.1 FILE statement for fixed-length input to **Customers** table

Field `f_of_5` is made from five sets of fields, with the characters in positions 10 and 11, and 15 to 20 being used twice. Field `f_of_3` also uses characters 2 and 13 to 20, and it uses characters 19 to 25 twice.

dbload command file – INSERT
The other type of control unit is the INSERT control unit, which comes in three forms. The simplest form is:

```
INSERT INTO Customers;
```

This takes the values from the preceding FILE statement and inserts the first field into the first column in the table, the second field into the second column and so on.

The next form consists of an INSERT specifying a list of columns. This makes sense with either of the first two FILE statements above, but it is not necessary to list all the columns if only some of the values should be transferred from the data file and the others should be set to NULL.

```
INSERT INTO Customers (Customer, Salut, Firstname, Surname, Address1, Address2,
     Address3, Postcode, Phone, Maxmoney, Enquiry, Lastmodel, Contactdate);
```

The third form of the INSERT control block uses field names instead of column names. This way, it is also possible to use constants. So to load the data from `custfix.unl` using new serial numbers for the customers and setting the contact date to 8 March 1991, the following statement could be used:

```
INSERT INTO Customers (f01, f02, f03, f04, f05, f06, f07, f08, f09, f10, f11, "08/03/1991");
```

If the FILE control block is for variable-length fields, the columns are implicitly given the names `f01`, `f02` and so on, and these names may be used in an INSERT control block. The final point to note, apart from the usual braces-surrounding-comments convention, is that it is possible to use one FILE control block for several successive INSERT control blocks. Also, one command file may have a sequence of FILE and INSERT control blocks.

dbload options

dbload is fussy about the way it is invoked; it must have a database, a command file and a log file specified, otherwise it prompts you for those names. The format of the command file has already been discussed; the log file is simply a record of what **dbload** says to the terminal while it is loading. The syntax for the basic use of **dbload** is:

```
dbload -d cars -c cars.cmd -l cars.log
```

There are numerous other options to **dbload** which control its behaviour in detail. The '-s' option performs a syntax check on the command file. The '-n' option is followed by a number and indicates the number of rows that should be loaded between messages. The default value is 100, but it could be reset on a heavily loaded system to reassure the user that **dbload** was still working. If the database has a transaction log, **dbload** loads the records in transactions of *n* records, where *n* is the number following the '-n' option. The '-e' option is followed by a number which indicates how many bad rows of data should be processed before the load is stopped. The '-i' option is followed by a number which indicates how many rows of data should be skipped before starting to load. This is very useful when a load fails part way through. The only other option, the '-p' option, tells **dbload** to prompt the user when it is about to abort, asking whether to commit the rows loaded since the last committed set of rows. Unless you set this option, the successfully loaded rows will be committed without question.

15.3.3 dbimport

The **dbimport** command is the opposite of the **dbexport** command; it creates and loads a database using the information created by **dbexport**. Like **dbexport**, the simplest use of **dbimport** is very simple:

```
$ dbimport cars
```

The directory `cars.exp` should exist in the current directory. If you are using INFORMIX-SE, the database `cars.dbs` should not exist in the current directory; if you are using INFORMIX-ONLINE, there should not be a database with the same name which you own in the system. The log file `dbimport.out` is created with a record of what was executed, and a copy of this file is sent to the screen. The export data is not removed.

As before, there are a number of options; in fact, there are even more options, but the main options are the same. The '-c', '-q', '-t', '-b', '-s' and '-f' options have the same meanings as before, except that the '-f' option indicates where the SQL statements are stored, rather than where they should be put. The analogue of the '-o' option to **dbexport** is the '-i' option; this specifies the directory where the export directory (`cars.exp`) can be found. In addition, if using INFORMIX-SE, the database can be created with a transaction log file specified using the '-l' option followed by the log file name (which should be an absolute path name, not a relative path name). If you are using INFORMIX-ONLINE, you can specify that the logging should be buffered, rather than unbuffered, by using `buffered` as an option. For both engines, if the database is to be a MODE ANSI database, this is specified by using the option '`-ansi`'; for more details about these, see Section 15.8.

15.4 Transactions

A transaction may be regarded as a list of operations which take place on the database which may be either committed or discarded as a single piece of work, depending on the outcome of the transaction. When a transaction is in progress, the database system keeps a record of all operations which modify the contents of a database, and it is possible to commit these changes to the database if everything goes according to plan, or to reverse the actions and leave the database untouched if something goes wrong. Transactions may only be used (explicitly) within an SQL script, although they are used implicitly within PERFORM.

Sometimes it is necessary to make changes to two tables such that if either change fails, the database should be left unchanged; one change should not succeed and the other fail. For example, in the **Cars** database, when a company record is deleted, the corresponding records in the **Models** table must also be deleted:

```
DELETE FROM Company WHERE Companies = 13;
DELETE FROM Models WHERE Maker     = 13;
```

If the first delete fails, the second will not be executed, so there is no problem. However, if the first succeeds but the second fails, the database will be left inconsistent; there will be some models made by a non-existent manufacturer.

To prevent this happening, INFORMIX-SQL provides transactions. A transaction is a unit of work which either succeeds entirely or fails entirely:

```
BEGIN WORK;      ( Start the transaction )
DELETE FROM Company WHERE Company     = 13;
DELETE FROM Models WHERE Maker        = 13;
COMMIT WORK;     ( Successful termination )
```

If either delete fails, the transaction can be terminated abnormally by ROLLBACK WORK; if the program terminates without explicitly committing a transaction, it is rolled back anyway.

15.4.1 Creating a transaction log

Standard Engine. Before transactions can be used, the database must have a transaction log. There are two ways of creating this, only one of which can be recommended. The non-recommended way is to create the database with a log:

```
CREATE DATABASE Cars WITH LOG IN "/usr/spool/dblog/cars.log";
```

This cannot really be recommended because it means that every table that is created and indexed will be recorded in the transaction log, which will grow very fast as a result. Also, operations like building a table cannot be included in a transaction, so it gives no advantages while the database is built – indeed, it will slow things down slightly and use a lot of space on the file system which contains the transaction log.

With versions 1.10 and 2.00, when you created a database using the menu system, you were asked whether you wanted to have a transaction log on the database, and if you said 'yes', the database was created using the WITH LOG IN notation. With version 2.10, this question is not asked – to add transactions to the database, you have to use the alternative method of adding a transaction log.

The recommended way of creating a transaction log, and the way of changing the name of the transaction log file, is to use:

```
START DATABASE Cars WITH LOG IN "/usr/spool/dblog/cars.log2";
```

The file must not exist and will be created empty, and all subsequent changes to the database will be recorded in this file. The START DATABASE statement will fail if anybody else is using the database when the statement is executed, and may only be executed by a DBA. Note that a START DATABASE statement makes the named database the current database.

It is not, regrettably, possible to specify a device such as a tape streamer as the transaction log file without some jiggery-pokery. The trick required to achieve this is to start the transaction log on the name of a non-existent file, to remove that file, and then to create (or link) the required device with the same name as the transaction log. The only thing to watch is that there are no transactions in progress while this process is going on.

15.4.2 What a transaction log does

When there is a transaction log present, all changes, whether in an explicit transaction or not, are recorded in the log. Any statement not inside a transaction is treated as a singleton transaction, as if there were a BEGIN WORK before it and either a COMMIT WORK after it (if it succeeded) or a ROLLBACK WORK (if it failed).

Because the transaction log records all the changes made to the database, it can be a powerful tool for helping with back-ups, as well as helping to maintain the integrity of the database by ensuring that either all or none of the changes of a related group are made. However, back-ups are the subject of a later section.

It must be pointed out that if all the changes made to the database are also being recorded separately on the transaction log, the database system will have to do more work for every operation which changes the database. This means that the database will slow down slightly. This is not normally a concern because of the advantages of a transaction log – the database can be kept in a state of referential integrity by making sets of DELETE (or INSERT or UPDATE) operations, and the database can be restored more easily in the event of a system failure.

If you are using INFORMIX-ONLINE or INFORMIX-TURBO, there will always be a transaction log on the database, but this will not be kept in a file – it is part of the database system itself. The full details of log handling in these systems is not described in this book.

15.4.3 Stopping a transaction log

Standard Engine.   Sometimes it is desirable (necessary) to stop using a transaction log. There are many reasons for this, but the most likely reasons are either that the log is no longer required, or because some large-scale changes are to be made and the log will grow too large if it is kept running. The only way to stop the log is to be a DBA and to execute the following statements:

```
DATABASE Cars EXCLUSIVE;
DELETE FROM Systables WHERE Tabtype = "L";
CLOSE DATABASE;
```

An alternative, equivalent condition is 'Tabname = "syslog"'. You should be very careful if you stop the log temporarily. The database should probably be backed up immediately before the log is stopped, and probably after the major changes are complete and just before the log is restarted. This technique works in version 4.00 as well, provided that the user who tries to delete the record is informix. If any other user tries to do it, even the person who created the database, the system will respond with error 274 'No DELETE permission'.

15.4.4 Differences between different versions of INFORMIX-SQL

There are, regrettably, some small but important differences between the different versions of ISQL in the behaviour of locks when there is a transaction log on the database. With version 2.00 and earlier, table locks could be applied to a table outside a transaction and they remained in force until they were explicitly released or the program finished. With version 2.10 and later, locks can only be applied inside a transaction and are automatically released when the transaction terminates – whether it terminates with a COMMIT WORK or a ROLLBACK WORK (which could be either implicit or explicit).

15.5 Audit trails

Standard Engine.   An audit trail is in some ways similar to a transaction log, but is a less powerful concept in at least two ways: it applies to a single table, and there is no concept of committing or rolling back changes. Like a transaction log, an audit trail can be used as a back-up technique – it is possible to restore a table from a back-up and then recover it using the audit trail. On a database consisting of many tables, this could take some time. Audit trails have been available in both version 1.10 and version 2.10, but were not part of version 2.00.

An audit trail is simply a list of all the changes made to a table. The audit trail file contains date, time and user ID information, as well as before and after images of the record changed. This structure is documented in the C-ISAM reference manual, but not in the ISQL manuals.

The advantage of an audit trail over a transaction log is that it only slows down updates to one table, instead of every table. It also grows less quickly than a transaction log. It is permissible, but foolish, to have an audit trail on every table, and even a transaction log as well, but that would make the database very much slower than with just the transaction log, which would be just as effective. Generally, though, audit trails are used in the absence of a transaction log to keep a back-up of the most critical (fastest changing) tables, leaving the other tables to be handled through the normal back-up procedures.

The three SQL statements to manipulate audit trails are:

```
CREATE AUDIT FOR Sales IN "/sphinx/john/cars.ext/sales.aud";
RECOVER TABLE Sales;
DROP AUDIT FOR Sales;
```

The CREATE AUDIT statement will create a new audit trail file. If the audit trail file name is the same as the existing one, nothing happens; if the name differs, an error is generated. (Unlike a transaction log, to change the name of an audit file, it must first be dropped and then restarted in the new audit file.) A back-up copy of the database should be made as soon as all the audit trails have been created, and before the first changes are made to the database.

If the table does get corrupted, it can be restored by carrying out the following actions:

1. Copying the file off the back-up.
2. Running RECOVER TABLE.
3. Running DROP AUDIT.
4. Running CREATE AUDIT to start the new audit trail.

If possible, the audit trail file should be located on a different device from that which holds the data, so that a hardware failure on one device does not damage the data on the other.

15.6 Locking

INFORMIX-SQL automatically locks rows of data during an INSERT, DELETE or UPDATE operation. If there is a transaction in progress, the locks remain in force until the COMMIT WORK or ROLLBACK WORK statement is executed. PERFORM also automatically locks a row of data when the user is updating it.

Sometimes the changes to be made are so large that it is necessary to stop all other users using the table until a sequence of changes are complete; at other times it is necessary to stop other people making changes while a sequence of changes are made, but it does not matter if the other people see the data at the same time; and sometimes it is just necessary to stop others changing the table while a particular set of checks are made. In these cases, the whole table must be locked, either in EXCLUSIVE mode (no one else can access the table) or in SHARE mode (other people can read the table but only the locking process can make changes to the table). When the lock is no longer required, it can be removed by unlocking the table; simply stopping the program also releases the lock. Any attempt to lock a table already locked by another user will fail. The statements are illustrated by:

```
LOCK TABLE Sales IN EXCLUSIVE MODE;
LOCK TABLE Stock IN SHARE MODE;
    ...
UNLOCK TABLE Stock;
UNLOCK TABLE Sales;
```

In versions 1.10 and 2.00, locks could be applied inside or outside a transaction. With version 2.10 and later, if there is a transaction log on the database, locks can only be applied inside a transaction, and they are automatically released by both COMMIT WORK and ROLLBACK WORK. The UNLOCK TABLE statement is not permitted in a transaction. In versions 1.10 and 2.00, if an UPDATE or DELETE statement encountered a row locked by some other user's UPDATE (say), the statement automatically failed. With version 2.10 and later, there is an option which makes the program wait for the row lock to be released:

```
SET LOCK MODE TO WAIT;
```

The only problem is that the program will wait until the row is released, and if the person who locked it has gone to lunch and left it locked, the program will wait until the person gets back and releases the row. Waiting for locked rows should be considered carefully before it is used.

15.7 Database back-ups

This whole section on back-ups only applies to INFORMIX-SE. The mechanisms for handling both INFORMIX-TURBO and INFORMIX-ONLINE are completely different and are not discussed in this book.

Standard Engine.   Both audit trails and transactions affect system performance and storage since extra files have to be opened and maintained, and both are also dependent on the quality of back-up routines undertaken. Back-ups should be made on a regular basis, at least once a day on rapidly changing databases. The time taken to run a back-up procedure is negligible compared to the time taken to recover from a disaster if no recent copy of the database exists.

There are approximately as many different ways of backing up a database as there are database administrators organizing the back-ups. The strategies for handling back-ups vary depending on:

- whether there is a transaction log on the database;
- whether the database is too big to fit on one cartridge tape (or floppy disk);

- what other back-ups are performed on the system;
- how rapidly the data changes.

Thus, this section can only offer guidelines, not an exact recipe for back-ups.

The crucial thing with back-ups – any back-ups – is to periodically test whether they work. That is, as part of the development of a database, the back-up strategy should be defined and actually tested, long before the system goes 'live'. The test should involve the following steps:

1. Perform a normal back-up.
2. Make a second, extremely carefully made back-up just in case something went wrong with the routine back-up.
3. Deliberately destroy the database (simply renaming it may be enough, if there is disk capacity to spare).
4. Recover the system from the routine back-ups using the chosen strategy.
5. Check the recovered system thoroughly.

If everything went well, you can sleep more easily, provided the back-up media are stored safely in a fire-proof safe, or off-site somewhere. If anything failed, the problem must be rectified and a new test made; the original system can be restored either by renaming the renamed database or from that extra carefully made back-up, and the test must be repeated. And after the initial test works, the test should be repeated periodically, even when the system has gone live, because there is nothing more frustrating than to have back-ups, to need to use them and to find that they cannot be used.

15.7.1 Back-ups without a transaction log

If there is no transaction log (and no audit trails), there is no choice but to back-up the entire database. The frequency with which this should be done will be determined by at least three factors:

1. The speed with which the database changes.
2. The importance of the database.
3. The ease of doing the back-up.

If the database is crucial to the operation of the company, it will be backed up more frequently than a less crucial one. However, if the database does not change (it is used for reference – SELECT – only), it only needs to be backed up once; if it changes substantially each day, it may need to be backed up daily. No one should be changing the database while it is backed up, which means that it could be inconvenient to do the back-up during the day. If the back-up will fit on to one tape (or one floppy), the back-up can be run automatically overnight. If it needs several floppies, the back-up must be done manually.

Although there is no such thing as a typical database, a database used as an important part of a business would be backed up daily on to a cycle of at least three sets of back-up media. If it does not change much, or only one or two tables change, it may be possible to do a weekly complete back-up and a daily incremental back-up of just those tables which have changed.

15.7.2 Back-ups with a transaction log

Using a transaction log on a database not only provides a method of ensuring that related changes are made but also provides a tool for backing up a database. After all, a transaction log records every change made to the database, so if it can be used to redo all the changes, only the log need be backed up. Of course, there *is* provision for recovering a database from a transaction log, so the back-up process can be simplified somewhat.

The basic technique for backing up a database with a transaction log is:

1. Stop anyone using the database.
2. Back up the entire database, except for the transaction log.
3. Empty the transaction log.
4. Release the database for use again.
5. Back up the transaction log daily until the next complete back-up.
6. Optionally, empty the transaction log after it is backed up.

The first back-up of the database should be made immediately after the log is started. On UNIX, it is sufficient to run the command:

```
$ cat /dev/null >/usr/spool/dblog/cars.log
```

to empty the log file after each full back-up. Step 6 is optional; emptying the transaction log each time it is backed up means that the log is smaller but makes the restoration process harder.

15.7.3 Restoring a database using a transaction log

The exact details of how to restore a database after a failure depend on the type of failure and on the type of back-up used. There are two types of failure to consider:

1. When the database is damaged but the log is intact.
2. When both the database and the log are damaged (or when there is no log).

There are also three back-up techniques to consider:

a. No transaction log.
b. Transaction log allowed to grow indefinitely.
c. Transaction log truncated at each back-up.

By definition, there is no case 1a to consider. With no transaction log (case 2a), the only method of restoring the database is to copy the entire database back on to the main disk system from the latest complete back-up. All the changes made since that back-up will be lost permanently.

When the database is damaged but the log is intact and is allowed to grow indefinitely (case 1b), the restoration process simply involves copying the entire database on to the main disk from the latest complete back-up and then bringing the database up to date using the log. The command to do this is:

```
ROLLFORWARD DATABASE Cars;
```

Rolling the database forward means that every completed transaction up to the point where the database failed is restored. Once the restoration is complete, the database must be started to a new log file; this avoids problems with the complete transactions on the log file. Note that only transactions which were not complete when the database failed are lost.

If the transaction log is truncated every time it is backed up (case 1c), the restoration process is more fiddly. After the database has been restored from the last complete back-up, carefully rename the current log. Then restore each incremental back-up of the log in turn and roll the database forward before doing the next. Finally, rename the log that was current when the database failed and roll the database forward again, and then start the database to a new log file.

If both the database and the log are damaged (cases 2b and 2c), the database must be restored from the back-up and rolled forward to the state when the last transaction log back-up was made. Any changes made after the last back-up of the transaction log are lost. The only difference is the number of times the database is rolled forward.

Whenever a back-up is made, the fact should be recorded. Ideally, the data should be stored in a database as well as on paper; it is very frustrating to have a complete set of back-ups that are unusable because the only information about what is on each back-up has been destroyed along with the other data on the machine. The information stored about the back-up should include:

- What was backed up.
- When it was done – date and time.
- Who did it.
- Which particular tape (or floppy) was used.
- Where the tape was stored.

There are two final points to be made about transaction logs. Whenever possible, the log file should be on a different UNIX file system from the database. If the database fails because of lack of space on the device, the transaction log will also fail if it is on the same file system, whereas if the log is on a different file system, it is unlikely that both will fail simultaneously. Transaction logs can grow fast – very fast if the database is active. The transaction log must be truncated periodically.

15.8 MODE ANSI databases

Version 4.00. The ANSI standard has a number of requirements which are not completely compatible with previous versions of Informix. Informix has introduced

MODE ANSI databases which conform to the standard, but there are some differences in the behaviour of the database as a result. The major differences are:

1. The database must have transactions.
2. The BEGIN WORK statement should not be used.
3. The COMMIT WORK statement must be used whenever any changes are made.
4. All database objects not owned by the user must have the owner's name prefixed to the object.

However, for people who wish to use them, it is possible to specify that a database should operate in ANSI mode. Once a database is operating in ANSI mode, there is no way of converting it to non-ANSI mode, other than using **dbexport** and **dbimport** to rebuild it.

There are two main ways of making a database operate in ANSI mode: one uses CREATE DATABASE with the option MODE ANSI tagged on (after the WITH LOG IN clause if using INFORMIX-SE); the other uses START DATABASE with the same option. You can also create a MODE ANSI database with **dbimport**.

```
CREATE DATABASE Cars
    WITH LOG IN "/usr/spool/logs/cars.log"
    MODE ANSI;
START DATABASE Cars
    WITH LOG IN "/usr/spool/logs/cars2.log"
    MODE ANSI;
```

All MODE ANSI databases have a transaction log, and all operations on the database are implicitly within a transaction; there are no singleton transactions as there are with non-ANSI databases. This will cause problems for people who are used to working with the SQL interface as it will be very easy to forget to commit all the changes made. If the data changes are not explicitly committed, they will be implicitly rolled back. However, most of the commands which alter the database tables and privileges cannot be rolled back. To protect users from this, ISQL detects if there is an incomplete transaction outstanding when you exit from the program and asks you to commit or rollback the work.

With a MODE ANSI database, you should not use the BEGIN WORK statement; it is not part of the ANSI standard. If you do use BEGIN WORK, you may only use it immediately after one of the statements CREATE DATABASE, DATABASE, START DATABASE, COMMIT WORK or ROLLBACK WORK; if it is used anywhere else, it causes an error.

The final major change with MODE ANSI databases is that all objects not owned by the user have to be prefixed by the owner's name; this includes, in particular, the system tables. For example, the following SELECT statement is correct:

```
SELECT Tabname
    FROM Informix.Systables
    WHERE Tabid >= 100;
```

If the 'Informix.' prefix was omitted, you would obtain a message that 'john.systables' was not a table in the database, assuming you were logged in as john. There is a variant on this notation where the user name is enclosed in quotes.

This preserves the case of the user name and therefore allows it to include capital letters, although all user names on UNIX are conventionally written in lower-case letters.

```
SELECT Tabname
    FROM "informix".Systables
    WHERE Tabid >= 100;
```

Because of this, if a database is to be a MODE ANSI database, all the tables should be created using CREATE SCHEMA statements. A new user should be created for the sole purpose of being the main DBA for the database. All the CREATE SCHEMA statements should specify this user in the AUTHORIZATION clause. Alternatively, a DBA can create tables on behalf of someone else using the notation:

```
CREATE TABLE ABC.Newtable
(
        ...
);

CREATE UNIQUE INDEX ABC.Pk_newtable ON ABC.Newtable(...);
```

Any SQL statements which may be executed by anyone other than the special DBA login (which means nearly everything) must have the user name prefix. (Note also that two different users can both have a table called by the same name, something which was impossible previously.) The *name.table* notation may also be used in a non-ANSI database, and the name must be correct, but its use is not mandatory. Both aliases (see Chapter 12) and synonyms (see Chapter 14) can be used to simplify complex statements.

To find out when you are using a non-ANSI construct in your work, you can set the environment variable DBANSIWARN:

```
DBANSIWARN=""; export DBANSIWARN
```

If you are using SQL, you will get a warning flashed up on the bottom of the screen: 'Warning: this statement is not compatible with ANSI standard SQL syntax'. If you use such a statement in a report, you will get a warning at compile time, but not at run-time. If you are using the ISQL menus to compile the report, the compilation will be deemed to fail even though there is only a warning issued; you can save the report even though there was an error, but you will also need to compile the report from the command line using **saceprep**.

PERFORM does not produce any warning on a MODE ANSI database. However, the syntax for specifying a table which has an owner as well as a table name is distinctly different from what is used normally in a form. An alias is specified as shown below:

```
TABLES
    tab1 = abc.companies
    tab2 = abc.models
END
```

The alias names are *tab1* and *tab2*; the owner of the tables is user abc. The names *tab1* and *tab2* are used in the ATTRIBUTES section of the form. As before, the END keyword is optional. There is no reason why the aliases should not be the same as the basic name of the table, as in:

```
TABLES
      companies = abc.companies
      models    = abc.models
END
```

This technique simplifies the form on two counts: first, it is intuitively obvious which table the alias is referring to; and second, the names in the ATTRIBUTES section of the generated form do not need changing.

The default permissions on a table in a MODE ANSI database are that only the owner has any privileges at all. This contrasts with a non-ANSI database where the default permissions grant all privileges to PUBLIC.

15.9 Summary

This chapter has discussed a variety of techniques for maintaining the data in a database. It started with mechanisms to unload bulk data from the database, and to load unloaded data back into the database. It then looked at transaction logs, which allow you to group several disjoint operations into one unit of work which either succeeds or fails as a unit. This was followed by a description of audit trails, a simpler, less powerful alternative to a transaction log, and a discussion of the techniques which can be used to back up a database. The final section discussed the MODE ANSI databases available with version 4.00, including the alias facility provided by PERFORM for working on MODE ANSI databases.

Miscellaneous aspects of INFORMIX-SQL

This chapter covers miscellaneous aspects of INFORMIX-SQL which did not have a convenient home in another chapter. In particular, it covers all the environment variables used by INFORMIX-SQL, the command-line interface to INFORMIX-SQL, the installation procedure, the other tools provided with INFORMIX-SQL, a summary of the system tables and a brief summary of the different versions of INFORMIX-SQL.

16.1 Environment variables

The four environment variables INFORMIXDIR, PATH, TERM and TERMCAP were introduced in Chapter 3. The environment variable DBDATE was introduced in Chapter 8, and DBMONEY was introduced in Chapter 9. There are a number of others which also affect the behaviour of Informix products. For completeness, they are all described here.

16.1.1 INFORMIXDIR

The Informix programs need to know where to look for other Informix programs, and also for the message files and other files. All the materials distributed with INFORMIX-SQL (or any other members of the Informix family) are stored in a set of sub-directories under one parent directory. Unless it is told otherwise, INFORMIX-SQL assumes that the parent directory is /usr/informix on UNIX. If the product has been installed somewhere else (eg /sphinx/informix), then INFORMIX-SQL *must* be told by setting the environment variable INFORMIXDIR so that it contains the name of the parent directory where the Informix product is installed, thus:

```
INFORMIXDIR=/sphinx/informix; export INFORMIXDIR
```

Note: if INFORMIX-SQL was installed in the default location, INFORMIXDIR does not have to be set. However, it generally makes it easier to set other environment variables if it is always set. This also means that new versions of the software can be installed and used separately from the old version. The best place to set this is in /etc/profile for Bourne and Korn shells on UNIX.

16.1.2 PATH

The command interpreter or shell must know where to look for the Informix commands. All the commands are stored in $INFORMIXDIR/bin (eg /sphinx/informix/bin), so the shell must be told to look in that directory too by adding the directory to the path, or the list of places where the shell looks for commands. A simple and reliable way to do that is:

```
PATH=$PATH:${INFORMIXDIR:-/usr/informix}/bin
export PATH
```

This simply says add $INFORMIXDIR/bin to the path, unless INFORMIXDIR is not set or is a null string, in which case, add /usr/informix/bin to the path.

16.1.3 INFORMIXTERM

If you have a version of INFORMIX-SQL prior to version 4.00, INFORMIX-SQL will always use the **termcap** system to control the terminal. For compatibility reasons, version 4.00 of INFORMIX-SQL will also assume that you wish to use the **termcap** system to control the terminal unless you tell it otherwise. If you wish it to use **terminfo** instead, you should set the environment variable INFORMIXTERM:

```
INFORMIXTERM=terminfo; export INFORMIXTERM
```

You can explicitly indicate that you wish to use **termcap** by setting:

```
INFORMIXTERM=termcap; export INFORMIXTERM
```

16.1.4 TERM

In common with most UNIX-based products, INFORMIX-SQL will work with almost any type of terminal, provided that it is told which terminal you are using and which control sequences clear the screen, move the cursor, change into reverse video, and so on. For INFORMIX-SQL to work, you must set TERM to an appropriate value. For example, if you are using a Wyse 50 terminal, set the TERM variable using:

```
TERM=wy50; export TERM
```

INFORMIX-SQL will let you know if it cannot find a description for your terminal. If you have any difficulty, consult your system administrator; if you are the system administrator, consult your operating system manuals, terminal manuals, Strang (1989) or your supplier.

16.1.5 TERMCAP

If you are using the **termcap** system, Informix will look for the terminal capability information in the file /etc/termcap. If that file does not exist, you should set another environment variable called TERMCAP:

```
TERMCAP=$INFORMIXDIR/etc/termcap; export TERMCAP
```

This file is distributed with the Informix products and contains the capabilities for the most common types of terminal. When it finds the **termcap** file, INFORMIX-SQL uses TERM to find the entry describing the terminal you are using.

16.1.6 TERMINFO

Similarly, if you are using the **terminfo** system, Informix will, by default, look for the terminal capability information in a file in a directory under the directory /usr/lib/terminfo. The directory name is a single letter, the first character of the value of the environment variable TERM. The name of the file is the full value of TERM. Thus, if TERM is set to wy50, the **terminfo** data will be found in /usr/lib/terminfo/w/wy50. Again, this information will sometimes be stored somewhere else, and in that case you would have to set another environment variable to tell Informix where to look:

```
TERMINFO=/usr/john/terminfo; export TERMINFO
```

16.1.7 DBDATE

The Americans interpret a date such as '06/09/91' as 9 June 1991. In the UK and Europe, the same value would be interpreted as 6 September 1991. INFORMIX-SQL can be told how to interpret dates and how to format them by default by setting the environment variable DBDATE. The default value is:

```
DBDATE="mdy2/"; export DBDATE
```

This indicates that the parts of a date are entered in the order month, day, year, and that dates should be displayed with a two-digit year and the separator should be '/'.
  A typical value for use in European countries would be:

```
DBDATE="dmy4/"; export DBDATE
```

This means that data should be entered and displayed in the order day, month, year (much more logical), and that the year should be displayed with four digits. There is another possible way of displaying dates which has two merits: (1) it is unambiguous, even shortly after the turn of the century, and (2) it can be sorted into date order using a simple alpha-numeric sort. The format is:

```
DBDATE="y4md-"; export DBDATE
```

This would print 6 September 1991 as '1991-09-06'. It is really useful when it comes to handling dates such as 1 February 2003 which would be printed as shown in Table 16.1.

DBDATE	Printed value
mdy2/	02/01/03
dmy2/	01/02/03
dmy4/	01/02/2003
mdy4/	02/01/2003
y4md-	2003-02-01

Table 16.1 DBDATE printing 1 February 2003

16.1.8 DBMONEY

Since INFORMIX-SQL is an American product, the default currency units are dollars '\$', and the default decimal indicator is the decimal point '.'. If this is not the currency you work in, you can set the environment variable DBMONEY to specify the currency units and decimal indicator. If you were working in Germany, this would be set as:

```
DBMONEY=",DM"; export DBMONEY
```

This indicates that the currency symbol preceding the money value is 'DM' for Deutschmarks and the decimal indicator is ',', so PERFORM would display a value of 12 000 Deutschmarks on the screen as:

```
12.000,00DM
```

Unfortunately, ACE does not understand DBMONEY as well as PERFORM, and it ignores a trailing currency symbol when it is printing with the PRINT USING format. Thus, in practice, the Germans would have to put up with using:

```
DBMONEY="DM,"; export DBMONEY
```

which would work in both PERFORM and ACE. In the UK, the normal setting is shown below, together with the appearance of £12 000:

```
DBMONEY="£."; export DBMONEY
£12,000.00
```

16.1.9 DBPATH

The environment variable DBPATH tells INFORMIX-SQL where to look for databases, forms, reports and SQL scripts. It is analogous to PATH in that it is an ordered, colon-separated list of directories to be searched. In version 2.00, the current directory was always searched first, then the directories on DBPATH. With version 2.10, the current directory is not searched unless it is listed in DBPATH; if there are two colons next to each other, or there is a leading or trailing colon, the current directory is searched at that point. Alternatively, if the name '.' appears between colons, the current directory is searched at that point. If no value is specified for DBPATH, only the current directory is searched.

The ISQL program uses DBPATH in two different ways, depending on whether there is a current database or not. If there is a current database, ISQL searches in the current directory and in the directory containing the database directory, and nowhere else. If there is no current database (that is, if there is no database name shown on the dashed line of the menus), all the directories on DBPATH are searched. If there were two form files with the same name in two directories listed in $DBPATH, the one in the first-named directory would be used in preference to the other; to run the second form, the full path name would have to be specified.

16.1.10 DBPRINT

When a report is sent to the printer, the printer to be used is specified by DBPRINT. On UNIX System V, the default value is 'lp -s'; on DOS, it is 'lpt1'. By setting this environment variable, the destination can be changed. For example, to send the output to a printer called 'beta' with the option '-onb', change it to:

```
DBPRINT="lp -s -dbeta -onb"; export DBPRINT
```

16.1.11 DBEDIT

If DBEDIT is set, the ISQL programs will not ask which editor you want to use but will simply run the editor specified in DBEDIT. Any editor may be used provided it produces 'flat ASCII' files – that is, files without embedded control sequences – and provided that it expects the name of its file as an argument on the command line. You could probably use **emacs**, **Uniplex** or **Wordstar** in non-document mode, if it takes your fancy. If you want to use **vi** without being asked about it, include the following in your .profile:

```
DBEDIT=vi; export DBEDIT
```

16.1.12 DBTEMP

By default on UNIX, temporary files are created in the /tmp directory. If, as on this machine, there is a separate mounted file system on /usr/tmp for temporary files, you will want to set DBTEMP so that temporary files are created there:

```
DBTEMP=${TMPDIR:-/tmp}; export DBTEMP
```

16.1.13 DBDELIMITER

When you unload data, a '|' character is used to separate the fields in each line unless DBDELIMITER is set to a different value. If you are importing data produced from a different database management system, you may well need to set this. Normally though, it can be forgotten.

16.1.14 DBMENU

DBMENU governs which user menu is run when you choose the **User-Menu** option. By default, its value is assumed to be:

```
DBMENU=main; export DBMENU
```

To run a different user menu, either invoke ISQL with the appropriate options or set DBMENU.

16.1.15 DBANSIWARN

As discussed in Section 15.8, this variable should be set if the database you are working with is a MODE ANSI database and you need to know when a non-ANSI construct is used. The value it is set to does not matter.

```
DBANSIWARN=""; export DBANSIWARN
```

16.1.16 DBLANG

This variable is set to allow you to have the error messages specified in several different languages on one machine. It specifies the name of a directory under $INFORMIXDIR where the message files are to be found. The default value is:

```
DBLANG=msg; export DBLANG
```

Note that $INFORMIXDIR is used as a prefix to the supplied value.

16.1.17 SQLEXEC

This environment variable is the way in which you control which database engine INFORMIX-SQL should use. You only need to set this if you have both INFORMIX-SE and INFORMIX-ONLINE (or INFORMIX-SE and INFORMIX-TURBO) installed on the system. If you wish to use INFORMIX-ONLINE, SQLEXEC does not have to be set at all; if you wish to use INFORMIX-SE, it must be set to the full path name of INFORMIX-SE, which means:

```
SQLEXEC=$INFORMIXDIR/lib/sqlexec; export SQLEXEC
```

If you wish, you may set it explicitly to use either INFORMIX-TURBO or INFORMIX-ONLINE. There is, in principle, no reason why you should not set it to any other program which uses the same interface – it reads its input from standard input and replies on standard output – but no other programs understand the commands, so INFORMIX-SQL will not work.

16.2 Command-line interface to INFORMIX-SQL

The main way of using INFORMIX-SQL is to type 'isql' to the command prompt and run the complete menu system. Some of the alternative methods have been mentioned in passing, but this section tries to assemble all the options together with as little repetition as possible. The interface has been changed, improved considerably, with different releases of INFORMIX-SQL.

16.2.1 Invoking the complete menu system

The simplest method of running ISQL is to type:

```
$ isql
```

It is frequently useful to be able to pre-select the database which is to be used, and this would be done by typing:

```
$ isql cars
```

While the copyright menu is on display, ISQL opens the database instead of just doing nothing. This can save a few seconds during start-up, especially since it means that ISQL will not subsequently ask you which database you wish to work with.

16.2.2 Using ISQL without any menus

ISQL has a mode of operation which does not use the full-screen facilities at all. In this mode, ISQL reads SQL commands from a file (or the keyboard) and executes each one in turn, echoing a success/failure message as each command is executed (or not). This mode is invoked by specifying a database and a script file. The database is either the real name of a database or a dummy argument '–' indicating that the database will be selected by the script. The script is specified as the name of a file which may have '.sql' as the suffix: if this suffix is present, it uses the file named, otherwise it appends '.sql' to the end of the file name given and uses that. If the program should read its standard input, it can be given another dummy argument '–'. Thus, all the following command lines will run ISQL in this mode:

```
$ isql cars dumpall
$ isql cars dumpall.sql
$ isql cars -
$ isql - mkcars.sql
$ isql - -
```

When the input is coming from the keyboard, this mode uses a '>' character as a prompt. It does not use a secondary prompt to indicate that it is waiting for the rest

Flag	Sub-menu
-f	**Form**
-r	**Report**
-t	**Table**
-d	**Database**
-u	**User-Menu**
-q	**Query-Language** (SQL)

Table 16.2 One-letter flags for ISQL

of the command. All SQL commands must end with a semicolon – ISQL does not act until it gets the semicolon. It prints its response on the *stderr* channel (defaulting to your screen), but the output from SELECT statements (including the headings) goes to *stdout*. The prompts are sent to *stdout* too.

There is no editing facility for correcting mistyped commands (or, if there is, I have not found it, and it is not documented anywhere), but there is one extremely useful facility available on UNIX, namely the shell escape. When '!' is typed as the first non-blank character of a command, what follows is interpreted as a shell command. This facility is available whether the command comes from the keyboard or a file. It means that a script such as mkcars.sql (which creates the complete **Cars** database) can document which table it is creating by including lines such as:

```
! echo "Creating table Customers."
```

As it is run, the script echoes messages which help to identify which statement caused the trouble if any statement fails.

```
Creating table Customers.

Table created.

Index created.

Index created.

Index created.
```

16.2.3 Invoking one of the ISQL sub-menus

It is possible to invoke any of the first-level sub-menus by starting ISQL with (optionally) the name of the database and a flag argument indicating the menu as shown in Table 16.2. In each case, ISQL will run as though the only facilities available are those which are part of the sub-menu specified. When you exit from the sub-menu, ISQL terminates too. The database to be worked with can be specified in front of the flag argument. Additionally, the flag '-s' (for *silent*) can be used to suppress unnecessary messages such as the start-up screen. This should precede the database name. Thus to run the **Form** menu on the **Cars** database silently, the following

Option	Sub-menu					
	Form	**Report**	**Query-Language**	**Table**	**Database**	**User-Menu**
Run	-fr	-rr	-qr	–	–	-ur
Modify	-fm	-rm	-qm	–	–	-um
Generate	-fg	-rg	–	–	–	–
New	-fn	-rn	-qn	–	–	–
Compile	-fc	-rc	–	–	–	–
Drop	-fd	-rd	-qd	-td	-dd	–
Use-Editor	–	–	-qu	–	–	–
Choose	–	–	-qc	–	–	–
Info	–	–	-qi	-ti	–	–
Save	–	–	-qs	–	–	–
Output	–	–	-qo	–	–	–
Create	–	–	–	-tc	-dc	–
Alter	–	–	–	-ta	–	–

Table 16.3 Two-letter flags for ISQL

command should be used:

```
$ isql -s cars -f
```

Changing this to:

```
$ isql cars -s -f
```

does not suppress the start-up screen and gives the full top-level menu.

16.2.4 Invoking one option of a sub-menu

Each of the one-letter flags listed in Table 16.2 can be supplemented by another letter to indicate which option(s) should be executed. The supplemental letters must be part of the flag argument and the acceptable letters are the initial letters of the options in the sub-menu. This gives the set of options shown in Table 16.3.

After the two-letter flag, the name of the object to be operated on can be specified in the normal way (ie without any extension). Thus, to generate a form called 'addcust', the command line could be either of these alternatives:

```
$ isql -s cars -fg addcust
$ isql cars -fg addcust
```

If the form name or database name was omitted, they would be prompted for, giving a minimal command line of:

```
$ isql -fg
```

If a command was given more than two letters, the options would be executed in turn. Thus, to modify and compile the form 'addcust' in one operation, the following command could be used:

```
$ isql -s cars -fmc addcust
```

However, not all such combinations work; for example, '-fgmcr' (which should generate, modify, compile and run the form addcust) only generated the form, though if the generate phase was interrupted, the modify phase was executed.

All this only applies to INFORMIX-SQL version 2.10 and later; the system was totally different (and undocumented) in version 2.00. However, as an instance of the difference, the '-q' option ran ISQL quietly and '-r' ran the **Query-Language** option.

Version 4.00. The '-q' and '-r' options can both also have the '-ansi' flag specified, in which case non-ANSI features will produce a warning, even if the environment variable DBANSIWARN is not set. (If the environment variable is set, the warnings will appear whether or not the '-ansi' option is used.)

16.3 Running forms and reports

Both forms and reports can be compiled or run direct from the UNIX command line without using ISQL and the options just outlined.

16.3.1 Running sformbld

The form compiler can be run direct from the command line. It has an orthodox, UNIX-style set of flags. There are three main options: '-s' to run silently, '-v' to run a verification check and '-d' to generate a default form. The silent mode is too effective; it suppresses error messages that the form failed to compile. The verify mode checks that the field lengths of character fields (in particular) are consistent with the lengths of the corresponding fields in the database. If it finds any inconsistencies, it produces a usable form, but it also produces a '.err' file with the current field length and the database field length both stated. This is very useful since it allows you to adjust the character fields by exactly the right amount.

The '-d' option is only half-documented. Its existence is documented; the fact that the first argument after the flag is the base name of the form is documented; and the fact that if there are not enough arguments, it will ask for the missing information is documented. What is not documented is that the command can be used with sufficient arguments that no questions are asked and a form is generated. The full syntax for the '-d' option should be:

```
sformbld [-s] [-v] -d [form [database [table1 ...]]]
```

This means that if you specify the '-d' option, the first argument, if present, is the name of the form, the second argument (if present) is the name of the database, and the third and subsequent arguments (if present) are the names of the tables on which the form is to be generated.

With versions up to and including version 2.10.00, the exit status was totally unreliable; it was typically non-zero (a failure condition in UNIX shell) even when the form compiled correctly. With version 2.10.03, the exit status seems to be set correctly. With version 2.10.03, **sformbld** is a link to (alternative name for) **isql**.

Version 4.00. There are two additional options which can be specified: '−c' followed by a number for the number of columns in the form, and '−l' followed by a number for the number of lines in the form.

16.3.2 Running sperform

A form can be run directly by invoking **sperform**. There is only one option; with version 2.00 it was '−q' and with version 2.10.00 it is '−s', both of which suppressed the start-up message. In version 2.00 and earlier versions of INFORMIX-SQL, this was a genuine, separate program from **isql**. With version 2.10.00, it is a simple (essentially one-line) shell script which invokes 'isql −fr' followed by the other arguments from the command line. With version 2.10.03, **sperform** is a link to (alternative name for) **isql**.

16.3.3 Running saceprep

A report can be compiled from the command line, just as a form can. The compiler is **saceprep**, and it too has an orthodox, UNIX-style set of flags. It can be run with '−s' to make it run silently, and with '−o' followed (after a space) by the name of the directory where the output file (the '.arc' *or* the '.err' file) will be placed. These arguments are followed by the name of the report to be compiled, without the '.ace' extension. Once again, up to version 2.10.00, **saceprep** was a separate program from **isql**, but with version 2.10.03 it is a link to **isql**.

Version 4.00. The '−ansi' option can be used on the command line. As usual, it compiles the report and warnings are generated if the SELECT statements in it do not conform to the ANSI standard.

16.3.4 Running sacego

Once compiled, a report can be run from the command line, just as a form can. Unlike a form, it can be mandatory that a report is run from the command line, because if the DEFINE section defines PARAM variables, these must be supplied as arguments to the report command line. One of the options is the ubiquitous '−s' which means, as usual, silent mode.

The other option is '−d' followed (after a space) by the name of a database. This database overrides the database specified at the top of the report file. It is, at first sight, an improbable facility; the structure of a database is normally sufficiently unique that a report designed for one database will not work on any other. However, as an example of when this facility is useful, there are a number of accounts packages which use an INFORMIX-SQL database structure for storing the data for one company. In a holding company which has a number of subsidiary companies, there will normally be a separate database for each of the companies in the group (to keep the auditors happy), and these databases all contain the same tables. This means that if a report is generated to produce a useful summary of the state of one company, the same report could be used on the other company databases with only one change – the name of the database – provided that the name of the company was stored somewhere in the database. The '-d' option to **sacego** means that one compiled version of the report can be used for all the databases. The chances are that a shell script would be used to specify on which company the report should be run this time; there is no need to make a special case out of the occasions when the company specified with the '-d' flag is the same as the company on which the report should be run this time.

In version 2.00 and earlier versions of INFORMIX-SQL, this was a separate program from **isql**. With version 2.10.00, it is a simple (essentially one-line) shell script which invokes 'isql -rr' followed by the other arguments from the command line. With version 2.10.03, **sacego** is a link to **isql**.

16.4 Installation of INFORMIX-SQL

The installation procedure for INFORMIX-SQL is essentially straightforward and is a model which other applications would do well to follow. There are four main steps to the installation process after the software and manuals have arrived:

1. Decide which directory to install ISQL in.
2. Create user `informix` and group `informix`.
3. Copy the software off the distribution media into the chosen directory.
4. Run the `installsql` shell script.

The materials that should arrive when you buy ISQL are a set of two manuals (one for version 1.10), either a set of floppy disks or a cartridge tape, a set of installation instructions, a serial number and key, and probably a licence registration form. The licence for this should be read, filled in and returned. The serial number and key must be kept safe – if the system has to be re-installed (for example, because the hard disk suffered a head crash), the serial number and key will be needed to make ISQL usable.

Choosing a directory in which to install ISQL is simple: any directory could be used as long as there is about 2 MB of spare space on the system. The standard directory is `/usr/informix`, and this will be assumed throughout the example.

Creating user `informix` and group `informix` need only be done the first time you install INFORMIX-SQL. Create an entry in `/etc/password` for a user called `informix` and make sure that the password field is set to "`No login`". The user number should be distinct from that used by any other user. The group number should be the same as the group number of group `informix` in `/etc/group`. The home directory was chosen in step 1. The entry in `/etc/passwd` will look like this:

```
informix:No Login:1200:1200:Informix Database:/usr/informix:
```

To create a group `informix`, edit `/etc/group` and add a new line with a different group number from any other group. The group should not be listed anywhere in the password file, and the group number for user `informix` should be the same as the group number for group `informix` in `/etc/group`.

```
informix::1200:informix
```

The next step is to copy the software off the media on to the hard disk. The details of this step vary from machine to machine and the only thing in common is that (on UNIX) either **tar** or **cpio** is used. The distribution notes and the media itself should indicate which format to use and how to get the files off the media. However, you may have to discover the correct name of the device that should be used.

The final step is to run the shell script `installsql`. You must be logged in as a superuser, the current directory must be the directory which the data was copied into – `/usr/informix` in this example – and you should type:

```
# ./installsql
```

It will tell you that you should be a superuser and gives you a chance to stop if you are not. Then it will ask for the serial number. Type the number you were given carefully. There are no spaces, the letters must be in upper case and there are six digits. Then you will be asked for the key – type that carefully too: it only contains letters and the letters must be in upper case. After that, `installsql` makes sure that every file in the distribution has the correct owner (normally `informix`, except for the database engine – and, in versions 1.10 or 2.00, `sperform` – which is owned by `root`), that they belong to the correct group (`informix`) and that they have the correct permissions. The programs which must be branded with the serial number and key are branded. When this is over, the directory and all the files underneath are installed correctly. The system is ready for use.

After all this, you may wish to modify the system-wide profile (`/etc/profile` for systems using the Bourne shell) to set up the default database environment variables. The most important ones are `INFORMIXDIR` (especially if you did not install ISQL in `/usr/informix`) and `PATH` – you will need to add `$INFORMIXDIR/bin` to the list of directories searched to find commands. You may also want to set `DBDATE`, `DBMONEY`, `DBTEMP` and `DBPRINT`.

What can go wrong? Occasionally, the media sent is faulty; your supplier should provide a replacement free of charge. Occasionally, the serial number or key has been mistyped and the software will not run – it complains about an invalid key; again, your supplier should provide a replacement free of charge. The only other thing to be careful of is that you have the correct version of the operating system. Also note that some more recent versions of UNIX do not allow you to just edit `/etc/passwd` and `/etc/group` – you have to use a system tool, normally `sysadmsh`, to change the files.

If you are installing both INFORMIX-SE and INFORMIX-NET, you must install INFORMIX-NET second. Similarly, if you are installing both INFORMIX-ONLINE and INFORMIX-STAR, you must install INFORMIX-STAR second. If you are using version 4.00, you must install both INFORMIX-SQL and either INFORMIX-SE or INFORMIX-ONLINE as no database engine is supplied with INFORMIX-SQL version 4.00.

16.5 Supporting tools provided with INFORMIX-SQL

When you purchase INFORMIX-SQL, you not only receive the user interface programs; you also receive a number of supporting tools. Some of these are solely for use by INFORMIX-SQL internally – these are **mkdbsdir** and **changrp** which make a database directory and set group permissions respectively. These are not always used – it depends on the operating system and even the version of the operating system. The other tools are **dbschema, bcheck, sqlconv, dbupdate, dbimport, dbexport** and **dbload. dbimport, dbexport** and **dbload** were discussed fully in Chapter 15.

16.5.1 dbschema

This wonderful tool is supplied with INFORMIX-SQL version 2.10 and later. It can be used to print out the schema of an Informix database in the form of a series of CREATE TABLE, CREATE INDEX, GRANT and REVOKE statements. The resulting output could be used to recreate the database, or as a way of documenting the database.

The basic options are '-d' followed by the database name – this is the only mandatory option – and '-t' followed by a table name which means that **dbschema** only prints out the CREATE statements for that one table instead of for the whole database. There are three auxiliary options:

- -o which allows the user to specify the name of the file where the output should go, instead of going to standard output.
- -s which can be used to specify the name of the user for which the synonym statements will be created.
- -p which can be used to specify the name of the user for which the permissions statements will be generated.

Both the '-s' and '-p' options can take the specification 'all', in which case the synonyms and permissions for every user are printed.

The only problem with this command is that it produces a heading on the same output channel as the main output from the command. If the output is redirected to a file, both the heading and the main output are sent to the file, and the heading must be removed before the file can be used.

16.5.2 bcheck

bcheck is not really a database tool; it works on individual C-ISAM files, checking that the data structures stored internally are self-consistent. With early versions of C-ISAM, this tool was very important, but ever since version 2.00 of ISQL (and, as far as I am aware, version 1.10 as well), the relevant version of C-ISAM has been so robust that it is seldom necessary to use this tool in earnest.

This program has six options. The '-y' and '-n' options are mutually exclusive: '-y' answers 'yes' to any questions posed by **bcheck** and '-n' answers 'no'. It is normal to run it first with '-n' to find out whether the file is damaged and then with '-y' if the C-ISAM file has to be rebuilt, although in most cases it would be simpler to run it with '-y' first. The only time the distinction is important is if you have other ways of repairing the damage than by using **bcheck**. The other options can be used in combination: '-i' checks just the index file, rather than both the index file and the data file; '-l' lists the entries in B+ trees (for more information on B+ trees, you will have to acquire a C-ISAM manual, or read the literature on data structures); '-s' resizes the index file node size (another obscure operation which is seldom necessary in practice); and '-q' (for *quiet*) suppresses the printing of the program banner.

After any options, it expects the name of one or more C-ISAM files. It does not mind whether the name is given without any extension, or with either a '.dat' or a '.idx' extension. If it is given several names, it runs on each C-ISAM file in turn. If you wish to check a complete database, execute a command such as:

```
$ cd cars.dbs
$ bcheck -n *.idx | more
```

Standard Engine. There are two SQL commands which have not been mentioned yet. These are CHECK TABLE and REPAIR TABLE, both of which need the name of a table after the command. Both these run **bcheck** on the named table, and you see the output from **bcheck**. The CHECK TABLE statement runs **bcheck** with the '-n' option:

```
CHECK TABLE Stock;
```

The REPAIR TABLE statement runs it with the '-y' option:

```
REPAIR TABLE Stock;
```

16.5.3 sqlconv

sqlconv is used to convert an INFORMIX 3.3 database into an INFORMIX-SQL database. Prior to version 2.10, the corresponding facility was called **dbconvert**. Since the conversion process requires some of the tools provided by INFORMIX 3.3 as well as those provided by INFORMIX-SQL, the explanation here is going to be brief – the reference manual documents the procedure very well.

The basic idea is that **sqlconv** generates two scripts, one in INFORMER to unload the data from the INFORMIX 3.3 database, and one in SQL to create the INFORMIX-SQL database and load it with the data from the old database. If there is lots of room on the disk, this can be done fairly quickly; if there is not much room, the scripts produced by **sqlconv** will have to be executed one step at a time, removing the parts of the old database as the new one is created.

16.5.4 dbupdate

dbupdate is used to convert ISQL 1.10 databases to ISQL version 2 (either 2.00 or 2.10, depending on which version is being used). It was not part of ISQL 1.10. It has three tasks:

1. To convert all-blank character fields to nulls.
2. To convert zero values in selected numeric columns to nulls.
3. To correct a bug in DECIMAL values.

By default it does all three tasks. It goes through each numeric column in the database asking whether zeros should be converted to nulls. Using the '-b' option means that blank character fields are left as blanks. Using the '-n' option leaves all the fields (other than the DECIMAL fields) unchanged and makes all the columns in the database NOT NULL. The normal use would be:

```
dbupdate old new
```

After this is complete, the old database must be removed because the data and index files of the user-defined tables in the two databases are linked. Once all the databases have been converted, **dbupdate** can be deleted – it will not be needed again.

When a database has been converted from version 1.10 and the '-n' option of **dbupdate** specified, any forms which use the database should be given a modified DATABASE statement:

```
DATABASE Oldcars WITHOUT NULL INPUT
```

This means that all the fields will default to zero or a blank so that if the user enters nothing in the field, at least some value will be inserted into the column. This should normally only be regarded as a short-term measure – either the columns should be made to accept nulls or the users should be trained to enter the correct data in the fields.

16.5.5 brand

brand is of no use once INFORMIX-SQL is installed and it can be removed. It is used to enable the software. When you supply the serial number and key, **brand** encodes the values you have supplied and modifies the programs to embed the code in them. When the programs run, they check that the serial number and key match: if the right key was used, the program will work; if not, it will produce an error message identifying the problem. If the serial number and key combination is wrong, the software must be re-installed completely, starting by copying the software off the distribution media, and this will copy **brand** back on to the machine again. Incidentally, the **installsql** script can also be removed once the product is installed.

16.6 The system catalogue

The system catalogue (catalog in American English) contains all the necessary information about the database in the nine tables created in an empty database. This section describes what information is stored in each of these system tables. A full list of the column names and types, and of the indexes on the system tables, is given in Appendix K of the reference manual; the description below gives some extra notes on that information.

16.6.1 Systables

This is the most crucial table of all because it defines where every other table is to be found – it is the only C-ISAM file that absolutely must live in the '.dbs' directory. It contains the names of all the tables (column **Tabname**), the number used to identify that table throughout the rest of the catalogue (column **Tabid**) and the path name of the C-ISAM file where the data can be found. The information about the row size, and the number of columns, rows and indexes is all derivable from other places either in the C-ISAM file itself or from the other parts of the catalogue (or both), but it is convenient to have them stored here as well. The UPDATE STATISTICS command, incidentally, updates the number of rows column (**Nrows**) by transferring some data from the index file to **Systables**. The table type indicates whether it is a real table (**Tabtype** is 'T' or a view ('V')). There is also a pseudo-table entry with type 'L' for the transaction log if the database has one. It is a pity that there is no entry for the name of the database – sometimes it would be useful to be able to identify the database from a program (or subroutine in a library).

This table can be changed by a DBA, but there are only two operations which should be done. One of these is to delete the transaction log record – it is the only way of stopping the transaction log. The other time it is necessary is if you transfer the database bodily and it turns out that one or more of the tables actually has an absolute path name stored in the **Dirpath** column. The best solution here is normally to delete the directory names from the data, leaving a relative path name which is relative to the database directory. The normal way of finding that you have this problem is that SELECT statements (and any other statement which accesses the C-ISAM file) fail to find the table, even though, according to the system catalogue, the table is there and has the correct columns and so on.

This table contains entries for itself and all the other tables in the system catalogue. Because it contains the path names of all these files, all the other system catalogue tables and all the user-defined tables, these can reside in any directory, but **Systables** must live in the database directory so that the database engine can find out where the other tables are.

Version 4.00. The extra table type 'S' has been introduced; it indicates a synonym. The mechanism for handling synonyms has been changed completely; for more details, see the section on **Syssyntable** later.

16.6.2 Syscolumns

This table documents the name of each column in the database, and the type, length and position of the data for the column in the record in the C-ISAM file. The column type is encoded; small numbers represent columns which allow nulls and large numbers (≥ 256) mean that the column does not accept nulls. The column length is simple except for DECIMAL or MONEY columns. In these, the number has to be treated as two 8-bit quantities; the first of these (the high-order 8 bits) represents the scale, and the low-order bits represent the precision. From these two numbers, the physical length on disk can be determined. Each column is assigned a number within the table indicating its position in the list when a statement such as:

```
SELECT * FROM Systables;
```

is expanded into a list of columns. The **Tabid** column is used to associate a table with the column.

One shell script which can be quite useful is called `collist`:

```
:    "@(#)collist.sh  5.2 90/12/31"
#
#   List columns for named table

case "$1" in
-d) DBASE=${2:?"$0: must specify database after -d"}
    shift 2;;
-d*)
    DBASE=`expr $1 : '-d\(.*\)'`
    shift 1;;
*)  : ${DBASE:=cars};;      # Supply your own default database here
esac

for table in $*
do
    echo " select systables.tabname, syscolumns.colno,"
    echo " syscolumns.colname"
    echo " from systables, syscolumns "
    echo " where systables.tabid = syscolumns.tabid"
    echo " and tabname = \"$table\""
    echo " order by syscolumns.colno;"
done | isql $DBASE - 2>/dev/null
```

This prints out the list of columns in each table specified as an argument. There is a default database which would need to be set depending on which project you are working on. You can specify the database by using the '-d' option.

16.6.3 Sysindexes

This is the last of the triumvirate of tables which describe the C-ISAM files. This table stores the names of the indexes, the number of the table which is indexed, information about the type of index and an ordered list of the column numbers which make up the index.

Position	Character	Meaning
1	s	SELECT
2	u	UPDATE
3	*	Column-level privileges
4	i	INSERT
5	d	DELETE
6	x	INDEX
7	a	ALTER

Table 16.4 The coding of **Systabauth.Tabauth**

16.6.4 Sysusers

This table simply lists users' login names and the level of database privilege that they are granted. The coding is simple: 'D' means database administrator, 'R' means resource-level privileges and 'C' means connect privilege. The priority of the person who created the database is 9; all other users are given privilege level 5. The password field is not used.

16.6.5 Systabauth

This table specifies the table-level access privileges. The table privileges are encoded in a seven-character column called **Tabauth**. The person giving the permission (the **Grantor**) is recorded, as is the person receiving the permission (the **Grantee**). The columns all either contain a minus sign '–' or a letter or asterisk '*', as indicated in Table 16.4. If the letter is in upper case (eg 'S'), then the person has been given the option of granting that privilege to other users. This is normally reserved for DBAs only, who do not need this permission explicitly since they have it implicitly – a DBA can always do any operation on any table. The '*' indicates that there is at least one record in the **Syscolauth** table indicating which columns this user has SELECT or UPDATE privileges on.

16.6.6 Syscolauth

This table contains a record of any column-level privileges granted to a user by anybody. It is similar to the **Systabauth** table, but it records both the **Tabid** and the **Colno**, and the **Colauth** field contains just two characters. The first of these can be 's' for select permission granted or '–' for permission not granted, and the second can be 'u' for update permission granted or '–' for permission not granted.

16.6.7 Syssynonyms

Version 2.10 and earlier. This table stores a list of the synonyms that users have created for themselves, defining the table which is meant by the synonym. `sqlexec` will not look at this table unless it fails to find a table name in **Systables**.

Version 4.00. This table is not used. It exists for backwards compatibility. For details of how synonyms are handled in version 4.00, see the discussion on **Syssyntable**.

16.6.8 Sysviews

A view has a record in **Systables** and **Syscolumns** defining its basic properties, and may have entries in **Systabauth** and **Syscolauth** defining who can use the view. However, a view also consists of a SELECT statement which defines the view, and the text of this is stored in **Sysviews**. If the statement is more than 40 characters long, there will be several rows of data containing the text of the SELECT statement.

16.6.9 Sysdepends

This table is used to record which tables or views a view references or depends upon. It is needed so that if a base table (that is, a table which is not a view, or a view which another view references) is dropped, all the views which are now invalid (because they reference a non-existent object) can also be deleted. If there are no views in the database, this table is empty.

16.6.10 Sysconstraints

Version 4.00. This table records the names of constraints, who owns the constraint, the table to which the constraint applies and the number of the index description in **Sysindexes** which contains the other information about the constraint.

16.6.11 Syssyntable

Version 4.00. This table is used to associate a synonym with the corresponding base table. The mechanism for handling this is that the user specifies the table name which is looked up in **Systables**; if the table type is 's', then the corresponding entry in **Syssyntable** is discovered to find the base table or view which actually corresponds to the table the user wishes to access. If the engine is INFORMIX-ONLINE, the synonym may actually be the name of a table in a database on a remote machine; this would also be defined in **Syssyntable**.

```
INFORMIX-SQL:  [Run] Create  Modify  Database  User-menu  Exit
Use a form, run a report or use RDSQL.

--------------------- cars ------------------ Press CTRL-W for Help --------
```

Figure 16.1 The main menu for INFORMIX-SQL version 1.10

16.7 INFORMIX-SQL: different versions

There have been four main versions of INFORMIX-SQL: versions 1.10, 2.00, 2.10 and 4.00. The basic operation of INFORMIX-SQL has not changed between these versions, but numerous details have changed. Versions 1.10 and 2.10 are now both archaic; there is almost invariably a newer version available for any given machine. Version 4.00 is the current version on the most popular machines and is being ported to other machines as fast as possible; where version 4.00 is not available, version 2.10 is the standard version.

16.7.1 Changes between versions 1.10 and 2.00

The main change between version 1.10 and version 2.00 was very noticeable because the ISQL main menu was reorganized. The main menu for version 1.10 is shown in Figure 16.1. The user had to decide to change something at the top level of the menu, and then decide what to change, whether it was a report or a form or whatever. With version 2.00, the interface was changed so that the user decided what he wanted to work with, whether it was a form or a report or whatever, and then decided what to do with it, which might be to change it, then compile it and run it.

Other changes were the addition of the schema editor which makes it easier for novice users to create and modify tables, the addition of null values to indicate that a value is unknown or not applicable, some extra security features to control who could do what with a database, and a set of transaction-handling facilities instead of audit trail manipulation commands. Outer joins, which allow you to

```
Query Next Previous Add Update Remove Table Screen Current Master Detail
      Output Exit                                ** 1: customers table**
   customer          [          ]
   salut             [     ]
   firstname         [          ]
   surname           [            ]
   address1          [                ]
   address2          [                ]
   address3          [                ]
   postcode          [          ]
   phone             [           ]
   maxmoney          [          ]
   enquiry           [ ]
   lastmodel         [          ]
   contactdate       [          ]
```

Figure 16.2 PERFORM menu: versions 1.10 and 2.00

conditionally select data from some tables, were also added. These do not affect the normal day-to-day use of INFORMIX-SQL. Another change was that the manual was split into two volumes; the amount of information was just too large to fit in one.

With version 1.10 (and 2.00), the interface to PERFORM was not a ring menu but rather consisted of a list of all the options which wrapped on to a second line at the top of the screen, as shown in Figure 16.2. It looked like a ring menu, except that no option was ever highlighted, and the list of options went on to the second line. It was not actually a ring menu, because although you chose the options using the initial letters just as you do in a ring menu, there was no moving highlight, and the cursor keys could not be used to select an option.

16.7.2 Changes between versions 2.00 and 2.10

One of the biggest changes between versions 2.00 and 2.10 was that PERFORM was rewritten to use the database engine **sqlexec** instead of accessing the C-ISAM files in the database directly. This required some changes inside **sqlexec**. The most visible effect is that PERFORM has now got a ring menu, whereas in the previous versions it had something which looked somewhat similar to a ring menu but was not actually a ring menu. This change is crucial, because it allows INFORMIX-SQL version 2.10 to work with INFORMIX-TURBO, which version 2.00 cannot do.

Another change was the re-introduction of audit trails, this time in addition to transaction logs. The concept of a clustered index was also introduced. When a clustered index is created, the data records are reorganized so that they are stored in the same order as is required by the index, which means that accessing all the records in the order indicated by the index is as efficient as possible.

The way that the database engine **sqlexec** handled enquiries was improved so that it could respond faster to enquiries. One of the ways it does this is by automatically creating an index on a table if there are no user-defined indexes which it can use to help speed up a particular operation. This is known as auto-indexing.

There were also some subtle changes in the way the system behaved; the form and report programs, which used to be distinct programs, became shell scripts which ran **isql** with appropriate options. This meant that when a form or report was run from within **isql**, instead of starting up a brand new program (and a brand new database engine), the current program continued running, using the same database engine which reduced the load on the machine. The schema editor used to be a separate program called **ised**; it no longer exists as a separate program but has been incorporated as part of **isql**. This also makes user menus more efficient.

16.7.3 Changes between versions 2.10.00 and 2.10.03

INFORMIX-SQL version 2.10.03 has some minor improvements over version 2.10.00. One such change is that the shell scripts called **sacego** etc have disappeared and been replaced by links to the **isql** program. This means that when you run **sacego** in version 2.10.03, you are running the same program as when you run **isql**. The program knows what you want it to do because (on UNIX at any rate) it can tell what you called it by looking at its arguments, and if it was called **sacego**, it will run the report as requested. The equivalent to version 2.10.03 under MS-DOS is version 2.10.06.

16.7.4 Changes between versions 2.10.03 and 4.00.00

Apart from anything else, all the products now bear the same version number. The INFORMIX-ONLINE product was introduced to replace INFORMIX-TURBO. There were major changes in the optimizer component of the database engine. The DATETIME and INTERVAL types were introduced. MODE ANSI databases were introduced, along with a number of other minor changes to improve the compatibility of INFORMIX-SQL with the ANSI standard. The handling of long fields has been improved with the WORDWRAP, COMPRESSED and RIGHT MARGIN keywords. The SET EXPLAIN command allows you to discover much more about how the optimizer processes a query, which in turn helps you to determine what indexes are needed. The behaviour of synonyms has been vastly improved; they apply to everyone. All table names can be prefixed by the owner name; if the database is a MODE ANSI database, this is mandatory. INFORMIX-ONLINE introduces the VARCHAR, BYTE and TEXT data types.

16.8 Summary

This chapter has covered a number of things which are difficult to put in anything other than a chapter labelled 'miscellaneous'. It gave a complete summary of the environment variables used by ISQL, talked about the command-line interface to ISQL, and described the installation procedure, miscellaneous supporting commands, the structure of the system catalogue and some details of the differences between the various versions of INFORMIX-SQL. None of this information is crucial for the average user to know; many DBAs get by with only the sketchiest knowledge of the material in this chapter.

This brings the book to a close, give or take the appendices. If you have understood everything in this book, you are very well equipped to go and create the forms, reports and scripts to handle any reasonable database problem using INFORMIX-SQL. If you understood everything in Part II, you should be perfectly capable of understanding and using the forms and reports produced by someone else, and if you have the source, you could almost certainly make minor modifications to the formats of reports and forms – the only suggestion I would make is that before you actually modify the source, you make sure that you have at least one back-up copy so that if anything goes wrong, you can restore the original.

Appendices

A
Answers to exercises

There are exercises in Chapters 3–13. There are no answers given for the exercises in Chapter 3 because the exercises ask you to create a database. Your solution is correct if you create a copy of the **Cars** database successfully. Similarly, there are no answers to the exercises in Chapter 10 because they are open-ended questions. The following pages provide the answers to the exercises in Chapters 4–9 and 11–13.

Chapter 4

1.

```
(
    @(#)company1.per    5.4 90/09/27
    Answer to Chapter 4 Question 1
)

DATABASE Cars

SCREEN
(

    ABC Cars Ltd: List of Car Manufacturers
    ========================================

Company number [f000]
Company        [f001           ]
Address        [f002                    ]
               [f003                    ]
               [f004                    ]
Postcode       [f005   ]

Telephone      [f006           ]

Notes
[f008                                    ]
[f010                                    ]
)
END

TABLES
Companies

ATTRIBUTES
f000 = Companies.Maker;
```

```
f001 = Companies.Company;
f002 = Companies.Address1, AUTONEXT;
f003 = Companies.Address2, AUTONEXT;
f004 = Companies.Address3, AUTONEXT;
f005 = Companies.Postcode, UPSHIFT, PICTURE = "AXXX #AA", AUTONEXT,
       COMMENTS = "Enter postcode";
f006 = Companies.Phone, DOWNSHIFT, COMMENTS = "Enter phone number.";
f008 = Companies.Notes1, AUTONEXT,
       COMMENTS = "Enter any general comments about this company";
f010 = Companies.Notes2,
       COMMENTS = "Enter any general comments about this company";
END
```

Chapter 5

1. Either of these answers would be satisfactory.

```
SELECT * FROM Stock;

SELECT Company, Modelname, Details, Stock.*
    FROM  Stock, Companies, Models
    WHERE Stock.Model  = Models.Model
      AND Models.Maker = Companies.Maker;
```

2.

```
SELECT * FROM Models WHERE Price > 10000;
```

3.

```
SELECT Company, Modelname, Details, Registration
    FROM  Stock, Companies, Models
    WHERE Stock.Model = Models.Model
      AND Models.Maker = Companies.Maker;
```

4.

```
SELECT DISTINCT Salut, Firstname, Surname, Company, Modelname, Details
    FROM  Customers, Models, Companies, Stock
    WHERE Customers.Lastmodel = Stock.Model
      AND Customers.Lastmodel = Models.Model
      AND Models.Maker = Companies.Maker;
```

5. The CREATE INDEX and DROP INDEX statements are not necessary for the statement to work – no indexes are *necessary* for SQL to work – but it does speed up this SELECT statement quite noticeably.

```
CREATE INDEX Price ON Models(Price);

SELECT Salut, Firstname, Surname, Price
    FROM     Models, Customers
    WHERE    Models.Model = Customers.Lastmodel
      AND    Enquiry = "S"
      AND    Price > 10000
    ORDER BY Price DESC;

DROP INDEX Price;
```

6.

```
SELECT DISTINCT Company, Modelname, Details, Maxspeed, Accel Acceleration
   FROM   Companies, Models, Stock
   WHERE Models.Model = Stock.Model
     AND Models.Maker = Companies.Maker
     AND Maxspeed > 100
     AND Accel < 10;
```

Chapter 6

1.

```
{
    @(#)stock1.ace        5.1 91/03/22
    List cars in stock
}

DATABASE Cars END

SELECT  Companies.Coname,
        Models.Modelname,
        Models.Details,
        Models.Price,
        Stock.*
   FROM      Stock, Models, Companies
   WHERE     Stock.Model = Models.model
     AND     Models.Maker = Companies.Company
   ORDER BY Coname, Modelname, Details
END

FORMAT

   PAGE HEADER
      PRINT "Report on cars in stock",
         COLUMN 60, "Page ", PAGENO
      SKIP 1 LINE

   PAGE TRAILER
      SKIP 1 LINE
      PRINT "ABC Cars Ltd", COLUMN 60, TODAY

   ON EVERY ROW
      PRINT
         COLUMN   1, registration,
         COLUMN  10, coname CLIPPED, " ",
                     modelname CLIPPED, " ",
                     details CLIPPED
      PRINT
         COLUMN  10, colour,
         COLUMN  18, condition,
         COLUMN  20, datebought,
         COLUMN  34, boughtfor,
         COLUMN  46, mileage

END
```

2.

```
{
    a(#)sales1.ace        5.1 91/03/22
    List of cars sold
}

DATABASE Cars END

SELECT  Companies.Coname,
        Models.Modelname,
        Models.Details,
        Sales.Registration,
        Sales.Boughtfor,
        Sales.Soldfor,
        Sales.Soldfor - Sales.Boughtfor Profit
    FROM     Companies, Models, Sales
    WHERE    Companies.Company = Models.Maker
    AND      Models.Model = Sales.Model
    ORDER BY Coname, Modelname, Details, Registration
END

FORMAT

    PAGE HEADER
        PRINT "Report on cars sold",
            COLUMN 60, "Page ", PAGENO
        SKIP 1 LINE
        PRINT
            COLUMN   1, "Reg.",
            COLUMN  10, "Make",
            COLUMN  34, 7 SPACES, "Cost",
            COLUMN  47, 1 SPACE,  "Sale value",
            COLUMN  60, 6 SPACES, "Profit"

    PAGE TRAILER
        SKIP 1 LINE
        PRINT "ABC Cars Ltd", COLUMN 60, TODAY

    ON EVERY ROW
        {
            Two lines of printing are used to ensure that
            cars with long names do not get muddled up
            with the prices
        }
        PRINT
            COLUMN   1, registration,
            COLUMN  10, coname CLIPPED, " ",
                        modelname CLIPPED, " ",
                        details CLIPPED
        PRINT
            COLUMN  34, boughtfor,
            COLUMN  47, soldfor,
            COLUMN  60, profit

END
```

Chapter 7

1.

```
(
    @(#)custom4.per     5.5 91/03/22
    Form for table Customers in database Cars
)

DATABASE Cars

SCREEN
(

            Customer details

Number    [f000]
Name      [f001 ] [f002      ] [f003           ]

Address   [f004                ]
          [f005                ]
          [f006                ]
Post code [f007    ]

Phone number [f008             ]
Type of enquiry [a]
Spending Power (estimated) [f009       ]
Last contact date [f011              ]

Model bought             [f010] [c000]
[c001          ]
[m000                ] [m001             ]
)
END

TABLES
Customers
Companies
Models

ATTRIBUTES
f000 = Customers.Number;
f001 = Customers.Salut,
       COMMENTS = "Mr Mrs Miss Ms or blank",
       INCLUDE = ("Mr", "Mrs", "Miss", "Ms", NULL);
f002 = Customers.Firstname;
f003 = Customers.Surname, REQUIRED;
f004 = Customers.Address1, AUTONEXT,
       COMMENTS = "Enter address";
f005 = Customers.Address2, AUTONEXT,
       COMMENTS = "Enter address";
f006 = Customers.Address3, AUTONEXT,
       COMMENTS = "Enter address";
f007 = Customers.Postcode, UPSHIFT,
       COMMENTS = "Enter post code",
       PICTURE = "AXXX #AA";
f008 = Customers.Phone, DOWNSHIFT,
       COMMENTS = "STD code, number, and extension";
a    = Customers.Enquiry, UPSHIFT, AUTONEXT,
       COMMENTS = "Q enquiry, S sale, C contact",
       INCLUDE = ("Q", "C", "S");
f009 = Customers.Maxmoney, REVERSE,
       COMMENTS = "2000 to 100000, or blank",
       INCLUDE = (NULL, 2000 TO 100000);
```

```
f011 = Customers.Contactdate,
       DEFAULT = TODAY, FORMAT = "ddd, dd mmm yyyy", NOENTRY;
f010 = Customers.Lastmodel =*Models.Model, QUERYCLEAR;
c000 =*Companies.Maker = Models.Maker;
c001 = Companies.Company;
m000 = Models.Modelname;
m001 = Models.Details;
END

INSTRUCTIONS

BEFORE REMOVE OF Companies Models
    COMMENTS BELL REVERSE "You can't do that!"
    ABORT

BEFORE EDITADD EDITUPDATE OF Companies Models
    ABORT

END
```

Chapter 8

1.

```
SELECT * FROM Models WHERE Price = (SELECT MAX(Price) FROM Models);
```

2.

```
{ 1st alternative }
SELECT MIN(Price), MAX(Price), AVG(Price)
    FROM  Models, Companies
    WHERE Models.Maker = Companies.Maker
      AND Company MATCHES "[A-M]*r*";

{ 2nd alternative }
SELECT Company, MIN(Price), MAX(Price), AVG(Price)
    FROM      Models, Companies
    WHERE     Models.Maker = Companies.Maker
      AND     Company MATCHES "[A-M]*r*"
    GROUP BY Company;
```

3.

```
SELECT AVG(Tanksize * Mpgat56) FROM Models;
```

4.

```
{ 1st alternative }
DELETE FROM Customers
    WHERE Contactdate < DATE("01/06/1989") AND Enquiry != "S";

{ 2nd alternative }
DELETE FROM Customers
    WHERE Contactdate < MDY(6,1,1989) AND Enquiry != "S";
```

5.

```
DELETE FROM Companies WHERE Maker NOT IN (SELECT UNIQUE Maker FROM Models);
```

6.

```
UPDATE Customers
    SET Maxmoney = 7500
    WHERE Maxmoney IS NULL OR Maxmoney = 0;
```

7.

```
{ 1st alternative }
SELECT Company, AVG(Tanksize * Mpgat56)
    FROM      Companies, Models
    WHERE     Companies.Maker = Models.Maker
    GROUP BY Company
    ORDER BY 2;

{ 2nd alternative }
SELECT Company, AVG(Tanksize * Mpgat56) Range
    FROM      Companies, Models
    WHERE     Companies.Maker = Models.Maker
    GROUP BY Company
    ORDER BY Range;
```

8.

```
INSERT INTO Customers
    VALUES (0, "Wright", "John", "Mr", "58 Elgar Road", "WOKINGHAM", "Berkshire",
            "RG12 0BL", "0734 508291", 37000, "S", 137, "05/01/1991");
```

9.

```
SELECT Company, COUNT(*), MIN(Price), MAX(Price)
    FROM      Companies, Models
    WHERE     Companies.Maker = Models.Maker
    GROUP BY Company
    HAVING    COUNT(*) > 2
    ORDER BY Company;
```

10.

```
UPDATE Customers
    SET Maxmoney = (SELECT Price FROM Models WHERE Model = Customers.Lastmodel)
    WHERE Enquiry = "S"
      AND (Maxmoney IS NULL OR
            Maxmoney < (SELECT Price FROM Models WHERE Model = Customers.Lastmodel)
          );
```

11.

```
{ 1st alternative }
SELECT COUNT(*) Num_sales, Lastmodel
    FROM       Customers
    WHERE      Enquiry = "S"
    GROUP BY Lastmodel
    INTO TEMP Sales_per_Model;

SELECT Company, Modelname, Num_sales, Price * Num_sales Value
    FROM      Companies, Models, Sales_per_Model
    WHERE     Model = Lastmodel
      AND     Maker = Company
    ORDER BY Value DESC;

DROP TABLE Sales_per_Model;
```

```
{ 2nd alternative }
SELECT Company, Modelname, COUNT(*) Num_sales, SUM(Price) Value
    FROM    Companies, Models, Customers
    WHERE   Company = Maker
    AND     Lastmodel = Model
    AND     Enquiry = "S"
    GROUP BY Company, Modelname
    ORDER BY Value DESC;
```

Chapter 9

1. Note the use of WHERE conditions on the aggregates to satisfy the conditions
    laid out in the question.

```
{
    @(#)report2b.ace      5.1 91/03/22
    Example report showing use of aggregates
}

DATABASE Cars END

OUTPUT
    PAGE LENGTH      23
    TOP MARGIN       0
    BOTTOM MARGIN    0
    LEFT MARGIN      0
END

SELECT  Customers.Salut,
        Customers.Firstname,
        Customers.Surname,
        Customers.Phone,
        Customers.Enquiry,
        Customers.Contactdate,
        Companies.Coname,
        Models.Modelname,
        Models.Details,
        Models.Price
    FROM    Customers, Models, Companies
    WHERE   Customers.Lastmodel = Models.Model
    AND     Models.Maker = Companies.Company
    AND     Customers.Contactdate BETWEEN MDY(6,1,1990) AND MDY(12,31,1990)
    ORDER BY Coname, Modelname, Details, Contactdate
END

FORMAT

    BEFORE GROUP OF Modelname
        SKIP 3 LINES
        NEED 4 LINES
        PRINT
            "Model: ", Coname CLIPPED,
            " ", Modelname CLIPPED
        PRINT
            COLUMN 1,  "Name",
            COLUMN 25, "Phone",
            COLUMN 38, "Model",
            COLUMN 60, "Date",
            COLUMN 72, 3 SPACES, "Price"
```

```
ON EVERY ROW
    PRINT
        COLUMN  1, Salut CLIPPED, " ", Firstname[1], " ", Surname CLIPPED,
        COLUMN 25, Phone CLIPPED,
        COLUMN 38, Details CLIPPED,
        COLUMN 60, Contactdate USING "dd mmm yyyy",
        COLUMN 72, Price USING "$$$ $$$."

AFTER GROUP OF Coname
    SKIP 1 LINE
    PRINT
        "Number of ", Coname CLIPPED, "s sold = ",
        GROUP COUNT WHERE Enquiry = "S" USING "<<<"
    PRINT
        "Value of sales = ",
        GROUP TOTAL OF Price WHERE Enquiry = "S" USING "$$$$ $$&.&&"

ON LAST ROW
    SKIP 2 LINES
    PRINT
        "Total number of cars sold = ",
        COUNT WHERE Enquiry = "S" USING "&<<<"
    PRINT
        "Value of sales = ",
        TOTAL OF Price WHERE Enquiry = "S" USING "$$$$ $$&.&&"

PAGE TRAILER
    PAUSE "Hit return to continue"


END
```

2. The report below satisfies the requirements.

```
{
    @(#)report2c.ace    5.1 91/03/22
    Example report illustrating a standard letter
}

DATABASE Cars END

OUTPUT
    REPORT TO PRINTER
    PAGE LENGTH 66
END

SELECT Customers.*, Models.*
    FROM    Customers, Models, Companies
    WHERE   Models.Model = Customers.Lastmodel
    AND     Models.Maker = Companies.Company
    AND     Companies.Coname = "Ford"
    AND     Customers.Enquiry = "S"
    AND     Customers.Contactdate < TODAY - 91    { 91 days = 3 months ago }
    ORDER BY Surname, Firstname
END

FORMAT

    ON EVERY ROW
        SKIP TO TOP OF PAGE
        SKIP 2 LINES
        PRINT
            COLUMN 41, Salut CLIPPED, " ", Firstname[1], " ", Surname CLIPPED
        PRINT
```

```
                    COLUMN 41, Address1 CLIPPED
            PRINT
                    COLUMN 41, Address2 CLIPPED
            PRINT
                    COLUMN 41, Address3 CLIPPED, 10 SPACES, Postcode CLIPPED
            SKIP 1 LINE
            PRINT COLUMN 41, TODAY USING "ddd dd mmm yyyy"
            SKIP 2 LINES
            PRINT "Dear ", Salut CLIPPED, " ",
                    Firstname[1], " ", Surname CLIPPED, ","
            PRINT
                "   Our records show that you bought a ",
                " Ford ", Modelname CLIPPED, " ",
                Details CLIPPED
            PRINT
                "from us on ",
                contactdate USING "dd mmm yyyy."
            SKIP 1 LINE
            PRINT FILE "newmodel.ltr"

        PAGE TRAILER
            PAUSE "Hit return to continue"


    END
```

A suitable sample letter might be:

```
Allow me to describe to you the new Ford Myth, a
fantastic new car...

The standard model comes with all the features you
would expect from a fully-equipped modern car.  Things
like:

    * an engine
    * steering wheel
    * brakes
    * lights
    * wheels

All of which are vital in any new car, as I'm sure you
would agree.  However, what really distinguishes this
car from the rest is the fantastic new fully automated
Personal Groomer installed in the passenger side of
the car, which allows the person sitting in the
passenger seat to be freshly manicured and groomed on
arrival at your destination.  Not that driving in this
car is a hardship, but with the hassles of modern
motorway driving -- the low speed, stop/start driving,
the tedium of waiting for the car ahead of you in the
middle lane to crawl past the lorry travelling in the
inside lane at all of 1 mph slower than the car ahead,
and that only on the steeper hills -- with all these
problems, anyone can arrive feeling wilted. And the
Personal Groomer takes care of that, enlivening you
instantly.

We at ABC Cars Ltd are proud to announce that we have
been selected by Ford to test market this new system,
and we can give you, one of our valued customers, the
opportunity to test drive one of these exciting new
models.  Please contact me on (0734) 580918 to arrange
a test drive.
```

```
Yours sincerely,

Heinrich Phillips
Marketing Director
ABC Cars Ltd.
```

In a full production report, the address handling would be made more sophisticated by the use of conditional printing; see the example report developed in Chapter 13.

This report also illustrates one of the problems with using ACE to handle text. The length of the model description printed in the first line of the body of the letter is of variable length, and that line could easily overflow the paper. Despite all its other properties, ACE is not a word processor or text formatter. On UNIX, the report could be piped through a simple formatting program which would wordwrap the longer lines. If this is not satisfactory, the structure of the letter would have to be changed so that the variable-length text was printed in a headline which would never run over the right-hand margin. If the report was really complex, it might be necessary to change the report so that it produced as its output a series of **troff** formatting commands so that when the report was filtered through **troff** and sent to a laser printer, the output would make full use of the range of facilities made available.

Version 4.00. Another powerful technique is to use a large CHAR variable (discussed in Chapter 13) which is assigned the words in the paragraph and then printed with the attributes CLIPPED, WORDWRAP and RIGHT MARGIN.

Chapter 11

1. This question has a small essay to go with the answer. The full form is big, and there is a lot to explain. Do not let the size of the answer scare you: most of the 300 or so lines of the form have been seen before in different contexts, although there are certainly some new ideas based on previously supplied information. The next five pages contain the listing of the form; the commentary which starts with the next paragraph continues after the listing.

   The answer supplied uses all six tables and has eight screen layouts. There is one main screen for each of the tables, and the extra two screens exist to hide sensitive data from the customer; they are clearly commented at the top of the layout. It does not have any composite joins, nor does it have any master/detail relationships.

   The salesman would be trained to use the **Table** option to switch between screens while the customer is present as this prevents the customer seeing the sensitive information. To see the sensitive information from the **Stock** table, use 3 S; to see the sensitive information about a sale, use 4 D.

   The hardest part of the answer is the transfer of information from the **Stock** table to the **Sales** table. The second hardest part is then making sure that the user cannot edit the transferred data.

```
{
    @(#)sales.per        5.5 91/03/22
    Answer to Chapter 11 Question 1
}

DATABASE Cars

SCREEN
{

        Stock List
        ==========

Registration   [f000    ]
Model Number   [f001] [f011]
Description    [f021              ]
               [f012              ]
               [f013              ]
Colour         [f002    ]


Notes
[f006                                      ]
[f008                                      ]
}

SCREEN
{

 [b1                                         ]
 [b]                                       [b]
 [b] Sales entry form                      [b]
 [b]                                       [b]
 [b] Registration [f000    ]               [b]
 [b] Model Number [p001] [f011]            [b]
 [b] Description  [f021            ]        [b]
 [b]             [f012            ]         [b]
 [b]             [f013            ]         [b]
 [b] Customer    [c000]                    [b]
 [b] Name        [c001 ][c002     ][c003    ] [b]
 [b] Sold for    [p003         ]           [b]
 [b] Date sold   [p004     ]               [b]
 [b] Terms       [p005]                    [b]
 [b] Colour      [p102    ]                [b]
 [b]                                       [b]
 [b2                                         ]
}

SCREEN
{

Sensitive Sales data -- do not show to the customer

Registration   [f000    ]
Model Number   [f001] [f011]
Description    [f021              ]
               [f012              ]
               [f013              ]

Condition      [p]
Datebought     [p103     ]
Boughtfor      [p104      ]
Mileage        [p105      ]

Notes
```

```
[p106                                                  ]
[p108                                                  ]

        Profit [profit   ]
        Markup [markup]%
)

SCREEN
(

Sensitive Stock data -- do not show to the customer

Condition     [a]
Datebought    [f003      ]
Boughtfor     [f004       ]
Mileage       [f005      ]
)

SCREEN
(

          Customer details

Number  [c000]
Name    [c001 ] [c002     ] [c003         ]

Address  [c004                    ]
         [c005                    ]
         [c006                    ]
Post code [c007     ]

Phone number [c008            ]

Type of enquiry [c]

Spending Power (estimated) [c009      ]
Model Number     [c010]

Last contact date [c011          ]
)

SCREEN
(

          Guide prices

Model Number     [f001] [f011]
Description      [f021                ]
                 [f012                ]
                 [f013                ]

Year [g001] Low [g002   ] High [g003   ]

Average [gavg   ]
Minimum [gmin   ]
Maximum [gmax   ]
)

SCREEN
(

          Model List
          ==========
```

```
Model          [f001]
Maker          [f011]
               [f021                ]
Modelname      [f012                ]
Details        [f013                ]
Price          [f014     ]
Maxspeed       [f015      ]
Accel          [f016 ]
Tanksize       [f017 ]
Urban          [f018       ]
Mpgat56        [f019       ]
}

SCREEN
{

        Company Details
        ===============

Company Number  [f011]
Company Name    [f021                 ]
Address         [f022                  ]
                [f023                  ]
                [f024                  ]
Postcode        [f025    ]
Phone           [f026        ]

Notes
[f028                                          ]
[f030                                          ]
}

TABLES
Stock
Models
Companies
Sales
Prices
Customers '

ATTRIBUTES

f000 =*Stock.Registration
     = Sales.Registration, QUERYCLEAR, UPSHIFT, AUTONEXT, PICTURE = "AXXXXXA";
f001 =*Models.Model
     = Stock.Model, QUERYCLEAR, NOENTRY, NOUPDATE;
     = Prices.Model, QUERYCLEAR;
{ Read the commentary on the answer to find out why this join cannot be made }
{    = Customers.Lastmodel, QUERYCLEAR; }
f002 = Stock.Colour;
a    = Stock.Condition, AUTONEXT, UPSHIFT,
        INCLUDE  = ('X', 'V', 'G', 'A', 'P'),
        COMMENTS = "Xcellent, Very good, Good, Average, Poor";
f003 = Stock.Datebought;
f004 = Stock.Boughtfor;
f005 = Stock.Mileage;
f006 = Stock.Notes1;
f008 = Stock.Notes2;
c000 =*Customers.Number
     = Sales.Customer, QUERYCLEAR;
p003 = Sales.Soldfor;
p004 = Sales.Datesold,
        DEFAULT = TODAY, NOENTRY, NOUPDATE;
p005 = Sales.Terms, UPSHIFT, AUTONEXT,
```

```
     INCLUDE = ('CASH', 'ACCE', 'BARC', 'HIRE', 'CHEQ'),
     COMMENTS = "CASH, ACCEss, BARClaycard, HIRE-purchase, CHEQue";

{ These are implicitly no-entry fields }
p001 = Sales.Model;
p102 = Sales.Colour;
p    = Sales.Condition;
p103 = Sales.Datebought;
p104 = Sales.Boughtfor;
p105 = Sales.Mileage;
p106 = Sales.Notes1;
p108 = Sales.Notes2;

f011 = Models.Maker = Companies.Maker, QUERYCLEAR;
f012 = Models.Modelname;
f013 = Models.Details;
f014 = Models.Price;
f015 = Models.Maxspeed;
f016 = Models.Accel;
f017 = Models.Tanksize;
f018 = Models.Urban;
f019 = Models.Mpgat56;

f021 = Companies.Company;
f022 = Companies.Address1;
f023 = Companies.Address2;
f024 = Companies.Address3;
f025 = Companies.Postcode;
f026 = Companies.Phone;
f028 = Companies.Notes1;
f030 = Companies.Notes2;

c001 = Customers.Salut,
       COMMENTS = "Mr Mrs Miss Ms or blank",
       INCLUDE = ("Mr", "Mrs", "Miss", "Ms", NULL);
c002 = Customers.Firstname;
c003 = Customers.Surname, REQUIRED;
c004 = Customers.Address1, AUTONEXT, COMMENTS = "Enter address";
c005 = Customers.Address2, AUTONEXT, COMMENTS = "Enter address";
c006 = Customers.Address3, AUTONEXT, COMMENTS = "Enter address";
c007 = Customers.Postcode, UPSHIFT,  COMMENTS = "Enter post code",
       PICTURE = "AXXX #AA";
c008 = Customers.Phone, DOWNSHIFT,
       COMMENTS = "STD code, number, and extension";
c    = Customers.Enquiry, UPSHIFT, AUTONEXT, DEFAULT = 'S',
       COMMENTS = "Q enquiry, S sale, C contact",
       INCLUDE = ("Q", "C", "S");
c009 = Customers.Maxmoney, REVERSE,
       COMMENTS = "2000 to 100000, or blank",
       INCLUDE = (NULL, 2000 TO 100000);
{ Read the commentary to find out why
  Customers.Lastmodel is not joined to Models.Model }
c010 = Customers.Lastmodel;
c011 = Customers.Contactdate,
       DEFAULT = TODAY, FORMAT = "ddd, dd mmm yyyy", NOENTRY;

g001 = Prices.Year_made;
g002 = Prices.Lo_price, FORMAT = "###,###";
g003 = Prices.Hi_price, FORMAT = "###,###";

gmin = DISPLAYONLY TYPE DECIMAL, FORMAT = "###,###";
gmax = DISPLAYONLY TYPE DECIMAL, FORMAT = "###,###";
gavg = DISPLAYONLY TYPE DECIMAL, FORMAT = "###,###";
```

```
b1   = DISPLAYONLY TYPE CHAR, REVERSE;
b2   = DISPLAYONLY TYPE CHAR, REVERSE;
b    = DISPLAYONLY TYPE CHAR, REVERSE;

profit = DISPLAYONLY TYPE MONEY;
markup = DISPLAYONLY TYPE DECIMAL, FORMAT = "###.##";

END

INSTRUCTIONS

{ Master/detail relationships as before }
Companies MASTER OF Models
Models MASTER OF Prices
Models MASTER OF Stock

{ You may only change Sales and Customers }
BEFORE EDITADD EDITUPDATE OF Models Companies Prices Stock
    ABORT

{ You may not update Sales -- just add }
BEFORE EDITUPDATE OF Sales
    ABORT

{ You may only delete Stock records }
BEFORE REMOVE OF Sales Models Companies Customers Prices
    COMMENTS BELL REVERSE "You may not change this table"
    ABORT

{ Finish border of Sales screen }
AFTER DISPLAY OF SALES
    LET b1 = "              ABC Cars Ltd"

{ Show range of prices }
AFTER DISPLAY QUERY OF Prices
    LET gmin = MIN OF g002
    LET gmax = MAX OF g003
    LET gavg = (AVG OF g002 + AVG OF g003) / 2

{ Show the company what we made on the deal }
AFTER EDITADD OF Soldfor
    LET profit = p003 - f004
    LET markup = ((p003 -f004) / f004) * 100

{ Transfer data to Sales record }
AFTER EDITADD OF Sales.Registration
    LET p001 = f001
    LET p102 = f002
    LET p    = a
    LET p103 = f003
    LET p104 = f004
    LET p105 = f005
    LET p106 = f006
    LET p108 = f008

{ Do not let user edit transferred data }
BEFORE EDITADD OF Sales.Model
    NEXTFIELD = f000

BEFORE EDITADD OF Sales.Notes2
    NEXTFIELD = p005

END
```

The control block:

```
AFTER EDITADD OF Sales.Registration
```

controls the transfer. The user enters the registration number in the field tagged f000; the joining condition verifies the number plate and also sets up the entries for the **Stock, Models** and **Companies** tables in the normal way. This initializes the fields f001, f002, a, f003, f004, f005, f006 and f008, which are then transferred to the **Sales** table fields by the sequence of assignments. Note that some of these **Sales** fields are on the hidden screen.

The two control blocks:

```
BEFORE EDITADD OF p001
BEFORE EDITADD OF p108
```

ensure that the user does not get to fiddle with the data transferred after the registration number was entered, and coincidentally ensure that the sensitive data is not shown either.

The specification on field p004 ensures that the **Sales.Datesold** field is set to today's date and is unchangeable. The field c000 occurs where it does to ensure that the cursor progresses in a logical fashion; it is verify joined to the **Customers** table, ensuring that the user must enter a valid customer number.

The fields b, b1 and b2 are an example of a useful technique for producing highlighted fields. Fields b and b2 are never assigned to, but because they are DISPLAYONLY fields with the REVERSE attribute, they appear in reverse video anyway, giving a border to the screen. The field b1 is assigned a value, which is a centred text string that appears in reverse-video, when the **Sales** screen is displayed. The overall effect is that the **Sales** screen has a reverse video border, which is quite striking.

The other control blocks are essentially simple; they prevent the form from being used for purposes for which it is not designed, such as amending **Sales** records, or fiddling with the **Companies, Models** and **Prices** tables. Note that the form permits the deletion of **Stock** records and the addition or amendment of **Customers** records (but does not allow **Customers** records to be deleted). This means that all the complex validation developed in Chapter 4 for adding a customer is present, whereas the validation for the **Companies, Stock** and **Models** tables is missing; the only attributes applied apart from verify joins are QUERYCLEAR (NOENTRY and NOUPDATE could be used but the control blocks stop data entry and updating anyway).

It would be useful to be able to display the maker and model information on the **Customers** screen, but this turns out to be impossible for a rather obscure reason. If the commented out join line near the attributes for field tag f001 is allowed to stand and some corresponding modifications are made elsewhere, PERFORM refuses to compile the form with the error message -2993, the message for which is 'There is a circular join path specified in the form'. The problem can be illustrated by looking at the diagram shown below, which is an expansion of part of the diagram of the connections

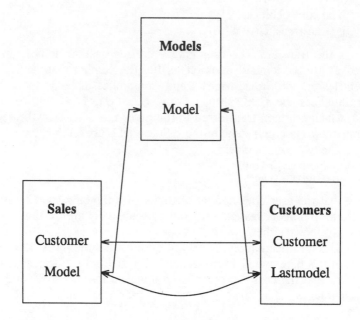

between the database tables shown in Chapter 2. The corrective action given in the error messages section of the reference manual is quite helpful – it reads:

> You cannot include a series of column joins that have the net effect of **table1.columnA** joins **table2.columnA, table2.columnB** joins **table3.columnB**, and **table3.columnC** joins **table1.columnC**. (A single join of **table1.columnA** joins **table2.columnA** joins **table3.columnA** is allowed.) Remove one of the joins so that this circular join path no longer exists.

The table shows the equivalences between the columns referred to in the error message and those in the form. There is indeed a loop which is shown by the lines made up of straight line segments.

Error message	Cars database
`table1.columnA`	**Sales.Model**
`table2.columnA`	**Models.Model**
`table2.columnB`	**Models.Model**
`table3.columnB`	**Customers.Lastmodel**
`table3.columnC`	**Customers.Customer**
`table1.columnC`	**Sales.Customer**

The other possible join between the **Sales** and **Customers** tables (shown by the curved line) does not cause this error message, but if it is specified, it causes a different problem: the **Sales** and **Customers** tables are then joined by two fields and PERFORM complains about a composite join which is not declared. The least unpleasant way of breaking the loop is to remove the connection between the **Customers** and **Models** table in this particular form. This is a very good reason for having more than one form to handle the database. (Alternatively, an INFORMIX-4GL program could be written to handle this task, but it would take longer than it took to produce this form.)

Chapter 12

1. This SELECT statement lists all libraries with any files defined as belonging to the library, and where the files have been defined in the **Files** table, gives the name of the file.

```
SELECT Library, Libfiles.Fileid, File
    FROM  Libraries, Libfiles, OUTER Files
    WHERE Libraries.Libid = Libfiles.Libid
    AND Libfiles.Fileid = Files.Fileid;
```

The results of this enquiry are:

Library	Fileid	File
libgeneral.a	1000	stdopt.4gl
libgeneral.a	1002	mktemp.c
libgeneral.a	1009	usertype.4gl
libgeneral.a	1010	decformat.c
libgeneral.a	1011	isfile.c
libgeneral.a	1012	isdir.c
libjl.a	1025	getpwd.c
libjl.a	1034	
libjl.a	1005	stderr.c
libjl.a	1006	setarg0.c

The following SELECT statement has no useful meaning. Notice that the joining condition has had to be changed so that library ID numbers are equated to file ID numbers. In as much as the results can be interpreted, for each library, it lists the numbers of the files included in the library, and it also lists the name of the file whose number happens to be the same as the number of the library, if there is such a file.

```
SELECT Library, Libfiles.Fileid, File
    FROM  Libraries, OUTER Libfiles, OUTER Files
    WHERE Libraries.Libid = Libfiles.Libid
    AND Libraries.Libid = Files.Fileid;
```

The results of this enquiry are shown in the following table.

Library	Fileid	File
libgeneral.a	1000	stdopt.4gl
libgeneral.a	1002	stdopt.4gl
libgeneral.a	1009	stdopt.4gl
libgeneral.a	1010	stdopt.4gl
libgeneral.a	1011	stdopt.4gl
libgeneral.a	1012	stdopt.4gl
libbunker.a		
libjl.a	1025	mktemp.c
libjl.a	1034	mktemp.c
libjl.a	1005	mktemp.c
libjl.a	1006	mktemp.c

2.

```
SELECT Company, Modelname, Details,
       P1.Year_made Year1, P2.Year_made Year2,
       P1.Lo_price, P1.Hi_price
   FROM     Companies, Models, Prices P1, Prices P2
   WHERE    Models.Maker = Companies.Maker
   AND      Models.Model = P1.Model
   AND      P1.Model     = P2.Model
   AND      P1.Year_made = P2.Year_made - 1
   AND      P1.Lo_price  = P2.Lo_price
   AND      P1.Hi_price  = P2.Hi_price
   ORDER BY Company, Modelname, Details, Year1;
```

Chapter 13

1.

```
{
    @(#)report3a.ace      5.1 91/03/22
    Customer Addresses
}

DATABASE Cars END

DEFINE
    VARIABLE aname    CHAR(30)
    VARIABLE salut2   CHAR(30)
END

OUTPUT
    PAGE LENGTH    23
    TOP MARGIN      0
    BOTTOM MARGIN   0
    LEFT MARGIN     0
END
```

```
SELECT Salut, Firstname, Surname, Address1, Address2, Address3, Postcode
   FROM    Customers
   ORDER BY Surname, Firstname
END

FORMAT

   FIRST PAGE HEADER
      SKIP 7 LINES
      PRINT COLUMN 35, "ABC Cars Ltd"
      SKIP 3 LINES
      PRINT COLUMN 35, "Customer List"

   PAGE HEADER
      PRINT COLUMN  5, "Customer List",
            COLUMN 40, TODAY USING "ddd dd mmm yyyy",
            COLUMN 70, PAGENO USING "Page <<<"
      SKIP 1 LINE

   PAGE TRAILER
      PAUSE "Hit return to continue"

   ON EVERY ROW
      IF PAGENO = 1 THEN
          SKIP TO TOP OF PAGE
      ELSE
          SKIP 1 LINE
      NEED 4 LINES
      { You cannot assign to any selected column }
      IF salut = "Esq" AND firstname[1] IS NULL THEN
          LET salut2 = "Mr"
      ELSE IF salut IS NULL AND firstname IS NULL THEN
          LET salut2 = "Mr"
      ELSE
          LET salut2 = salut
      IF salut2 != "Esq" AND salut2 IS NOT NULL THEN
          LET aname = salut2 CLIPPED, " ", firstname[1]
      ELSE
          LET aname = firstname[1]
      IF salut2 = "Esq" THEN
          PRINT COLUMN 15, aname CLIPPED, " ",
                surname CLIPPED, ", Esq"
      ELSE
          PRINT COLUMN 15, aname CLIPPED, " ",
                surname CLIPPED
      IF address1 IS NOT NULL THEN
          PRINT COLUMN 15, address1
      IF address2 IS NULL THEN
          PRINT COLUMN 15, address2
      IF address3 IS NOT NULL THEN
          PRINT COLUMN 15, address3 CLIPPED,
                10 SPACES, postcode
      ELSE IF postcode IS NOT NULL THEN
          PRINT COLUMN 15, postcode

END
```

2. This answer only illustrates the changes to the DEFINE, INPUT and SELECT sections. Note that the report no longer uses any parameters. The FORMAT section is unchanged.

```
{
    @(#)report3b.x        5.1 91/03/22
    Address label generating report
    Changes from previous version only
}

DATABASE Cars END

DEFINE
    { Restrict data selected by report }
    VARIABLE early        DATE
    VARIABLE late         DATE
    VARIABLE cust_match   CHAR(30)
    VARIABLE maker_match  CHAR(30)
    { ... }
END

INPUT
    PROMPT FOR early       USING "Earliest date: "
    PROMPT FOR late        USING "Latest date: "
    PROMPT FOR cust_match  USING "Pattern for surnames: "
    PROMPT FOR maker_match USING "Pattern for makers: "
END

{ ... }

SELECT  Customers.Salut,
        Customers.Firstname,
        Customers.Surname,
        Customers.Address1,
        Customers.Address2,
        Customers.Address3,
        Customers.Postcode
    FROM     Customers, Models, Companies
    WHERE    Customers.Lastmodel = Models.Model
      AND    Models.Maker = Companies.Company
      AND    Customers.Address1 IS NOT NULL
      AND    (Customers.Address2 IS NOT NULL OR Customers.Address3 IS NOT NULL)
      AND    (Salut IS NOT NULL OR Firstname IS NOT NULL)
      AND    Contactdate BETWEEN $early AND $late
      AND    Surname MATCHES $cust_match
      AND    Coname MATCHES $maker_match
    ORDER BY Surname, Firstname
END

{ ... }
```

Schemas for the Cars database

These schemas were used to create the database used in this book. The primary and foreign keys are documented in a manner which can be used to generate SQL scripts which check the integrity of the database.

Companies

```
(
     @(#)companie.sql      5.2 91/03/22
     Database Cars: Table Companies
)

CREATE TABLE Companies
(
     Maker              SERIAL(1)      NOT NULL,
     Company            CHAR(15)       NOT NULL,
     Address1           CHAR(24),
     Address2           CHAR(24),
     Address3           CHAR(24),
     Postcode           CHAR(8),
     Phone              CHAR(16),
     Notes1             CHAR(60),
     Notes2             CHAR(60)
);
(
     Company    - Company number
     Coname     - Company name
     Address1   - 1st line of address
     Address2   - 2nd line of address
     Address3   - 3rd line of address
     Postcode   - Postcode (UK)
     Phone      - Telephone number
     Notes1     - Free format text
     Notes2     - Free format text
)
(
     PRIMARY KEY Companies(Maker)
)
CREATE UNIQUE INDEX Pk_companies ON Companies(Maker);
CREATE UNIQUE INDEX I1_companies ON Companies(Company);
```

Customers

```
{
    @(#)customer.sql     5.2 91/03/22
    Database Cars: Table Customers
}

CREATE TABLE Customers
{
    Number          SERIAL(1000)   NOT NULL,
    Salut           CHAR(5),
    Firstname       CHAR(10),
    Surname         CHAR(15)       NOT NULL,
    Address1        CHAR(24),
    Address2        CHAR(24),
    Address3        CHAR(24),
    Postcode        CHAR(8),
    Phone           CHAR(16),
    Maxmoney        MONEY(6,0),
    Enquiry         CHAR(1)        NOT NULL,
    Lastmodel       INTEGER,
    Contactdate     DATE
);
{
    Number      - Customer number
    Salut       - Salutation
    Firstname   - Personal name
    Surname     - Family name
    Address1    - 1st line of address
    Address2    - 2nd line of address
    Address3    - 3rd line of address
    Postcode    - Postcode (UK)
    Phone       - Telephone number
    Maxmoney    - Estimated spending power
    Enquiry     - Type of enquiry
    Lastmodel   - Model enquired about
    Contactdate - Date contacted
}
{
    PRIMARY KEY Customers(Number)
    FOREIGN KEY Customers(Lastmodel)
        REFERENCES Models(Model)
}
CREATE UNIQUE INDEX Pk_customers ON Customers(Number);
CREATE INDEX F1_customers ON Customers(Lastmodel);
CREATE INDEX I1_customers ON Customers(Surname);
```

Models

```
{
    @(#)models.sql      5.1 90/08/19
    Database Cars: Table Models
}

CREATE TABLE Models
{
    Model           SERIAL(1)      NOT NULL,
    Maker           INTEGER        NOT NULL,
    Modelname       CHAR(20)       NOT NULL,
```

```
    Details              CHAR(40),
    Price                MONEY(6,0),
    Maxspeed             SMALLINT,
    Accel                DECIMAL(3,1),
    Tanksize             DECIMAL(3,1),
    Urban                DECIMAL(3,1),
    Mpgat56              DECIMAL(3,1),
    Enginesize           SMALLINT
);
{
    Model       - Model number
    Maker       - Company number
    Modelname   - Name of model
    Details     - Details about model
    Price       - Price of new car
    Maxspeed    - Top speed (mph)
    Accel       - Time to accelerate 0-60 mph
    Tanksize    - Tank size (gallons)
    Urban       - Fuel consumption, steady 56 mph, mpg
    Mpgat56     - Fuel consumption, urban cycle, mpg
    Enginesize  - Size of engine (cc)
}
{
    PRIMARY KEY Models(Model)
    FOREIGN KEY Models(Maker)
        REFERENCES Companies(Maker)
}
CREATE UNIQUE INDEX Pk_models ON Models(Model);
CREATE INDEX F1_models ON Models(Maker);
CREATE INDEX I1_models ON Models(Modelname);
```

Prices

```
{
    a(#)prices.sql       5.3 90/08/19
    Database Cars: Table Prices
}

CREATE TABLE Prices
{
    Model                INTEGER       NOT NULL,
    Year_made            SMALLINT      NOT NULL,
    Lo_price             DECIMAL(6,0)  NOT NULL,
    Hi_price             DECIMAL(6,0)  NOT NULL
);
{
    Model       - Model number
    Year_made   - Year to which prices apply
    Lo_price    - Lower guide price
    Hi_price    - Higher guide price
}
{
    PRIMARY KEY Prices(Model, Year_made)
    FOREIGN KEY Prices(Model)
        REFERENCES Models(Model)
}
CREATE UNIQUE INDEX Pk_prices ON Prices(Model, Year_made);
CREATE INDEX F1_prices ON Prices(Model);
```

Sales

```
{
    a(#)sales.sql        5.2 91/03/03
    Database Cars: Table Sales
}

CREATE TABLE Sales
(
    Registration        CHAR(7)        NOT NULL,
    Customer            INTEGER        NOT NULL,
    Model               INTEGER        NOT NULL,
    Soldfor             MONEY(8,2)     NOT NULL,
    Datesold            DATE           NOT NULL,
    Terms               CHAR(4)        NOT NULL,
    Colour              CHAR(8),
    Condition           CHAR(1),
    Datebought          DATE           NOT NULL,
    Boughtfor           MONEY(8,2),
    Mileage             INTEGER,
    Notes1              CHAR(60),
    Notes2              CHAR(60)
);
{
    Registration     - Registration number
    Customer         - Customer number
    Model            - Model number
    Soldfor          - Amount sold for
    Datesold         - Date when sold
    Terms            - Method of purchase
    Colour           - Colour of car
    Condition        - Condition of car
    Datebought       - Date car bought
    Boughtfor        - Buying price
    Mileage          - Mileage when bought
    Notes1           - Free format text
    Notes2           - Free format text
}
{
    PRIMARY KEY Sales(Registration, Datesold)
    FOREIGN KEY Sales(Customer)
        REFERENCES Customers(Customer)
    FOREIGN KEY Sales(Model)
        REFERENCES Models(Model)
}
CREATE UNIQUE INDEX Pk_sales ON Sales(Registration, Datesold);
CREATE INDEX F1_sales ON Sales(Model);
CREATE INDEX F2_sales ON Sales(Customer);
```

Stock

```
{
    a(#)stock.sql        5.1 90/08/19
    Database Cars: Table Stock
}

CREATE TABLE Stock
(
    Registration        CHAR(7)        NOT NULL,
```

```
        Model                INTEGER          NOT NULL,
        Colour               CHAR(8),
        Condition            CHAR(1),
        Datebought           DATE             NOT NULL,
        Boughtfor            MONEY(8,2)       NOT NULL,
        Mileage              INTEGER,
        Notes1               CHAR(60),
        Notes2               CHAR(60)
);
{
        Registration     - Registration number
        Model            - Model number
        Colour           - Colour of car
        Condition        - Condition of car
        Datebought       - Date car bought
        Boughtfor        - Buying price
        Mileage          - Mileage when bought
        Notes1           - Free format text
        Notes2           - Free format text
}
{
        PRIMARY KEY Stock(Registration)
        FOREIGN KEY Stock(Model)
            REFERENCES Models(Model)
}
CREATE UNIQUE INDEX Pk_stock ON Stock(Registration);
CREATE INDEX F1_stock ON Stock(Model);
```

Models2

This table was used to illustrate COMPOSITES in Chapter 11:

```
{
        @(#)models2.sql      5.1 90/08/19
        Database Cars: Table Models2
}

CREATE TABLE Models2
(
        Model                INTEGER          NOT NULL,
        Maker                INTEGER          NOT NULL,
        Modelname            CHAR(20)         NOT NULL,
        Details              CHAR(40),
        Price                MONEY(6,0),
        Maxspeed             SMALLINT,
        Accel                DECIMAL(3,1),
        Tanksize             DECIMAL(3,1),
        Urban                DECIMAL(3,1),
        Mpgat56              DECIMAL(3,1),
        Enginesize           SMALLINT
);
{
        PRIMARY KEY Models2(Maker, Model)
        FOREIGN KEY Models2(Maker)
            REFERENCES Companies(Company)
}
CREATE UNIQUE INDEX Pk_models2 ON Models2(Maker, Model);
CREATE INDEX F1_models2 ON Models2(Maker);
CREATE INDEX F2_models2 ON Models2(Model);
CREATE INDEX I1_models2 ON Models2(Modelname);
```

Stock2

This table was used to illustrate COMPOSITES in Chapter 11:

```
{
    @(#)stock2.sql       5.1 90/08/19
    Database Cars: Table Stock2
}

CREATE TABLE Stock2
{
    Registration      CHAR(7)        NOT NULL,
    Maker             INTEGER        NOT NULL,
    Model             INTEGER        NOT NULL,
    Colour            CHAR(8),
    Condition         CHAR(1),
    Datebought        DATE           NOT NULL,
    Boughtfor         MONEY(8,2)     NOT NULL,
    Mileage           INTEGER,
    Notes1            CHAR(60),
    Notes2            CHAR(60)
);
{
    PRIMARY KEY Stock2(Registration)
    FOREIGN KEY Stock2(Maker, Model)
        REFERENCES Models(Maker, Model)
    FOREIGN KEY Stock2(Maker)
        REFERENCES Companies(Maker)
}
CREATE UNIQUE INDEX Pk_stock2 ON Stock2(Registration);
CREATE INDEX F1_stock2 ON Stock2(Maker, Model);
CREATE INDEX F2_stock2 ON Stock2(Maker);
```

C
Useful programs

These programs may be of use to you. The first can be used to experiment with USING clauses in reports, and the second is a simple restricted shell that can be used to contain users within a user-menu.

Formatting DECIMAL values

To help produce the lists of formats shown in Chapter 9, the following two tables were created:

```
CREATE TABLE Formats
(
    Seq SERIAL(1) NOT NULL,
    Fmt CHAR(20)  NOT NULL
);

CREATE TABLE Decimals
(
    Seq SERIAL(1) NOT NULL,
    Val DECIMAL   NOT NULL
);
```

These were each filled with some data (it didn't take long to generate a default screen for the two tables), and the report shown below was then run:

```
{
    @(#)ckusing.ace      5.1 91/03/08
    @(#)Report to demonstrate formats with PRINT USING
}

DATABASE
    Cars
END

OUTPUT
    PAGE LENGTH      23
    TOP MARGIN        0
    BOTTOM MARGIN     0
    LEFT MARGIN       0
END

SELECT  Formats.Fmt,
        Formats.Seq      Seq1,
        Decimals.Val,
        Decimals.Seq     Seq2
```

307

```
FROM Formats, Decimals
{ There is no WHERE clause quite deliberately }
ORDER BY Seq1, Seq2

END

FORMAT

PAGE HEADER
    PRINT "Decimal formats illustrated"
    SKIP 1 LINE
    PRINT
        COLUMN  2, "Format string",
        COLUMN 20, 5 SPACES, "Decimal value",
        COLUMN 45, "Formatted value"

ON EVERY ROW
    IF (Fmt MATCHES "*DB*" AND Val <= 0.0) OR
       (Fmt MATCHES "*CR*" AND Val >= 0.0) OR
       NOT (Fmt MATCHES "*[DC][BR]*")
    THEN
        PRINT
            COLUMN  2, Fmt CLIPPED,
            COLUMN 20, Val,
            COLUMN 45, Val USING Fmt

AFTER GROUP OF Seq1
    SKIP 1 LINE

END
```

Note that this report is quite clever; it reads in the format string as a variable, prints it as a variable and uses it in the USING clause of a print expression. This can be very useful, and a similar trick can be done with column numbers. When the report was run, the environment variable DBMONEY was set to:

```
DBMONEY="£."; export DBMONEY
```

The reason that the strings of asterisks are longer than any of the formatted output is that the variable used in the USING statement is 16 characters long, and there are 16 asterisks in the output.

Restricted shell for use with INFORMIX-SQL

This shell is not guaranteed to be completely tamper-proof; there are many things that could go wrong if someone was very determined to break out. On the other hand, it certainly keeps casual users well under control. The methods of breaking this would require odd environment variables (such as IFS) to be set.

```
/*
    @(#)isqlsh.c    2.1 88/09/10
    @(#)Basic restricted shell for use with ISQL
    @(#)Author: J Leffler, Sphinx Ltd.
    @(#)May be freely adapted for use
*/

#include <stdio.h>
#define SHELL       "/bin/sh"
```

```
#define ALLOC(x)    malloc((unsigned)(x))

static struct
{
    char    *name;
    char    *path;
} cmdlist[] =
{
    { "date",       "/bin/date"                     },
    { "ls",         "/bin/ls"                       },
    { "sperform",   "/usr/informix/bin/sperform"    },
    { "sacego",     "/usr/informix/bin/sacego"      },
    /* Add any other commands here as required */
    /* Leave the next line at the end of the list */
    { (char *)0,    (char *)0                       }
};

extern  char    *malloc();
extern  char    *realloc();
extern  char    *strtok();
extern  char    **parse();

static  char    sccs[] = "@(#)isqlsh.c  2.1 88/09/10";

main(argc, argv)
int     argc;
char    **argv;
{
    int     i;
    char    *cmd;
    char    **nargv;
    char    **argvp;

    if (argc <= 1)
        return(0);  /* No command -- succeeded */

    /* Check whether command is valid */
    cmd = argv[1];
    if (strcmp(cmd, "-c") == 0)
    {   /* Invoked as 'isqlsh -c "cmd args"' */
        argv = parse(argv[0], argv[2]);
        cmd = argv[1];
    }

    for (i = 0; cmdlist[i].name != (char *)0; i++)
        if (strcmp(cmd, cmdlist[i].name) == 0)
            break;

    if (cmdlist[i].name == (char *)0)
    {
        fprintf(stderr, "%s: invalid command %s\n",
                argv[0], argv[1]);
        return(1);  /* Invalid command -- failed */
    }

    /* Try executing command as a.out program */
    /* NB: cannot use execvp as it fails on Xenix if */
    /* command is a.out program but is not readable */
    argv[1] = cmdlist[i].path;
    execv(cmdlist[i].path, &argv[1]);

    /* Failed -- must be a shell script */

    /* Allocate space for revised command list */
```

```
    nargv = (char **)ALLOC((argc+2)*sizeof(char *));
    if (nargv == (char **)0)
        return(1);  /* No memory -- failed */

    /* Set revised argument list */
    argvp = nargv;
    *argvp++ = SHELL;
    *argvp++ = cmdlist[i].path;
    for (i = 2; i < argc; i++)
        *argvp++ = argv[i];
    *argvp = (char *)0;

    /* Execute command */
    execv(SHELL, nargv);
    return(1);  /* Cannot execute -- failed */
}


/*
    Parse command supplied as argument after -c option
    NB: this version does not handle quotes or backslashes
*/

char    **parse(arg0, argstr)
char    *arg0;
char    *argstr;
{
    int     argc;
    char    **argv;

    /* Need 2 arguments: 1. shell name, 2. terminal null */
    argv = (char **)ALLOC(2*sizeof(char *));
    if (argv == (char **)0)
        exit(1);    /* No memory -- failed */

    argc = 0;
    argv[argc++] = arg0;
    while ((argv[argc++] = strtok(argstr, " \t"))
                                        != (char *)0)
    {
        /* Found another argument -- get space for it */
        argv = (char **)realloc(argv,
                            (argc+1)*sizeof(char *));
        if (argv == (char **)0)
            exit(1);    /* No memory -- failed */

        /* Subsequent calls to strtok need */
        /* null first argument */
        argstr = (char *)0;
    }

    return(argv);
}
```

D
References

References from Informix Software Inc

These reference materials are all from Informix; they refer directly to the INFORMIX-SQL product or to the Informix family of products. When you buy INFORMIX-SQL, you receive the reference manual and user guide automatically. Although only one edition of Tech Notes is listed here, there have been a number of other ones, most of which cover some useful points.

ISI (1987). Tech Notes Spring 1987. Informix Software Inc:

> Discusses outer joins and query optimization.

ISI (1990a). *Informix-SQL Reference Manual*. Informix Software Inc, (Version 4.00, Part No. 200-411-0002-0):

> The reference manual for INFORMIX-SQL version 4.00.

ISI (1990b). *Informix-SQL User's Guide*. Informix Software Inc, (Version 4.00, Part No. 200-411-0001-0):

> The user guide for INFORMIX-SQL version 4.00.

General references

These books and articles are not directly related to INFORMIX-SQL.

ANSI (1986). *Database Language SQL*. ANSI X3.135-1986:

> The ANSI version of the ISO standard for SQL.

311

Bourne S. R. (1987). *The UNIX System V Environment*. Addison-Wesley:

> Nothing to do with databases, but it is a good general introduction to UNIX.

Codd E. F. (1970). *A relational model of data for large shared data banks*. *CACM* **13** (6):

> The original article on relational databases.

Codd E. F. (1990). *The Relational Model of Data*. Addison-Wesley:

> A definitive view of what a relational database system should provide.

Date C. J. (1983). *An Introduction to Database Systems: Volume II*. Addison-Wesley:

> Not as important as Date (1986) or Date (1990). This book has many other references in it.

Date C. J. (1986). *Relational Database: Selected Writings*. Addison-Wesley:

> This book contains a collection of 'philosophical' writings on relational databases and SQL, but it is not an introductory text. It has a useful chapter on database design.

Date C. J. (1989) *Relational Database: Writings 1985-1989*. Addison-Wesley:

> This is a companion volume to Date (1986). It has extensive discussions of topics such as foreign keys and nulls. It also has an amusing and yet profound description of some rules for handling relational databases contributed by Andrew Warden.

Date C. J. (1990). *An Introduction to Database Systems: Volume I*, 5th edition. Addison-Wesley:

> This is a good introduction to database systems in general, and relational systems in particular.

Fleming C. C. and von Halle B. (1989). *Handbook of Relational Database Design*. Addison-Wesley:

> One of many books describing a method for designing databases.

ISO (1987). *Database Language SQL*. IS 9075-1987:

> This is the ISO version of the ANSI standard for SQL.

NCC (1986). *SSADM Manual Version 3*, Volumes 1 & 2. G. Longworth & D. Nicholls, NCC Publications:

A widely used design methodology.

Strang J. (1989). *Reading and Writing Termcap Entries*, 3rd edition. O'Reilly & Associates, Inc, 632 Petaluma Avenue, Sebastopol, CA 95472, USA:

Nothing to do with databases, but if you are in difficulties setting your terminal up on UNIX, this may well help you. You will still need the manual for your computer and for the terminal.

Index